PEACHES

PEACHES
A CHRONICLE OF THE STRANGLERS 1974–1990

soundcheck books
the stories behind the sounds

First published in Great Britain in 2014
by Soundcheck Books LLP, 88 Northchurch Road, London, N1 3NY.

Copyright © Robert Endeacott 2014

ISBN: 978-0-9575700-4-7

All rights reserved. No part of this book may be reproduced or transmitted in any form or by any means, electronic or mechanical, including photocopying, recording, or any information storage and retrieval system without permission in writing from the publisher.

This book is sold subject to the condition that it shall not, by way of trade or otherwise, be lent, resold, hired out or otherwise circulated without the publisher's prior consent in any form of binding or cover other than that in which it is published and without a similar condition being imposed on the subsequent purchaser.

Every effort has been made to contact copyright holders of photographic and other resource material used in this book. Some were unreachable. If they contact the publishers we will endeavour to credit them in reprints and future editions.

This title has not been prepared, approved or licenced by the management, or past or present members of The Stranglers and is an unofficial book.

A CIP record for this book is available from the British Library

Book design: Benn Linfield (www.bennlinfield.com)
Printed by: Bell & Bain, Glasgow

CONTENTS

Acknowledgements	IX
Author's Introduction	XI
1 The Early Days	1
2 1974: The Official Birth	3
3 1975: The Band Developing	5
4 1976: The Stranglers Burn Up Time	10
5 1977: Getting A Grip On The Charts	19
6 1978: Black & White ... And Read All Over	47
7 1979: Flying Near Straight With Perfection	63
8 1980: Black & Blacker	79
9 1981: The Gospelinblack And Beyond	94
10 1982: Recovery	107
11 1983: Fresh Start?	115
12 1984: All Quiet On The Stranglers Front	130
13 1985: Consequences	135
14 1986: Slumbertime?	142
15 1987: Static On Tour	153
16 1988: M.I.B. M.I.A.	158
17 1989: The Twilight	164
18 1990: And Now, The End Is ...	167
Summing It All Up	179
Bibliography	181
About The Author	182

Dedicated to Mum & Dad, God bless you both,
and to Stranglers fans everywhere

ACKNOWLEDGEMENTS

It has been a huge pleasure dealing with each and every one of you.

Dean Abbott, Chris Archer, Keith Asken, Chris Band, Gareth Barber, Simon Barraball, Steve Beddoe, Mike Bellwood, Ian Bond, Dean Bourne, Keith Bowe, Matt Brown, Dave Brydon, David Buckley, Steve Bullock, Steve Burns, Adam Burton, Jim Cadman, Mark Campbell, Owen Carne, Ronnie Carnwath, Gill Cory, Phil Coxon, Barry Cridland, Brian Crook, Richard Cusworth, Paul Davies, Mike Edwards, Ian Ellis, John Ellis, Samantha Emery, Sophie Cater Emery, Chris Dalston, Steve Flanagan, Sam Gibbard, Phil Godsell, Ian Gomm, John Goodall, Dom Grace, Al Hillier, Sam Holliday, Philip Johnson, Leonor Jonker, Gary Kent, Paul Kent, Nic Kent, Simon Kent, Ed Kleinman, Jon Leeming, Ian Lever, Mark Luff, Donald MacKay, Rob Mackenzie, Jim Malone, Ian McCabe, Alan McDonald, Bongo McDonald, Martin McGowan, Davy McLaughlin, Patrick McLaughlin, Grant McNab, Ron Moger, Anne-Marie Mondan, Graeme 'Mully' Mullan, Gareth Noon, Bernie Nussbaum, Andy Oddy, David Peace, Dom Pilgrim, Nick Quantrill, Jim Radley, Ava Rave, Mark Ray, John Robb, Paul Roberts, Pete Robinson, Duncan Round, Adam Salem, Jake Slaughter, Andy Stafford, Tony Stubley, Lee Turtle, Eric Vonk, Baz Warne, John Wheelhouse, Sil Wilcox, Guy Westoby, Robert Williams, plus Adam Pope, Liz Green, Johnny I'anson and Rozina Breen and all their colleagues at BBC Radio Leeds who would always play Stranglers records given the chance. And every bootlegging monkey out there, and everyone who has offered to help but who I've forgotten.

And of course, *all* The Stranglers, past, present and future.

■ ■ ■ ■ ■ ■ ■ ■ ■ ■ ■ ■ ■ ■ ■ ■ ■ ■ ■

AUTHOR'S INTRODUCTION

One of the main things I loved about all the Punk/New Wave scene was the do it yourself, decide for yourself, attitude. BE yourself. Not that The Stranglers were Punk, they just took timely advantage of the new sensation, creating superior sounds at the same time. Years on, I still love Jean-Jacques Burnel's response on Channel 4's *Punk Top Ten* programme: 'Were we Punk? Could I give a fuck?' 'He was also asked if The Stranglers' lyrics were more intelligent and musical than the others ... 'Oh come on, are you deaf or what? Course they're fucking more musical than them'. I've been saying it for years, Monsieur Burnel should write a book.

Seeing The Stranglers in concert was/is always a thrill, I just wish I'd seen them in the 1970s (I'm not sure, but I think my first time was in 1981). At least I've been able to listen to numerous bootlegs to help ease the regret. Gigs were special and the band always left us wanting more. Hugh Cornwell's guitar string-ends waving around like cat whiskers from the machine head, JJ Burnel karate-kicking; the coolest bassist of all time, creating growling bass effects like a shipwreck shifting on the ocean floor. His riffs *speak* to me, they really do. At the back, keyboard god Dave Greenfield hovering over the proceedings like a mad/genius scientist, along with the sentinel Jet Black slamming away some of the most powerful and perfect drum backbeats ever heard. The Stranglers are the first group who really got into my head and soul, always possessing the uncanny ability of creating the most stirring heavy, gritty, *dramatic* sounds as well as some of the softest and sweetest melodies around.

The main reason for calling this book *Peaches* is due to my near-obsession with collecting live versions of one particular line from that song: Hugh often altered the 'skewer' line to fine comic effect. Their wit was just another facet of the band which really appealed to me.

I'm extremely grateful to all the people who have helped with this quest and it's essential that I mention four specific books which have been useful *and* inspirational. *No Mercy* (David Buckley), *The Men They Love To Hate* (Chris Twomey), *A Multitude Of Sins* (Hugh Cornwell) and *The Stranglers: Song By Song* (Hugh Cornwell and Jim Drury), all great reads. Also the excellent *Strangled* magazine as well as Jim Radley's supreme *Burning Up Time* forum, and Gary Kent's splendid www.strangled.co.uk site. AND of course the unbeatable official site, www.strangled.net.

Just like with most jobs, writing a book takes dedication and hard graft. I know though that I am far from being the most qualified Stranglers fan to write about the band. Yes, I've seen them more times than I recall but there are countless fans around the world who have spent more money and time on the band than I ever could, so this book is, in some way, a tribute to the fans too.

Thanksinblack, *Robert Endeacott*, 2014.

1 THE EARLY DAYS

Typical of the disparate souls who will become The Stranglers, how such an unlikely set of musicians first came together is no conventional 'How The Band Met' story. Those four youngish men in the first line up hadn't gone to school or college or university together, they hadn't grown up near each other and they certainly hadn't been manufactured into a soulless cash cow boy band either, unlike McLaren's Sex Pistols for instance (Ah, the Sex Pistols, brilliant but, in truth, just a dirtier, spottier, spittier version of The Monkees of the 1960s. The Pistols were the 1970s *Punkees*!). The much more arduous journey of The Stranglers begins in the early 1970s, involving various dubious elements along the way, like American draft dodgers (not George W. Bush), armed robbery, a shooting, busking, drugs busting and an ice-cream van. All before the scout hut, the off licence and the *millions* of gigs.

NOTABLE BIRTHDAYS
(In case you fancy sending any of them a card, except Hans, of course, who sadly left us in 1995).
Jet Black: 26th August 1938 (born Brian John Duffy). Hugh Cornwell: 28th August 1949. Dave Greenfield: 29th March 1949. Jean-Jacques Burnel: 21st February, 1952. Hans Wärmling: 22nd July, 1943. John Ellis: 1st June, 1952. Paul Roberts: 31st December 1959. Baz Warne: 25th March 1964.

By 1973, a stocky bearded 35-year-old, born in Ilford as Brian John Duffy, but known as Jet Black, runs a number of small businesses in Guildford, including an off licence and a fleet of ice cream vans. Inventive, intelligent, pragmatic yet entrepreneurial, he is the kind of bloke who grafts until he makes a success of whatever he is working on. Making it big in commerce though is not his life's motivation and he needs a new challenge. As a teenager he made it to semi-professional level as a band drummer, playing numerous gigs across London in the 1950s and 1960s, as well as at the home of Barbara Andrews, mother of a certain Julie Andrews. By the 1970s, he'd packed in drumming, selling his kit to Barbara, but, come 1973, he decides to pick up the drumsticks again.

Around the same time, a 24-year-old biochemistry graduate, Hugh Cornwell, is studying and working in Lund, southern Sweden, as you do, and busking as a singer and guitarist. With his friend Hans Wärmling he forms Johnny Sox, briefly renamed Wanderlust. Wärmling, a prolific guitarist/writer, has experienced moderate fame in the Swedish band Jackie Fountains and reportedly in a latter-day line up of the much better known Spotnicks.

During his teens in Highgate, London, the wiry, sharp-witted Cornwell shared a little limelight with schoolmate and future folkie Richard Thompson in their band Emil & The Detectives, even once supporting 1960s teen *chanteuse* Helen Shapiro. A stunning guitarist, Thompson taught Cornwell bass. Thompson will fare very well in his own musical career, as part of Fairport Convention, also as a duo with (now ex-) wife Linda and as a solo artist. Cornwell occasionally busked in Bristol while studying at the city's university and supplements his income by entertaining customers in eateries owned by his friend, the late TV chef Keith Floyd.

Johnny Sox consists of Cornwell, two Swedes (Wärmling and Jan Knutsson, who didn't last very long) and two American draft dodgers, Gyrth Godwin and drummer 'Chicago' Mike. A mysterious benefactor regularly hangs around them too: the half Swedish, half Hawaiian post office and bank robber Axl C who gives the band money, as well as a Ford transit van, in gratitude for putting him up and for not grassing him up, too. Late in 1973, Cornwell convinces his bandmates that if they are serious about succeeding then they need to move to the bright lights of London. The live music scene there is expanding rapidly and bands such as Brinsley Schwarz, Ducks Deluxe and Dr Feelgood are impacting greatly on the pubs and clubs circuit.

Cornwell's aspirations for London, however, encounter an early obstacle – Hans Wärmling stays in Sweden. Chicago Mike has things on his mind too: the American government has lifted the moratorium on draft dodgers, so he can now return home without the worry of a jail sentence for not fighting in Vietnam, or any other place the US wants to try and bully the crap out of in the world's playground.

2 1974: THE OFFICIAL BIRTH

Differing versions of events exist around who actually founded the band. From my point of view, that of a simple fan, I don't care so much about who started it all, I'm just bloody glad some bugger did. I am though very confident that The Stranglers would never have happened had Jet Black and Hugh Cornwell not met.

In John Robb's exemplary *Punk Rock, An Oral History*, the main protagonists are asked about the gestation of The Stranglers. Hugh Cornwell recalls that early in 1974, Chicago Mike left Johnny Sox, meaning they suddenly need a drummer. They advertise and Jet Black turns up with a Beatles' haircut, a suit and a beard, plus the added bonus of the use of his off-licence in Guildford for digs and rehearsals if required. A good friend of Jet's lives in the house too, a charming old chap in his seventies called George. All that the new residents have to do, Jet says, is work for their keep while he continues with his own work.

Plenty of rehearsing gets done but not much actual work, and Gyrth reportedly drinks a lot of the off licence stock too. Gyrth and Jan then have a falling out one evening in a club – Gyrth gets drunk and disorderly and so Jet lays into him for not doing any work and not being committed enough to the band. He heads back to Sweden where his wife and child live. Then Jan departs too, so now there are two. But, as one door closes another one opens (unless of course it's a prison cell or a tomb): before his exit, hitch-hiking Gyrth thumbs a lift off the enigma that is Jean-Jacques Burnel; a Harley Davidson-loving, karate-obsessed London-born French man, who prefers 'John' to Jean. He is working as a delivery driver in London, *and* he is virtually a skinhead at the time.

Burnel, although a trained classical guitarist, isn't contemplating a career in music until this encounter. Saving up to pay for a trip to the States to be a motorcycle mechanic, he plans to move to Japan to try and earn a black belt in karate, but Gyrth invites him back to Jet's Jackpot off-licence, where he meets the others. Shortly after Gyrth and Jan exit stage left, never to return, Hugh visits Burnel as he wants two singers in the band, plus, of course, a bassist. The two discuss matters over a bottle of wine; Jean-Jacques takes little persuading to quit his job and join. Meanwhile, Jet has sold all but one of the ice cream vans, the remaining vehicle is to be used for transporting gear and people to and from gigs. That's right: gigs, though Hugh and JJ have expressed doubts that any actually took place at this stage.

Reports therefore that January 1974 saw Johnny Sox play, as a trio in a few London gigs including the Brecknock Arms (Camden), the Lord Nelson (Holloway Road) and the Newlands Tavern (Nunhead), are debatable. Nevertheless, the three rehearse and write virtually every day whilst working in a variety of jobs to keep them in food and financially afloat.

11th September '74. On this date seven years before, The Beatles began shooting their Magical Mystery Tour film, and this day marks the start of an equally bizarre journey of sorts, as Jet Black registers the band's name. Our trio eventually agree on The Stranglers moniker after watching movies on TV, every one of them with strangling in it apparently. The Guildford Stranglers and Oil & The Slicks, as well as The Chiddingfold Chokers, are other names bandied around, with varying degrees of seriousness. The band's HQ changes too, with Jet renting an end-terrace house in Chiddingfold in place of the off-licence which is up for demolition as part of the 'redevelopment' of Guildford town centre. The band hold regular rehearsals in Bramley Village Hall and Shalford Scout Hut as well as a cricket pavilion in Brook, Surrey.

3 1975: THE BAND DEVELOPING

Early 1975 and visiting his old friend Hugh Cornwell in England, Hans Wärmling is invited to join the band. His acceptance brings the band up to a quartet: Cornwell, Wärmling, Burnel and Black. The number of gigs increases as time passes, as does the band's skills as musicians and songwriters. Self-confidence grows, even if some gigs are demoralising disasters and much of the live set consists of cover versions. Landlords and managers of most venues prefer covers, simply because audiences do too. The band has written dozens of their own songs by now and as a result pay for demo tapes to send to record labels for consideration. Or inconsideration more like: neither record deal nor big break looks likely, despite the hard graft. This frustratingly slow progress alas proves too much for Hans, who quits. He 'jumps ship' but undoubtedly received help in his trajectory as well, after dropping the band in the crap soon before an important gig, a Jewish wedding. Whilst his departure might seem a tad hostile, he has always been highly regarded by the other three as a person and as a musician.

March '75. Although the band have officially been manager-less, Brian Crook, an old school pal of JJ's, steps into the breach to fill the gap. Brian told me 'I first met the Stranglers after JJ joined. He introduced the guys (Hugh, Jet and Hans) and proceeded to tell me they needed a manager. I was happy to oblige … they had already been signed up by Reg McClean, a Jamaican Londoner who ran his own label in Chiswick called Safari Records. They had recorded "Strange Little Girl" and "My Young Dreams" as demos, I appeared on the scene around this time trying to get gigs and impress upon them the need for a "Promo kit". They were only interested in coming by their next meal, it was hard times for the guys sharing slices of cheese on toast and half a bitter at the local pub'.

SAFARI

The Safari development seems to be very promising news for the band. McLean claims he wants a short-term recording deal with the band who record the aforementioned batch of demo tracks at Trans World Studios (TW Studios) in Fulham, which McLean finances. Those tracks are 'Charlie Boy', 'I Know It', 'Chinatown', 'Make

You Mine', 'My Young Dreams', 'Wasted' and 'Strange Little Girl'. Apparently impressed, McLean promises that 'My Young Dreams' will be released as a single in April 1975. But it isn't and so Brian Crook is asked to investigate. He told me: 'The band needed to get out of the Safari contract so I was introduced to Reg and I got myself a job in the label. I promoted singles around the UK in radio stations, clubs and record shops, and whilst doing this I disposed of all "contracts" and removed all sign of The Stranglers in the record company's offices … they were now free to move on to the "Derek Savage days"'.

FIRST DEMOS

Here is fan Chris Band's assessment:

A good set of songs, though 'I Know It' and 'Make You Mine' lack the distinctive prominent bass and keyboards. They do showcase some decent harmonies, and here Hugh Cornwell and JJ Burnel's vocal styles are very melodic without any of the aggression which they would become (in) famous for. 'Chinatown' has a cinematic feel, and although it's a Hans Wärmling song, perhaps it sowed the seed for the other band members to create more epic, sweeping tunes of later years. The arrangements begin to get bolder and more experimental with 'My Young Dreams', 'Charlie Boy', 'Wasted' and, most obviously, 'Strange Little Girl' which is the standout track.

TRANS WORLD STUDIOS

TW Studios becomes popular with the band, not only because it has a near-permanently open kebab house nearby but also because there is a guitar shop upstairs which rents out equipment. The band sometimes borrow gear for free (providing the owner's Alsatian allows them to). Some good comes out of the sessions, as the man running the recordings is Alan Winstanley and he will feature prominently in Stranglers' folklore. Two other demo recordings are known to exist from this era, but whether they are made at the same sessions seems unlikely: 'White Wedding' and 'Country Chaser'. According to the *No Mercy* biography, McLean promises to find the band gigs if they hire out their PA for him, and, indirectly, to his credit, one of the band's most famous songs emerges because of that little agreement. Hugh and JJ take the PA out with the speakers and set it all up for some black singers in Acton Town Hall. On one occasion, the pair are the only white people there, and the sounds and experience inspire them to write 'Peaches' later that night. It is their attempt at rap/reggae.

May '75. 'Soft rock' band The Stranglers place an ad in *Melody Maker* again. They get a sax player (unreliably reported as being called Igor) who doesn't last long at all – and they get a long-haired and moustachioed chap called Dave Greenfield, a keyboard player based in Germany who heard about the ad from his aunt. A big talent, intelligent, with years of band

7 • 1975: THE BAND DEVELOPING

experience, Greenfield can write songs and play both guitar and keyboards (presumably not at the same time, though you never know) and he's not a primadonna. Recalling the phone conversation with Jet Black prior to his audition, Dave asks, not unreasonably, why he is called Jet – 'Because I'm the fastest thing on two legs' comes the reply. With Dave's arrival though came a departure too. Brian Crook explains: 'Dave appeared ... well it was plain to see that this was the missing piece of the jigsaw, the odd gig here and there in pubs and working men's clubs quickly showed that this band had a future. I wasn't able to help them in the way a professional manager could help and realised this and, besides, my best mate was in the band, I needed to be realistic about the future'.

Islington's legendary Hope & Anchor, home of pub rock, where The Stranglers played many early gigs. (*Fin Fahey*)

BIRTHPLACES

None of the band actually hails from Guildford – Jet Black is from Ilford, Essex. Jean-Jacques Burnel (of French descent) is from Notting Hill and Hugh Cornwell is Kentish Town. Compared to the new addition, Dave Greenfield, they are all 'bloody northerners', as he comes from Brighton, Sussex.

Summer '75. The Stranglers have gained backing from the Albion Agency, a tiny booking partnership in Wandsworth, formed by Derek Savage and Dai Davies. A select few friends chip in to help too, arranging and publicising gigs and generally spreading the word about how good this band is. Before Albion, Jet Black's pal Charles Edwards also helped manage the band's affairs. Another unofficial backer is Garry Coward-Williams, a 15-year-old schoolboy and amateur photographer. The band take him under their wing and he even lives with them for a short while in their Chiddingfold digs. Hugh gives him the nickname Chiswick Charlie and his schoolmate Duncan, also a fan, becomes Duncan Doughnuts.

TEAM STRANGLERS

Also that summer, Ian Grant joins Albion as a partner. Savage and Davies ask him to watch a certain band - The Stranglers - who have been mithering them, and if he likes them then Albion will take them on. Grant does, so Albion do. Grant sees them supporting eccentric [the late] Viv Stanshall at the now defunct Nashville Rooms in West Kensington. Grant brings in publicist Alan Edwards too: a masterstroke. Edwards, realises he needs to devise creative ways to get gigs for an unknown band, so purportedly books dates for other bands like the 101'ers and Eddie & The Hot Rods, without telling them, only to then call the venues later to advise that they have cancelled, but he could offer them ... The Stranglers instead!

Artist Kevin Sparrow is also recruited. He creates the distinctive Stranglers logo (even if some folks think it looks like the Walt Disney insignia).

24th August '75. A pleasant Sunday afternoon at Watchfield disused airfield in Wiltshire, where the band play at the relocated Windsor 4 Free Festival. This sees Dave Greenfield's Stranglers debut. Stage time is set for 5p.m. Their reception and set list is lost in the mists of time.

November '75. Stranglers gigs include the Nashville Rooms, the Windsor Castle pub, the Railway Arms, Redhill, Surrey (affectionately called The Nob) , the Cart & Horses in London, the Target Club in Reading, the New River Arms, Turnford, Hertfordshire, and last, but by no means least, the legendary Hope & Anchor in Islington. The Nashville, the Hope & Anchor and also the Red Cow in Hammersmith will be crucial to the band's development (and indeed many other bands. AC/DC's first ever UK gig is at the Red Cow). The Hope & Anchor is run by Fred Grainger, a fan of the band, and Dave Robinson. The latter was Jimi Hendrix's ex-roadie and a former manager of Brinsley Schwarz. He will go on to form Stiff Records with Jake Riviera. The Stranglers' first gig there is disappointing to say the least, as the audience consists of one man and his dog. Actually, that's a lie; he didn't have a dog. Legend has it that the band buy him his ale all night to persuade him to stay for the duration.

15th November '75. The first known bootleg recording of the band comes from the Redhill gig, recorded on a tape recorder belonging to Hugh Cornwell. Christened 'The Stranglers At The Nob', the set list included 'Peaches', 'Go Buddy Go', 'Choosey Susie' and cover versions such as 'Fun Fun Fun', 'Rock 'n' Roll Music' and a certain 'Walk On By'. There was 'If' too, made (in) famous by Telly Savalas, plus Slade's 'Flame' and the popular ditty 'I Saw Her Standing There', in which an early example of Hugh's witty wordplay is heard — 'I couldn't dance with her mother — oooh!'

21st December '75. Advertised as The start of a 25 year residency, The Stranglers play at the Hope & Anchor, watched by Chas de Whalley, a freelance journalist with the *New Musical Express*. The turnout is a marked improvement since their last gig there as there are six people watching, including Chas. He likes what he hears and so writes a very positive review. Consequently, Albion ask him to write a promotional leaflet for the band; he duly obliges: '... all the punk poise of the original Electric Prunes, the acid ingenuity of the early Doors, tempered with the dark twentieth century gothic horror of Lou Reed's classic Velvet Underground.' High praise indeed. The Stranglers have plenty of quality acts to keep them company at the Hope & Anchor, with Graham Parker & The Rumour, Dr Feelgood, The Steve Gibbons Band, The 101'ers and The Kursaal Flyers all appearing regularly. Many bands stayed there for the night too, and the mighty Phil Lynott often dossed there.

4 1976: THE STRANGLERS BURN UP TIME

The band play over 200 gigs this coming year, few of them passing without incident. They suffer plenty of concert misfortune too, due to old/faulty equipment and the county of Kent. Why Kent? Well, Kent is the most frequent setting for their mishaps, as if ley lines there cause instruments to falter or the ice cream van to break down. And when they do manage to perform, they often don't get paid or are told to get out of town unless they play something the punters knew. Objects being thrown at them, bar tables for example, aren't a rarity either.

On a more positive note, devoted fans are starting to emerge. One such gig-regular is a late-20s lad called Dave, quickly nicknamed by Hugh as 'Dagenham Dave'. His girlfriend Brenda, an illustrator, would also be renamed, as Bren Gun. Dave hails from Manchester but having worked at Ford's motor plant in Dagenham, gains the new moniker. Clearly smitten with the band, they hold him in high esteem too. A scaffolder by trade, but also a well read, intelligent and entertaining rogue never short of a few quid to buy his favourite band drinks. And he isn't afraid of aggression, or of upsetting people with his forthright views. There are, it could be said, distinct similarities between himself and the band. He isn't the only tough lad around, a certain set of lively individuals from Finchley take strongly to The Stranglers' music too.

The Albion Agency men are working very well for the band, helping them acquire higher-profile gigs as the sweaty year of 1976 steams on. The Stranglers support a fair few more-established acts as well as being backed themselves too, with The Vibrators and John Mellor's (that's Joe Strummer to you) band the 101'ers appearing occasionally on the same bill. The London pub rock scene has been buzzing, so many quality acts popping up around the capital, and The Stranglers cause more commotion than most, and that includes the Pistols. Out amongst the audiences watching The Stranglers on a pretty regular basis are stars in the making such as Glen Matlock, Steve Jones and Paul Cook, and future Pretenders front person Chrissie Hynde. Paul Cook isn't shy of asking Jet Black for tips on percussion, while Ms Hynde is quoted as saying she will become the lead singer for The Stranglers one day – the band tell her they don't even need her as a roadie!

Song-wise, 1976 sees the premiere of the band's epic 'Down In The Sewer', one of their most popular tracks ever. Also during this period, Hugh Cornwell and JJ Burnel often wear make-up on stage, primarily eyeliner – nothing too Alice Cooper or Sweet-esque. Artist Kevin Sparrow causes furore with his poster advertising the gigs at the Hope & Anchor – underneath a large photograph of a murdered woman lying on the ground runs the legend 'Fact: Stranglers seen leaving 3.00 a.m. with 17-year-old nympho schoolgirl!' Nowadays such a design would be banned before the ink had even dried. Note: it has been said the poster features one of the Boston Strangler's victims, but that is unconfirmed.

January '76. Stranglers gigs virtually every night, taking in more than a dozen venues, sometimes two different ones in a single night. These include the Speakeasy, Ronnie Scott's (Upstairs At Ronnie's) in London W1, the Duke Of Lancaster in New Barnet and the Alhambra in Brighton, as well as the regular stints at the Red Cow and Hope & Anchor.

February '76. Fewer gigs, but eight different venues including Camden Lock's Dingwalls, a couple of colleges and a club in Leicester called the Freewheeler. On Sunday 29th the band play two gigs, their customary Hope & Anchor residency, plus the Roundhouse which is said to be their first major gig, with Deaf School, Nasty Pop and Jive Bombers. The Stranglers, however, walk off after just one song due to the PA system cutting out. Thankfully there are no repercussions as the venue's regular promoter, John Curd, is a fan.

March '76. In addition to playing over a dozen different venues, The Stranglers spend a few mid-March days at Foel Studios in mid-Wales recording new demos of 'Peaches', 'Bitching', 'Tomorrow Was (The Hereafter)' and a fledgling 'Down In The Sewer', but without the grand finale. The studio and sessions are run by Ian Gomm, former Brinsley Schwarz guitarist and all round good bloke. The Stranglers are the first clients at the new studio, and Gomm does them a freebie as Dai Davies knows the Brinsley's of old. The ice cream van breaks down on their return to London.

On the gigs front, pubs, colleges, the Nashville and the Marquee are played, and the Red Cow and Hope & Anchor slots as usual. Confusion exists over the official date the band is supported by debutantes The Vibrators, but 11

March 1976 seems favourite. John Ellis, a founder Vibrator, recalls – 'The first time I met The Stranglers was at the very first Vibrators gig. We had only been playing together for two weeks, but I got us a gig at Hornsey College of Art supporting them. I think there were about four people in the audience. I didn't take much note of them. We were busy doing our thing, getting the gear in and out etcetera. We usually got on well with them. There was always a little bit of argy bargy between bands, mostly good humoured'.

23rd March '76. The Stranglers play at the Nashville, along with the Sex Pistols.

27th March '76. Recording and mixing demos in Pebble Beach studio in Worthing. This costs £1,000, and is funded by Bell Records' Andrew Bailey. The tracks are 'Go Buddy Go' and 'Bitching', reportedly re-recorded for United Artists on 22 July too.

April '76. Only twelve gigs this month, but the band are spreading their wings to such far flung outposts of the empire as Rebecca's in Birmingham, the Raven Hotel (apt name) in Corby and the Boat Club in Nottingham.

13th April '76. Two sets at London's Speakeasy, 10.30p.m. and 1.30 a.m.

May '76. 'Heatwave Britain' and the band slog through nineteen gigs in eighteen different venues in the South and Midlands, including one at the Grey Topper in a little place called Jacksdale, Nottinghamshire. Despite being a small village, the Topper puts on many top gigs, recounted in the superb *The Palace And The Punks* by Tony Hill. Not just up and coming bands like The Stranglers (who play 'Great Balls Of Fire' in their set) but established names like The Sweet, Mud, Bay City Rollers, Hot Chocolate, Ben E. King, Geno Washington, and Desmond Decker and Jimmy Cliff (on the same weekend), as well as Judas Priest and Saxon.

1st May '76: At Purley Halls, a private function held by Young Conservatives, someone has the jolly corking wheeze of hiring The Stranglers. Prior to their set, Jet announces, 'Listen, you're not going to like us so you may as well fuck off now.' For the only time in my life, it actually makes me wish I'd been a (very) young Tory, so I could have witnessed the event. The audience of over 300 rapidly decreases to fewer than ten.

16th & 17th May '76. The Stranglers support Patti Smith, an eye-catching coup if ever there was one. Kris Needs of *ZigZag* saw most of it: 'The minute I entered the old engine shed I was aware that something far different and 100 times more exciting was going down. There were these two depraved looking geezers hacking dementedly at their guitars, while a bearded character with a plaited ponytail coolly produced unbelievable soaring melodies from a battered Hammond organ. Holding this avalanche of lunatic genius together was a thickset drummer who behaved more like he was hammering the roof on a garden shed – occasionally standing up for added force. They built to an awesome climax then stopped suddenly. A short gap. The guitarist announces a number called 'Down In The Sewer', and they career into a song about making it with rats. I was absolutely stunned...'

Reports concerning the Patti Smith support slot say that on the first night the band are met with a hostile audience reaction which carries over into the second night. Until that was, they played 'Tits', their less than subtle homage to ... well, tits – pretty obvious really. The audience realise that much of the material is nowhere near as heavy as they'd assumed and, in fact, is often tongue-in-cheek irreverence. According to Jet Black, the night is the turning point of their career. Around the time of their sound check, Hugh Cornwell meets actor Adam 'Batman' West who is in the same building doing promotional work for the great Tony Wilson's Granada TV show *So It Goes*. Hugh tries to persuade West to join the band on stage during the gig, dressed in his full Batman regalia. Alas, Mr West isn't allowed, though he is up for it. In Hugh's *A Multitude Of Sins*, there is a suggestion that the famous thespian had some kind of white powder around his nose.

Afterwards, a worse for wear Joe Strummer declares his absolute love for Patti Smith and makes a bit of a tit of himself. Good to know it happens to the best of them too. The 101'ers had performed on the same bill and Joe implores Cornwell and Burnel to tell him why his band isn't as good as theirs. Regardless of whatever answers he got, Strummer will do just fine, forming the Clash soon after.

22nd May '76. At Kettering Central Hall, the band support Ricky Valance. Yes, Ricky Valance of 'Tell Laura I Love Her' fame; how many Ricky Valances do you know?

3rd June '76. The Stranglers work on two new demos in the Riverside Studios in Chiswick, namely 'Grip' and 'Peasant In The Big Shitty'.

17th June '76. The band feature in the Midsummer Music Festival at Walthamstow Assembly Hall, appearing with Ian Dury & The Kilburns, and the Sex Pistols. Garry Coward-Williams, roadie-ing for the band as well as photographing, recalls the admission price was 90p and that fewer than 30 people show their faces. Quite an average gig apparently, the most excitement being when Hugh nearly gets electrocuted from a faulty microphone. How shocking (sorry, couldn't resist!).

25th June '76. At the Three Rabbits pub, coins are incessantly chucked by the unappreciative audience. Still, that nets the band about a fiver from the projectile pennies.

4th July '76. As well as a five night stretch at the Hope & Anchor, The Stranglers perform at the Roundhouse supporting The Ramones and The Flamin' Groovies in a Fourth of July American bicentennial commemorative concert. This is 'da bruvvers' first ever UK date (possibly their first European date period).

5th July '76 – The Dingwalls Incident. The following night, at Dingwalls it's the same bill, but a much smaller venue. Dingwalls has been described as more like a Wild West saloon than a respected London venue, and certain events after the gig help add to that image. Because they admit to having smoked dope rather than doing the more fashionable speed/uppers and the like, it seems The Stranglers aren't really 'in' with the punk fraternity. And having a keyboardist with a moustache (canyoufuckingbelieveit?) doesn't help either. Tonight, The Stranglers support the Flamin' Groovies and the Ramones again. After their slot, Joe Strummer congratulates Hugh on the band's performance just as events are turning sour. According to No Mercy, Dagenham Dave coerces JJ Burnel in to drinking two bottles of red wine in quick succession; JJ did not drink much alcohol, so therefore feels the effects.

Consequently, an under-the-influence JJ lurches past Steve Jones and Paul Cook from the Sex Pistols and Paul Simonon from the Clash. Simonon spits on the ground and JJ thinks he is spitting at him, which apparently isn't the case, it's just a habit he has at the time. AConsequently, JJ sticks one on Simonon who, along with Jones and Cook jumps on top of JJ. All three are unceremoniously bundled out of the place by the bouncers. Outside in the car park it gets more serious, a face-off between The Stranglers' entourage and a hotchpotch of Clash and Pistols folk and ... Chrissie Hynde, while an innocent Simonon and a drunk Burnel take centre stage. Johnny Rotten makes a derogatory comment and so Dagenham Dave (or it might have been Dave Greenfield, though he is normally quite a peaceful guy) slams him against a van door. That commotion seems to ease the tension and no actual fisticuffs occur. Meanwhile, Hugh watches the proceedings from the inside of the ice cream van with a girl he's been chatting up. With the Finchley Boys in tow, this is a one-sided contest and Team Stranglers are triumphant, though they are not best popular with the Pistols and the Clash thereafter.

TIME FLIES

June 2010, riding his cherished Triumph Scrambler near Swiss Cottage, JJ Burnel encounters another Triumph biker, this time a black Bonneville. They meet at traffic lights and compliment each other's choice of motorcycle. JJ then thinks he recognises the other man and asks if he is called Paul Simonon. Indeed he is. They shake hands and then the lights change and they're off. It has only taken them 34 years to press the flesh.

30th July '76. The band play a concert for inmates of Chelmsford Prison, an event not well known in rock history, probably because it was The Stranglers and not the *pioneering* Sex Pistols who didn't actually play there until September (but to much more acclaim). Not that The Stranglers are being completely ignored, there are journalists taking notice ... Chas De Whalley dubs them 'Punk Floyd', likening some of their material to Syd Barrett-influenced Pink Floyd.

August '76. Only eight gigs as the band are busy writing and rehearsing. Notable appearances are at the Nashville, and The Penthouse in Scarborough, while on August 17th – regarded as one of the seminal dates of the burgeoning British Punk 'movement' – the 100 Club. Another important part of the scene is Mark Perry's *Sniffin' Glue* fanzine, and August's edition (only its second) reports positively about the band: 'The group consists of a very straight looking drummer, who keeps a very sound beat throughout; an organist who looks like he's just come home from Woodstock; a bass player who looks like a Ramone and a singer/guitarist who just looks scruffy. Together they add up to one of the most original groups I've ever seen on the pub circuit.'

September '76. Similarly quiet, though, oddly enough, the band plays at a wedding in Southend-on-Sea on Saturday 4th. Meanwhile, record labels are sniffing around the growing-ever-hotter Punk/New Wave scene, with The Damned and Sex Pistols leading the race to be the first signed up. The Damned win that contest as Stiff Records sign them and the alleged first ever UK punk single, 'New Rose', soon follows in October. Meanwhile, EMI carry on 'umming and arring' about whether or not to sign the Pistols, but The Stranglers' situation isn't looking too gloomy, their reputation as a great live band – even if gigs are often beset by ropey equipment – is growing. One man in particular follows their progress with great interest: Andrew Lauder, head of United Artists' A&R. However, every time he's seen the band play, something has gone wrong with the equipment.

October '76. Dr Feelgood's third album for UA, *Stupidity*, enters the charts at No. 1. Being live rather than a studio album adds ammunition to the belief amongst some labels that such releases are a sure route to success (as well as being cheaper to produce). The Stranglers are busy on the live circuit again, and on Friday the 9th they play Roehampton Digby Stuart College, which is run by the local convent. They're also listed as playing the 'Village Disco' in Bournemouth.

1st October '76. The band drive to Liverpool to play the opening night of Eric's Club. Myth has it that the Sex Pistols play on the same night with them. It is, however, just a myth.

10th October '76. The Stranglers perform at the Nashville, with the gig recorded and thus becoming one of their earliest ever bootlegs. They play as a tight unit and even the poor quality of the recording can't disguise how good they are. Hugh Cornwell keeps his sardonic repartee to a minimum, probably because he knew it was being recorded and he needed to be politer than normal. After the first song he tells the audience 'It's our first Saturday night here'. Set list: 'Grip', 'Sometimes', 'Bitching',

'Peasant In The Big Shitty', 'Hanging Around', 'Peaches', 'Ugly', 'London Lady', 'Down In The Sewer', 'Walk On By' and finished with a seven minute long 'Go Buddy Go'.

23rd October '76. In the days following, The Damned's classic debut single 'New Rose' is released, The Stranglers support Patti Smith again, twice at Hammersmith Odeon and once at Birmingham Odeon. With luck, Ms Smith will have known they were called The Stranglers by now, and not The *Strangers*. *Sounds'* Jonh [sic] Ingham's contrary review (30th October 1976) of the Saturday night Hammersmith gig: 'They were much improved from my last experience of them, and there is a lot in their playing, particularly Jet Black's drumming, to recommend them, but I find the Doors reference tedious and the subject matter of their songs uninteresting. Still, as each number started I could remember the whole tune; having only heard them once, it says something for staying power'. The gig is recorded and the set list is 'Grip'; 'Sometimes', 'Bitching', 'Peasant In The Big Shitty', 'Hanging Around', 'Peaches', 'Ugly', 'Down In The Sewer' and 'Go Buddy Go'. It's clear that a few keen Stranglers fans are there, and Patti Smith fans respond to every track with polite applause also.

November '76. By late November, The Stranglers have played another mix of venues, including the Marquee, the Valley Football Club in Redditch, Bradford University (where JJ Burnel studied a few years before), Newcastle Poly, Teesside Poly, and universities in Bangor, Manchester and Glasgow.

14th November 1976. Torrington Arms gig, Woodside Park, London. A dozen or so wild looking lads arrive before the gig, as Hugh and JJ stand at the bar, suddenly suspecting they're going to get chinned. But the motley collection of young men is there to *watch* The Stranglers, not to assault them. And so the relationship begins between the band and the Finchley Boys. According to the Finchley crew, The Stranglers were the first ever band to not back down in the face of their 'intimidating' audience tactics. The next day, the band play at Oxford Poly as support to The Flamin' Groovies, along with The Vibrators and The Damned. Two nights later they play the Nashville, supported by Chelsea, and on the last night of the month, the 100 Club again.

17th November '76. At the band's Bradford Polytechnic gig, there's some trouble. JJ Burnel tells Leeds' *New Pose* fanzine, '… some idiot chucked the glass, it shattered over a couple of girls at the front and went over us y'know so we found him afterwards and beat the shit out of him. Cos he was an idiot'.

18th November '76 – Fforde Grene Hotel, Leeds. One lucky Leeds teenager, Steve Flanagan, went to the gig with his mates:

> The band introduced themselves in joke Hovis-style northern accents as being 't'Stranglers from t'London' then went straight in to the fantastic 'Grip', speedily followed by 'Ugly', 'Bitching', 'London Lady' and 'School Mam' dedicated by Hugh Cornwell 'to the 250 million students in Leeds', during which he rubbed

his neck vigorously for a while before dribbling saliva. 'Hanging Around' was voted the best number of the set by my drinking partners but the encore 'Go Buddy Go' was also brilliant. Getting an encore at the Fforde Grene was a real achievement, as the vast majority of the regulars were denim clad tossers hoping to catch the next Wishbone Ash. In fact, my main memory of the evening was of one such slob requesting that the band 'Fuck off'. Jean-Jacques Burnel challenged him to come up to the stage, with a genuine menace which he was clearly prepared to back up when he unhitched his bass guitar, ready to wrap it round someone's head.

30th November '76. The 100 Club. On the bill with The Stranglers are Clemen Pull and Lee Kosmin Band. Quite a crowd, including Dagenham Dave and a load of the Finchleys. Dave joined in with some of the pogoing the Finchleys had been undertaking, but it descends into serious violence. It's said that Dave outfought eight, maybe even more, of the Finchley Boys, before finally giving in. He is hospitalised with broken ribs and cuts and bruises, but his pride is hurt more. The fight convinces him he is being forced out of The Stranglers 'family'. The band play on during the fighting, though JJ implores them to stop. Soon after his release from hospital, the band visit Dave at his flat near Lancaster Gate to see how he's recuperating, but when his relationship with girlfriend Brenda comes to an end – she leaves him – he sinks into a deep depression.

December '76. Kris Needs in *ZigZag* mag sums up The Stranglers' year perfectly in the November issue: 'In a year of solid gigging in the Smoke they've built a fanatical following with their rancid brand of manic rock ... The Stranglers' untamed originality is a force 9 gale of bad breath which could knock the already battered music scene into a cocked hat...' Although the increasing publicity is welcome, it is likely that the Pistols' outrageous appearance on Bill Grundy's *Today* TV programme on the 1st of this month helps the cause of most punk/new wave bands.

4th December '76. The Stranglers play in a UA rehearsal room in a private session for Andrew Lauder. And because the equipment actually works, Lauder finally finds out for himself how good the band are.

6th December '76. United Artists sign the band. Such controversy! The *Evening Standard* runs the headline '£40,000 contract for another punk group' while Lauder receives abusive phone calls from musicians outraged that more 'talentless punks' have jumped the queue for pop success (Lauder is known as a bit of a hippy at this time having signed Hawkwind, Can and Man). UA's initial plans for the band are to make their debut album a live one, undoubtedly encouraged by the success of Dr Feelgood's *Stupidity* LP. The Stranglers' joy at having been signed at last is however tempered by the news that Jet's ice cream van has coughed its last rev, the engine having seized up with the clock showing 77,000 miles travelled. R.I.P.

11th December '76. The band play at Aylesbury Friars club, Jet Black is hit by a glass bottle thrown from the audience and it smashes into numerous pieces. He carries on drumming unperturbed.

12th December '76. Officially, The Stranglers' first Scottish gig takes place at Tiffany's in Edinburgh on December 13th but they in fact appear tonight at Strathclyde University in Glasgow. Ian Gillan's band cancel so The Stranglers step in as replacements. You can well imagine how the gig went down, punters having forked out lots of that strange currency to see a well-known heavy rock band, but get a not well known 'punk' band instead. And one that goads them for liking heavy rock in the first place too, no doubt. The band end up barricading themselves in their dressing room afterwards whilst angry Jock fans try to beat a way in.

T-SHIRTS

Hugh Cornwell and JJ Burnel are regularly seen wearing specially designed t-shirts with amended versions of Ford Motors' blue & white logo on. And so 'Trotsky', 'Fuck' and reportedly even 'Truck' insignia in the Ford style often appear on their chests. Also quite common is a screen print of the pop artist Colin Self's 'Guard Dog on a Missile Base, No.1' design, plus a much less appealing image involving male genitalia wearing sunglasses.

5 1977: GETTING A GRIP ON THE CHARTS

In the year in which the two sevens clash, the great comedian Groucho Marx dies and no one laughs. Elvis Presley dies his ignoble death too and certainly some people do laugh. Marc Bolan dies and nobody notices because they are too busy laughing about Elvis. It was also the year Stranglers acolytes Alan Edwards and Tony Moon get together to produce *Strangled* mag, an excellent effort at keeping the band better in touch with the increasing number of followers. 1977 is the year too of the Silver Jubilee being rammed down our throats so we can all celebrate the Queen's health and prosperity, seeing as how she's led and looked after us all so well for 25 years. This year is yet another one of tremendous hard labour for The Stranglers too. Working and gigging virtually all the time, whilst trying to partake in the necessary 'evil' of grabbing media attention in an age where the old adage of there being no such thing as bad publicity certainly rings true in the music biz.

STRANGLED MAGAZINE

Strangled starts life in 1976 as Sideburns, founded by Tony Moon and friend Tony Cunningham, to cover lots of bands, not just The Stranglers. In fact, Moon is a bigger fan of Dr Feelgood. Incidentally, the famous quote 'This is a chord, this is another one, this is a third. Now go out and form a band!' comes from *Sideburns* and not, as has often been said, *Sniffin' Glue*.

January 1977. The idea of their debut album being a selection of live cuts is scrapped in favour of studio recordings made earlier in the month. Martin Rushent produces. Rushent has been a successful engineer for many artists from Stone The Crows to the Sensational Alex Harvey Band, but he has only produced a couple of albums prior to The Stranglers. The band take just two days to record their first single as well as enough material for the album plus some for the follow up, if there is to be one! Gigs include Maidenhead Skindles Hotel, Croydon's Red Deer, the Royal College of Art (along with The

Adverts), the Roxy Club in London with Cortinas supporting, and on the 30th they play at the Rainbow.

(Image courtesy of Duncan Round)

LES 'FRENCHIES'

The Roxy gig is filmed for French television, along with a brief interview with Frenchman Jean-Jacques Burnel. Top fan and journalist Anne-Marie Mondan of *Rock Interviews* translates: 'What do your songs talk about?' JJ: 'Oh, they talk about life, especially in London because we are Londoners, but they also talk ... there's one song about hitting your girlfriend, there is a song which says the Queen is all shit, because what's the Queen for, what the hell does she do? We don't think she's got anything to say. There are lots of things, political stuff now ... It means a lot of actions, lots of aggression of what needs to be attacked.' 'What needs to be attacked?' 'People's brains, they're too apathetic, they are too lethargic. They need shaking up now, because, especially here in England, they've done bugger all for years.' 'Do you like hippies?' 'No.' 'Do you like the Rolling Stones?' 'No'. 'Why?' 'Because they are ... a pleon, yeah that's it, they are ... they have nothing, no value in this world we're living in. They are the result of another period of time. They're dead, they're products of show business, they should be in the Folies Bergère!'

28th January '77. The vinyl birth of The Stranglers takes place with the startling debut single '(Get A) Grip (On Yourself)' backed with 'London Lady'. In the history of popular music, it's hard to find a more dynamic debut single ever. The mighty 'wall' of guitars is Martin Rushent's influence, while the inclusion of saxophone on 'Grip' is a mutually agreed idea which simply adds another layer of energy to the song. Playing the sax is Eric Clark, a Welsh miner friend of Dai Davies.

5th February '77. Tony Parsons' *NME* review: '... a stunning double-sided single of distinctive, intelligent, contemporary rock 'n' roll that sounds like Roxy Music would have if that old capped-tooth smoothie Bryan Ferry had been influenced by the Doors.'

THE DOORS

Hugh Cornwell isn't unhappy for the band to be compared with The Doors as he likes them a lot, especially Robbie Krieger's guitar work. That though is not an admission that The Stranglers have copied Jim Morrison and co, as he tells *Melody Maker*: 'I don't rush back after a gig and put on *Strange Days* for some new ideas to rip off. We do have the same line up as The Doors, but Dave had never heard of them until he met us. He was more into Yes and stuff like that'.

CON-VENTION

So what happened, why doesn't 'Grip' storm the charts? The public and media like it very much, after all. A few factors are involved but I don't think it's too unkind to blame the Germans, they have plenty to answer for and I don't just mean lederhosen. The disco group Silver Convention are German, and the fault lies with them or at least some associates, together with the organisations who compile and publish the charts, the British Market Research Bureau and *Music Week* (then called *Record Retailer*). Sales figures of the Silver Convention's disco single 'Everybody's Talkin' 'Bout Love' somehow get mixed up with those of 'Grip'. Their painful ditty goes to No.25 and charts for five weeks, while 'Grip' is hanging around for four weeks, peaking at just No.44, having sold over 15,000 copies by its second week. *Record Retailer* says sorry with a front page apology, but the damage has already been done, the initial momentum of the single has been derailed.

John Robb. 'Grip' certainly did grip, and inspire, the future punk icon, writer, journo and entertainer:

> Growing up in Blackpool I was floored by punk rock. It really connected with me. The thrill of the music, the look, the attitude, the politics: it all made total sense to my 16-year-old mind. The endless stream of bands and great singles made it an amazing time to be a teenager. But there was one band that really made a connection ... The Stranglers. The Stranglers were different. They were darker and more twisted, the music was more aggressive and yet it had a perverse, romantic feel to it.

30th January '77. As told by *Punk Diary*: 'The Stranglers are having trouble with the GLC [the Greater London Council} over everything from stage dress (and undress) to language ... Some members of the GLC Public Committee saw the band at the Croydon Red Deer and had restrictions written into their contract with the Rainbow, assuring that certain words 'would not appear on their apparel or over the amplifications while opening up for Climax Blues Band'.

In *No Mercy*: Jet describes events at the Rainbow gig – 'We got on stage and Hugh's got this Fuck t-shirt on which he'd been wearing for months, and to our utter astonishment some GLC inspector at the back of the venue happens to see it through his binoculars. He sent word to Dai Davies to tell him to get it off immediately, because it might provoke a riot. We're steaming away and our manager is crawling along the back of the stage on all-fours saying "Jet Jet Jet, tell Hugh he's got to get the t-shirt off immediately or they'll pull the power!" So Hugh puts it on back to front, then of course he turns around and they pull the switch!'

They can't however keep a good Strangler down ... the band hold 'secret' gigs under different names like 'The Old Codgers', 'The Shakespearos' and 'Bingo Nightly & The OAPs'.

1st February '77. The Stranglers' first ever gig on foreign soil (not counting Wales, Scotland or Tyneside) takes place in Germany at Hamburg's Market Halle. Chris Twomey's *The Men They Love To Hate* states gigs take place in France, Belgium and Holland as well, none of them to especially keen receptions, especially Hamburg, where only six people attend, four of whom are press, and still there are objects thrown at the band.

VIVE LA (PUNK) ROCK

In France a punk scene is already pretty well established, so it is almost inevitable the band would become popular there. More so with Jean-Jacques Burnel's presence. Anne-Marie Mondan says: 'Punk and new wave generally sprang from economic and political troubles, like high unemployment rates and low income in difficult situations. Some young people wanted to rebel, they were angry and against politics, they had no jobs, no money, no hope. When a context is like this, of course, musicians are here to think aloud what other people think quietly. And they write lyrics and play!' Typical of The Stranglers' journey though, they would still have to really graft to garner a big following there.

9th February '77. Truly terrible news – the suicide by drowning of Dagenham Dave. He jumps off London's Tower Bridge into the Thames.

12th February '77. The band play at Glasgow University's Queen Margaret Union. It's unlikely that even Hugh can remember precisely when he began to improvise on 'Peaches' and the 'worse places to be' line – but this gig is one of the first recorded examples. Set list and quotes from fan Chris Band:

'(Get A) Grip (On Yourself)'. 'Sometimes' (before which Cornwell advises, 'This is called "Sometimes", it's about beating up your girlfriend when she won't listen to anything'). 'Bitching',

'School Mam' (which segues dramatically in to 'Peasant In The Big Shitty'), 'Straighten Out', 'Hanging Around', 'Peaches (replacing the 'skewer' line with 'Or like being stuck in Aberdeen in a snowdrift'), 'Ugly', 'London Lady' and finally 'Down In The Sewer', the perfect finale.

13th February '77. A shortened bootleg recording also exists of this Miniqui Hall, Falkirk gig. Despite the tape's poor sound quality, there is no mistaking the tightness of the band. Their attitude towards the audience seems as aggressive as the songs, as if they're getting their retaliation in first. Recorded tracks are 'Something Better Change', 'London Lady', 'Hanging Around', 'I Feel Like A Wog' and 'Straighten Out'.

24th February '77. The Rock Garden gig in Middlesbrough is a good example of a hostile audience reception towards the band. Someone in the audience moans about a slight delay before 'Sometimes', prompting Jet Black to snarl, 'Shut up cunt, haven't you ever seen a broken string before?' Hugh Cornwell later berates the audience for being corpses glued to their chairs, unable/unwilling to dance; maybe Jet's friendly manner petrified them. Set list: 'Grip', 'Sometimes', 'Bitching', 'School Mam', 'Peasant In The Big Shitty', 'Straighten Out', 'Hanging Around', 'Ugly', 'London Lady', 'Sewer', 'Something Better Change', 'Go Buddy Go'.

1st March '77. The band's first ever session for John Peel's show on Radio 1, to be transmitted on March 7th. Tracks are 'Hanging Around', 'I Feel Like A Wog', 'Goodbye Toulouse' and 'Something Better Change'. It will be the first opportunity for many listeners to hear this disturbing band in what is a superb debut session. The Stranglers have worked so much to create the buzz, but Peel certainly helps increase the anticipation for their imminent first album.

In *The Peel Sessions* book, 'I saw them supporting Patti Smith at the Hammersmith Odeon and people were getting up and walking out, always a good sign', said Peel. The DJ knows the band aren't the finished article yet, commenting on constraints facing them while criticising Jon Anderson's prog rockers Yes at the same time in *Sounds' John Peel Column*, 'The Stranglers have the right idea and are struggling to find the technical skills necessary for the expressing of that idea, whereas Yes have no idea at all yet have awesome personal abilities and vast technical resources at their disposal for bringing this intellectual vacuum to the waiting millions'.

5th March '77. A gig at Manchester's Electric Circus venue. *NME* journo Paul Morley reviews it positively, adding: 'Skeletal framework, very monochrome, Burnel's bouncing screwball bass fights Black's brain cell pulping constant bash, Greenfield's keyboard spills all over the place, and Cornwell's guitar adds plenty of interference plus some sassy lead. Plus everything's CATCHY. It's ridiculous. At Manchester they didn't play 'Walk On By' or 'Go Buddy Go' but there was still so much good stuff'.

24 • PEACHES

Touring this month also takes in Birmingham Barbarellas, Huddersfield Polytechnic, Wolverhampton Lafayette, Hawick Town Hall, Wakefield Unity Hall, York University, Ulverston Penny Farthing and Liverpool C.F. Mott College, amongst others. And on 16th March they're at the Affair in Swindon, with an unsubstantiated claim that local boys XTC support.

A prized possession: an autographed membership card to The Electric Circus. (*Image courtesy of Duncan Round*)

NUDE SHOCKER

April 1977 sees reporter Chas De Whalley appearing in all his glory in *Sounds*, dekegged (a.k.a. 'debagged'). These journalists eh, always trying to make headlines! Well, you know what I mean. The Stranglers are the guilty reporter-strippers, for reasons not entirely clear.

1st April '77. The Stranglers play Leeds Polytechnic, supported by another up and coming band advertised as 'The Jams'. Wonder if it was a case of The Stranglers 'Kick Out The Jams'?

7th April '77. The band are recorded by the BBC playing live at the Paris Theatre, London.

15th April '77. *Rattus Norvegicus*, the band's debut album, is released. And so it all really begins.

1977: GETTING A GRIP ON THE CHARTS

RATVERTISING

Naturally UA are hell bent on heavily promoting their dangerous new, not-really-punk artistes, and their ingenious advertising campaign perfectly complements the spirit of Punk. With a hint of reverse psychology which parasites like Saatchi & Saatchi would have been proud of, their advertisements utilise both negative and positive vibes, almost as if they were saying 'Here's our latest album, like it or fucking lump it'. Full page ads use various press quotes such as, 'a Force Nine Gale of Bad Breath' (Kris Needs, *ZigZag*); 'When was the last time you heard an angry psychedelic band?' (Giovanni Dadomo, *Sounds*); 'Stopping them is going to be about as easy as playing yoyo with a bulldozer' (*Album Tracking*); 'Their music is taut, intelligent and infectious' (Barry Cain, *Record Mirror*); 'Known in some quarters as Bullshitters of the first order.' (Chas de Whalley, *Album Tracking*); 'Make no mistake about it, these guys are going to make records that will be played till they wear out.' (Phil McNeill, *NME*), and 'They even smoke dope' and 'They're erudite, intelligent - just a little pretentious' from Mick Brown of *Sounds*. Also 'The Stranglers are colourfully outrageous and their music is amazing.' (Bob Hart, *The Sun*); 'Too middle class to be punks,' (Mick Brown, *Sounds*) and 'Spouting nihilistic kindergarten polemics,' (Phil McNeill, *NME*).

STRANGLERS IV – RATTUS NORVEGICUS
Released: 15th April 1977.
Label: United Artists Records.
Charted at No.4
Side One: 1 'Sometimes', 2 'Goodbye Toulouse', 3 'London Lady', 4 'Princess Of The Streets', 5 'Hanging Around'.
Side Two: 1 'Peaches', 2 '(Get A) Grip (On Yourself)', 3 'Ugly', 4 'Down In The Sewer' (a) 'Falling', (b) 'Down In The Sewer', (c) 'Trying To Get Out Again', (d) 'Rats Rally'.

In a few words – what the *Ford* are the songs about? Part 1
'Sometimes': About an ex-girlfriend (Cathy) of Hugh Cornwell's who was unfaithful to him; they argued and he slapped her. The aggression in the song refers to the atmosphere at many of the band's gigs too.
'Goodbye Toulouse': Relates to a Nostradamus prediction about the demise of Toulouse, France, said to be sited on a fault line and with a nuclear reactor nearby too. Written by Burnel, sung by Cornwell.
'London Lady': Burnel being indiscreet about a one night stand with a certain female music journo, when there was a lot of 'loose flesh' around; it contains drug references as well.

'Princess Of The Streets': Burnel singing his woes about a former girlfriend, his first love. In the original version there was one more verse existed, sung a cappella, but it was left out of the recording.

'Hanging Around': Co-written by Burnel and Cornwell, about inner-city life and gigging and socialising in the Nashville, and 'codes' in the late lamented gay bar the Coleherne in the Earl's Court Road. Gary Coward-Williams and Duncan Doughnuts feature too.

'Peaches': Lusty lyrics about women's bottoms and men's letching on beaches towards said bottoms. Controversial but it could have been worse, they could have called it 'Arses'.

'(Get A) Grip (On Yourself)': A general comment on what was happening around the band, playing music but earning so little it felt like they were being punished and suffering for their art.

'Ugly': Another experimental song about women from Burnel singing 'in character'.

'Down In The Sewer': An epic tale of rats' survival paralleled with that of the band's struggles. The sewer is London, the rats are the band and people they met whilst gigging who picked up lots of sexually transmitted diseases. The lyrics are from outsiders' perspective, with a few drugs references too.

Notable songs of the time not on the vinyl album:

'Go Buddy Go': A little ditty written by the then schoolboy Burnel, a self-explanatory story about a party and a pal, called Bob, the chords of the chorus heavily influenced by Hendrix's 'Hey Joe' and the middle eight from Hugh added later.

'Choosey Susie': A former girlfriend of JJ's, the same lady as featured in 'Princess Of The Streets'.

○

RATTUS 'TAILS'

The album is originally going to be called *Dead On Arrival* and the planned release date brought forward by a month. The title *Rattus Norvegicus*, Latin for the brown rat, comes about thanks to UA's art director Paul Henry unearthing a dazzling image of a rat silhouetted against a glorious orange sunset. The Rat has been the prominent insignia of The Stranglers ever since. On the album cover, the 'IV' was added to the band name just to confuse the public. Chas De Whalley in *Sounds* (16th April 1977) gives the LP a very healthy four out of five stars. Kris Needs' review in *ZigZag* (May 1977) is even more glowing: 'They've come a long way since I first saw them supporting Patti Smith a year ago. All that untamed potential has been refined and channelled into yet another of the year's great debut albums...and what a great year for debut albums!'

Producer Martin Rushent sums up the malevolent persona of the LP: 'There was something sinister and evil about the band that I didn't want to hide. Whether that was real or whether they were putting it on, I don't know. But it seemed to work. Their songs used to spit at you and I wanted that to come across ... I thought if it was all tarted up in echoes and flashy production techniques it would dilute the impact. I wanted the record to sound dirty, aggressive and subversive.'

John Robb's review of *Rattus Novegicus*:

Belligerent, nasty and over the top ... Fantastic! The album cover is also perfect, a movie like picture of these strange looking people, with make-up on, that made them look even stranger and harder and freakier. Side One is stuffed with short, sharp shock songs – 'Sometimes' neo jazz belligerence, 'London Lady''s riffing action, 'Princess Of The Streets' bellicose howl and 'Hanging Around''s euphoric pop, great hooks and snarling attitude.

Side Two builds and builds from the almost conventional 'Grip' to the jagged bass line of 'Peaches'. Hugh smirks his way through 'Peaches' and that curious enunciation of 'clitoris – no one even knew what a clitoris was in those far off days, when men were apes and boys were confused chimps.

The next track is the dark and violently strange 'Ugly', a seething mash up of this insane riff and JJ's mental acid trip that saw a free association of lyrics about class and girls and, bizarrely, Ozymandias. When 'Ugly' ends you'd hold your breath for the opening salvo of 'Down In The Sewer', a perfect depiction of city life in decaying Britannia where buildings look like open sewers. It is social commentary but instead of making everything a checklist of punk clichés they sang about running as rats in a decaying sewer. The band are the ultimate rat pack, hunch-shouldered in their gang and doing their rat walk on stage over a seething backbeat.

The glorious twanging guitar solo still sounds as soaring and effortlessly brilliant as it did the first time I thrilled to it. The intro itself would have been enough to make a full song for most bands but The Stranglers weren't finished yet, there was that insane mid-section with the zigzag bass riff that was yet another masterpiece from Burnel. It built the foundations for Hugh's sneering vocal and those weird sound effects of rats' chattering teeth and sewer sounds and the song's general psychedelia, building up to the return of the twanging guitar section and then the end, Dave Greenfield's rolling keyboards of 'Rats Rally', one of the greatest keyboard sections in the history of rock 'n' roll. Greenfield is easily the best ever keyboard player in UK music, technically brilliant but never backing off from a tune. You just want 'Rats Rally' to go on forever!

17th April '77. The Stranglers play the Roundhouse. *The Guardian* covers it : 'Outside, a crowd of several hundred trying to get in, and inside startled GLC officials eyeing the latest punk ladies' fashions of a transparent plastic mac and very little else. All this for a band no one had heard of until a couple of months ago but who now have a big fat recording contract and advance sales of 15,000 on their first album ...'

Set list and comments from fan Chris Band:

> 'Dagenham Dave' (Hugh introduces this new song, a tribute, 'This is a dedication to a friend ... It's about a black guy who was a bit over the top in every respect, he just couldn't find anything in life to make him hold his interest so he committed suicide about six weeks ago, threw himself off Tower Bridge and they found him in the Thames about four weeks later. So this is a little reminder to ya').'School Mam', 'Peasant In The Big Shitty' (this rattles along at quite a pace, frantic psychedelia anyone?), 'Straighten Out', 'No More Heroes' (which Cornwell describes as their latest song 'Whatever Happened To The Heroes'), 'Peaches' (including the adjustment of '... like being stuck outside the Roundhouse ... trying to get in without a ticket'), 'I Feel Like A Wog' (which Cornwell explains is '... about victimisation, that's the name of the game in this country), 'Hanging Around', 'Ugly' (JJ Burnel really goes for it on the delivery with this, virtually screaming the lyrics out at times, it's ultra-intense), 'London Lady', 'Sewer', 'Grip', 'Something Better Change'.

(*Image courtesy of Duncan Round*)

18th to 30th April '77. Not all the gigs actually happen, but the band has been scheduled to play a total of nine dates, including Paris, Helsinki and Geneva. They do play the Petit Theatre in Le Havre on the 20th.

1977: GETTING A GRIP ON THE CHARTS

23rd April '77. The transmission date of the band's appearance at the Paris Theatre, London, supporting Dave Edmunds' Rockpile. It's *BBC Radio 1's In Concert* and six tracks are broadcast: 'Sometimes' ('This is a song about male and female violence when words don't mean anything anymore,' explains Hugh), 'Dagenham Dave' ('... an epitaph for a friend), 'Peaches' ('...worse places to be, like sitting in a disused cinema', which indeed the theatre was), 'I Feel Like A Wog', Straighten Out', 'London Lady'.

The Stranglers have another date with the BBC this month for *The Old Grey Whistle Test* television programme. The 'appearance' though is in fact a hastily arranged video clip. A school of thought (well, two of us) being that 'Whispering' Bob Harris was 'bricking It' as he was scared of Punk/New Wave bands and that the invitation to The Stranglers was rescinded at short notice, but that is purely a theory. Mind you, the month previously Harris had nearly been beaten up by some of the Sex Pistols' chums at the Speakeasy, but was saved by Procol Harum's road crew, who happened to be drinking there. Perhaps they came to poor Bob's aid when they saw him turn 'A Whiter Shade Of Pale'? We shouldn't joke, because Harris' pal George was actually glassed, so Harris wasn't going to be best disposed to all things punk.

RATTUS SALES

Rattus Norvegicus sells outstandingly well, exploding onto the album charts with more vigour than a particularly substantial projectile vomit. Its chart performance is better than probably anyone had realistically hoped for, even though The Damned and Clash's debut albums had reached No.36 and No.12 respectively. With this, The Stranglers haven't necessarily needed to use gimmicks, a new trend in selling vinyl, but, regardless, one is provided in the form of a free single with 10,000 copies of *Rattus*: 'Choosey Susie' b/w a live version of 'Peasant In The Big Shitty', in a gaudy orange and (annoyingly) plain card picture sleeve. By the first week of May, the album is the fourth bestselling in the UK. The Stranglers are in the esteemed company of Abba, The Shadows and the Eagles, having sold over 30,000 albums in approximately three weeks. More astonishing is that it reaches No. 46 in the charts after less than two full days' sales figures AND a bomb scare at EMI's distribution centre - where UA records are distributed from - to delay its initial shipping.

6th May '77. Their new single 'Peaches' and 'Go Buddy Go' is out today. Hopes are that it will have the same impact on the charts which 'Grip' should rightly have had. The version of 'Peaches' on *Rattus* is too graphic for release as a single (you simply cannot say 'shit' on a record, though you can obviously release shit records, as many have proved) and so a sanitised version is recorded for the single. Even then, it would seem that the rulers of the pop world – the disc jockeys – are generally loath to play it. Fortunately, 'Go Buddy Go' is popular too, so that gets good airplay. The single will feature for fourteen weeks in the charts, peaking at No.8 and selling more than a quarter of a million copies. The Sex Pistols' 'God Save The Queen' is out around this time too, while another radically different and subversive act hit the charts for the first time as well, outselling and outplacing The Stranglers in fact. They all should have teamed up, it would have made classic entertainment, The Stranglers, Pistols … and The Muppets!

Rats on the move. May sees The Stranglers on the road with The *Rattus Norvegicus* Tour – also billed as 'Rats On The Road' – at venues in London, Edinburgh, Canterbury, Cardiff, Paris, Guildford and Bournemouth. The tabloids, never a beast to worry about causing the British public to soil itself or splutter their cornflakes over the breakfast table by printing scandal and outrage, are still enjoying the hideous infestation of Punk Rock. It works too, with various bands suffering gig cancellations imposed by local authorities who believed the media's misreporting of horrendous violence at concerts.

14th May '77. The *NME*'s 'TS' reviews 'Peaches' and 'Go Buddy Go', not very kindly or indeed accurately, with a barely veiled accusation that the band are charlatans and fake punks and the songs being rip offs of The Downliners Sect and Chuck Berry. Meantime, the cleaned up pressing of 'Peaches' somehow implies that the band are meekly conforming to the 'system' they despise.

14th May '77. The band play tonight at Edinburgh's Herriot-Watt University. Ali Macdonald attended and Stranglers fan Donald Mackay got his impressions:

> It wasn't a big venue, with about 400 people there … It was just a wee hall with a stage at chest level. The Stranglers was the hottest, sweatiest gig I've ever been at. I was three rows from the front, slightly on Hugh's side [the right as you look at the stage] and we were just bouncing about. There was a lot of pogoing – you couldn't not! The two frontmen really stood out for me, Jean-Jacques Burnel and Hugh Cornwell to the fore with their guitars, moving around. Cornwell did most of the vocals, though they both sang. The crowd was familiar with the songs, with 'Peaches' and 'Grip' the stand out tracks on the night, as well as 'Hanging Around'. It was quite a short set actually, probably a good thing as you couldn't possibly survive all that sweating for three hours!

19th May '77. At Coventry's Tiffany's, tired of one individual in the crowd throwing beer cans at him, and having ignored his request to stop it, JJ Burnel jumps off the stage to smack the culprit in the face.

26th May '77. The Stranglers' first ever appearance on *Top Of The Pops*, fondly remembered by fans for their comically bad miming to 'Go Buddy Go' and the suitably yob like Burnel and Cornwell swapping their bass and lead guitars respectively.

28th May '77. At the Canterbury Odeon, fans queuing for the gig are hassled by 50 or so local thugs. JJ recalled the incident in *No Mercy* – 'So myself, a Hell's Angel and Dennis Marks from the Finchleys went out and confronted them. I went berserk and went for them with a mike stand and initially they all backed off. But when they realised there were only three of us they started getting stuck in. By that time a few Finchley Boys had come out of the hall

31 • 1977: GETTING A GRIP ON THE CHARTS

to help us and eventually it all broke up. But I remember one of the Finchleys telling me that a guy was just about to stab me in the back and he just managed to stop him'.

29th May '77. Trouble at their Guildford Civic Hall gig where fans wreck £700 worth of seating. It might have been something to do with Cornwell mentioning that they had wanted the seats removing beforehand so the fans could enjoy the gig more. Anyway, they are banned as a consequence.

June '77. Their appointment diary contains plenty of alterations and crossings out due to the 'Punk paranoia' of local authorities cancelling scheduled gigs – like in Torquay, Leeds, and Blackburn for instance. They did play the famous Wigan Casino on the 4th, and the gig at Glasgow's City Halls takes place too, descending into a 'disastrous riot' according to Martin Kielty's *Apollo Memories*, due to vindictive bouncers getting overly physical with audience members.

6th June '77. The Manchester Electric Circus is a great gig. The band is TIGHT and the bass especially has not only loudness but real meat to it too. Set list: 'Grip' (a haymaker of an opener), 'Yeah, fucking hell yeah!' shouts someone in the crowd), 'Sometimes', 'I Feel Like A Wog' (with Hugh Cornwell's intro, '... it's about intimidation, you probably know all about that up here in Manchester'), 'Dagenham Dave' (Cornwell says Dave was from Manchester and 'one of the greatest blokes you could meet'), 'School Mam', 'Peasant In The Big Shitty' (what anyone thought of the maniacal vocalist Dave on hearing this for the first time would have been 'interesting'!), 'Peaches', 'No More Heroes' – '... about being your own hero'), 'Hanging Around', 'Straighten Out' (Hugh says to the sound crew, 'Can we have more vocals on the fucking mic, I can't hear a fucking thing up here'. He then coolly responds to an audience question – 'Yeah we're London and proud of it'), 'London Lady', 'Sewer', 'Ugly'(arrives with a slap to the chops and carries on assaulting the senses, JJ Burnel's voice isn't meant to be pretty after all). Final track is 'Something Better Change', a stunning anthem to get even the laziest off their arses.

9th June '77. Like indigestion, the band are repeated on Top Of The Pops with 'Go Buddy Go'.

23rd June '77 – 'Battle of Cleethorpes'. A dozen or so local dockers are fishily in attendance for the Winter Garden's gig. It becomes abundantly clear that they are there just to cause trouble, throwing missiles at The Stranglers and their support band London, as well as reportedly beating up at least one young woman in the audience. It all cumulates in The Stranglers, ably protected by the Finchley Boys – their unofficial security team – having a rare old set to with said stevedores ending in serious violence. Despite their cowardly antics, some of these Lincolnshire louts were genuine tough nuts, and even karate kid JJ Burnel struggles to make much impact on one man-mountain in particular. Legend has it that the Finchleys later have some t-shirts made to mark the occasion, bearing the words 'I Survived The Battle Of Cleethorpes'. The same night, 'Go Buddy Go' is on *Top Of The Pops* again.

London's Roundhouse, 1977. (TracksImages.com/Alamy)

26th June '77. It's a Sunday and the band close the month's gigging with two performances at the Roundhouse, at 4p.m. and 8p.m. Set list: 'Grip' (a superb rendition), 'Sometimes' (after which, Hugh says, 'Right that's enough of that album, we've got more interesting things to play you'), "I Feel Like A Wog" '... about intimidation in the twentieth century all over England'), 'Dagenham Dave', 'Dead Ringer' (Cornwell introduces it with, 'This is a new song, it's called 'Dead Ringer' which means you're a fucking good likeness to someone I thought you were', Dave Greenfield sings it), 'Bitching', 'Peaches' (with new 'worse places to be' line '... like being stuck outside the Roundhouse without a ticket'), 'No More Heroes', 'Hanging Around', 'Something Better Change'.

CAPITAL

The band also feature in session on Nicky Horne's Capital Radio show this month, playing 'Goodbye Toulouse', 'I Feel Like A Wog', 'No More Heroes', 'Dagenham Dave' and 'Hanging Around'. 'I Feel Like A Wog' is particularly mesmerising in this version as Cornwell sings and Burnel whispers menacingly at the same time. That added sinister element improves an already brilliant track.

27th June '77. The band re-enter the recording studio; they believed they'd had enough material to fill two albums, but not so. Notwithstanding, the new LP takes more than two weeks to record, compared to less than a week for the first. 'Overspill' tracks from the *Rattus* sessions are 'School Mam', 'Something Better Change', 'Bitching' and 'Peasant In The Big Shitty'. Unfortunately, according to producer Martin Rushent, the sessions are much more fraught this time, with the band being too 'self-conscious' and not as easy to work with, JJ especially. The presence of too much booze and too many acolytes in the studio slows up the work as well.

1977: GETTING A GRIP ON THE CHARTS

July '77. No gigs for the band. The first week is spent recording, the rest of it meant to be a well-earned break, except a Strangler's lot is not an 'appy one. Life is always full of twists and surprises, not necessarily pleasant ones. Jean-Jacques Burnel, because he holds two passports, one French and one British, discovers to his great alarm that he has been called up by the French government to carry out two years' Army National Service. Fortunately, the band's lawyers exploit a loophole in the legislation and so he need only provide proof of a permanent residency in the UK to avoid extradition and the call up. Meanwhile, at United Artists, Andrew Lauder has been busy too, signing up Buzzcocks on a reported £75,000 contract.

23rd July '77. The Stranglers release their third double A side single – 'Something Better Change' b/w 'Straighten Out'. It will peak at No. 9 and spend eight weeks in the charts, faring marginally poorer than the Pistols' 'Pretty Vacant' out at a similar time. Tony Parsons' review of 'Something Better Change' in the NME, tries to ridicule the band but really only succeeds in making himself look self-righteous. It began 'I was garrotting my best girl as we were listening to *Rattus Norvegicus* the other morning ...' and it frankly doesn't improve. 'The public and media don't have much to be offended by with this latest Stranglers offering, though casually racist radio advertising could have caused problems, ads on Capital Radio poking fun at Arabs wanting to buy *everything* ("out now on United Arab Republic" records) and takeaways and Chinese people's perceived mis-pronunciations of "United Artists Lecords" and "Snap, clackle and plop" which makes very little sense anyway.'

August '77. The Stranglers have plenty of work to do even when not gigging, writing or recording. Hugh and Jet spend the 5th to 20th August in America, helping promote *Rattus Norvegicus*, which A&M Records are releasing there, while JJ apparently is on his motorbike carrying out similar promotional duties in Europe. Dave Greenfield the slacker stays here and gets married!

1st August '77. The band appear as part of the Rotterdam Festival. The set list is consistent with previous gigs this year, though a couple of remarks from Hugh add something different. During the third song 'Straighten Out', an audience member near the stage gets a bit too giddy. Hugh reproaches him, 'Oi, if you wanna play with a cock go out and wank in the toilets, don't use this mike stand alright!'. The new 'Peaches' line is, '... like Stockholm... or Gothenburg... or even Malmo'.

MUTATIONS

A curiosity of a single is released on UA called 'Mony Mony' by Celia & The Mutations. Celia is soloist Celia Gollin and her 'new' backing band The Mutations is in fact the barely kept secret of The Stranglers. The B-side is Celia singing their own 'Mean To Me'. Not a bad single but with practically no publicity work to help sales, it won't trouble the charts.

13th August 1977. Jim Evans interviews Jet Black in the latest *Record Mirror*. Asked how he feels about having two Top 30 hits ['Something Better Change' at No. 16, 'Peaches' still at No. 28] Jet responded, 'It's good. We've worked for it ... Now that we've got where we have, it's nice to be able to say a big "up yours" to all those who put us down, knocked us over the last year or so.' And asked if The Stranglers are Punk he answered, 'We're new wave but not punk. But we started a lot of the "punk" style. Like abusing the audience, throwing beer at them. Johnny Rotten and Joe Strummer were always at our early gigs, picking up tips.'

18th August '77. *Top Of The Pops* plays 'Something Better Change' over the show's Top 30 countdown.

27th August '77. With the Drones and London as support, a special gig as a thank you from The Stranglers to the Finchley Boys, is held at the Wilmot Youth Centre in the district. The building's capacity is supposedly 300; the attendance probably nearer 700.

Bitching. Meanwhile, rock god guitarist Pete Townshend is a bit pissed off with the band, specifically Hugh Cornwell, for criticising the Who. He told *Melody Maker* (17 September 1977), '... if people knew what the Who had done, well, I'd be embarrassed about it, listing our achievements and showing the fucking big mouth in The Stranglers how much I've given to charity, how much we've given to our roadies, how much I've spent on other groups to try and help them. Let him see if he can do it, keep up for 15 years, THAT's what commitment is all about, but I don't want a knighthood for it.' Just as well, really, because he hasn't got one.

30th August '77. Another brilliant session for John Peel's show on Radio 1. Tracks are 'Dead Ringer', 'No More Heroes', 'Burning Up Time' and 'Bring On The Nubiles'.

September '77. In addition to faring well in the *Melody Maker*'s readers' poll – top in the Brightest Hope category for instance – this will be a month of high drama for the band. A small but very eventful European tour takes place, and a new single AND album of the same name come out.

2nd September '77. The band play Amsterdam's Paradiso Club. Dutch fan Eric Vonk recalls:

> Hugh Cornwell greets the crowd with a swipe at prog rock, 'There's a gig on featuring The Grateful Dead, Pink Floyd and Yes and there're all going to use the same equipment and it's going to take place in the Archaeology Department at the Rijksmuseum'. Set list: 'Grip', 'Ugly', 'Straighten Out', 'Nubiles' (forget the lyrics and just try and take in the amazing Greenfield keyboard noises like the maddest, loudest, most beautiful-est futuristic fairground ride ever going), 'Peaches' ('... worse places to be, like in... the United States Of America'), 'I Feel Like A Wog', 'Dagenham Dave', 'Hanging Around', 'Dead Ringer', 'No More Heroes', 'Something Better Change', 'Burning Up Time', 'London Lady', 'Sewer', 'Five Minutes'.

1977: GETTING A GRIP ON THE CHARTS

SWEDEN

By September 14th, the band have also performed in Rotterdam, Frankfurt, Hamburg and the Swedish capital Stockholm. Three more gigs are scheduled for Sweden, including one in the town hall of Klippan near Malmo, but events cause the band to be thrown out of the country beforehand: for their own safety, say the Swedish police. It turns out that Klippan is the stronghold of the Raggare, a nefarious band of US obsessed, heavy drinking bigots who regard most bands, most people in fact, as enemies. Likened to Hell's Angels, but preferring 1950's American cars swathed in Confederate flag designs and the like to motorbikes, around 500 of them arrive on the afternoon of the proposed Stranglers gig. They aren't there to watch the concert. Overcoming the venue's perimeter fencing and the security guards, they aim to set about the band's equipment on stage as well as the six roadies who attempt to stop them doing it.

The four Stranglers, meanwhile, are in their cellar dressing room, unaware of the chaos above. The police arrive in numbers and clear the hall of the shithead hooligans, but only after much of the equipment has been wrecked. And then they tell the crew that they will have to fend for themselves once they leave, with hundreds of the Raggare now waiting for them in the town square. One of the crew, Alan McStravich, in *The Men They Love To Hate*, said that they are prepared to take drastic measures to protect themselves and the remnants of the equipment but are '... caught by the police making petrol bombs ...' The crew get back to the hotel for their belongings and are then given an armed escort all the way to Stockholm where the police stay until the roadies are on a boat back to England.

16th September '77. 'No More Heroes' single is released. Part of *NME*'s complimentary review says, 'The Stranglers now set the standard against which the rest of the new bands have to measure themselves'.

22nd September '77. The band perform the new single on *Top Of The Pops*. It's a brilliantly daft appearance from the start, with Burnel wafting smoke away from the amps and speakers with a newspaper rather than 'playing' his bass — to Cornwell's blistering guitar solo, which he somehow manages with only one hand on the strings while twiddling his other hand's fingers in mid-air. The single fares well, highest chart placing of eight in a nine week spell. Alas, 'classics' from pop legends such as Danny Mirror, Meri Wilson and Baccara get in the way of it going higher.

23rd September '77. *No More Heroes* the album is released. Two albums within just a few months of each other! Advance orders are said to be 62,000 copies. The LP sleeve is one of the most iconic images of the era. Designed again by Paul Henry, it is in fact a late rushed replacement for his original photo design of JJ Burnel lying naked on top of a replica of Leon Trotsky's tomb. It's a striking image, but it contains only one Strangler so it was rejected, they are a democratic group after all.

NO MORE HEROES
Released: 23rd September 1977.
Label: United Artists Records.
Charted at No.2
Side One: 1 'I Feel Like A Wog', 2 'Bitching', 3 'Dead Ringer', 4 'Dagenham Dave', 5 'Bring On The Nubiles', 6 'Something Better Change'.
Side Two: 1 'No More Heroes', 2 'Peasant In The Big Shitty', 3 'Burning Up Time', 4 'English Towns', 5 'School Mam'.

In a few words – what the *Ford* are the songs about? Part 2

'I Feel Like A Wog': Deliberately provocative title, it is in fact an anti-racist song, dealing with alienation, immigration, Cornwell feeling like a foreigner, combined with memories of a night the band spent in Hamburg. The word 'wog' originally was an acronym of Western Oriental Gentleman [or possibly Wily], so there you go.

'Bitching': Amidst references to Hell's Angels and the band renting out their own PA, this song refers mainly to venues the group played in, some run by disrespectful people who treated them poorly. Fred Grainger and Bill Phelan – both mentioned in the song – ran the Hope & Anchor and Duke Of Lancaster pubs respectively, and both treated the band very well.

'Dead Ringer': This refers to other punk/new wave bands of the time being false and not genuine.

'Dagenham Dave': Homage to the band's great supporter who committed suicide.

'Bring On The Nubiles': A very juvenile song, in more ways than one in fact, not intended to promote any particular activity whatsoever, despite the insinuations. The strict definition of nubile is a woman ready for marriage, which isn't what the band had in mind here!

'Something Better Change': Although an all-time favourite anthem for many, the song itself has no real deep meaning and, according to Cornwell, was generally intended just to antagonise.

'No More Heroes': Not the band acting all disaffected and nihilistic, it's more a maligning of the lack of people worth idolising. Elvis Presley and Groucho Marx died while the band were in America; Hugh Cornwell admired both men. He was enthralled by Leon Trotsky as well, also name-checked, and so travelled from the US to Mexico to see the revolutionary's former home in Mexico City.

'Peasant In The Big Shitty': Reportedly written by JJ whilst tripping on acid so it's unclear what the lyrics really mean.

'Burning Up Time': JJ Burnel on a Brighton train to see a girlfriend, the lyrics also refer to the Finchley Boys. Unsurprisingly, the drug speed was an influence too, and the song was written very quickly.

'English Towns': Supposedly a tribute in parts to The Doors. Jim Morrison talks of his crystal ship being filled with 1,000 girls, whereas The Stranglers talk of no love in the same number of girls. It's probably more fun in LA than in most English towns!

'School Mam': Cornwell taught biology at a college for a short while, and though this story is fictional, the woman in charge (the school ma'am) was something of an ogress.

Notable songs of the time not on the vinyl album:
'Straighten Out': The breakdown of society and order, plus (possibly) some allusion to cannibalism
'Five Minutes': Shocking true story from JJ about a sexual attack by a gang of men on a female friend of his, living in the same digs.

✪

John Robb's review of *No More Heroes*:
… the wreath on the cover, another piece of great iconic Stranglers artwork along with the band pics on the back where they look like they'd been struck by lightning. Not as atmospheric as *Rattus* which made you want to have a shower after listening to it, but it is their most punk record with anthem-like songs and lyrics meant to offend: 'Bring On The Nubiles' and 'I Feel Like A Wog' which were easily assimilated when you knew the band's REAL philosophy and you read *Strangled* explaining the BIG IDEA that they were laughing at the shock they were creating. The band were certainly not racists, 'Wog' was a tongue in cheek social analysis of them in an awkward social situation.

As I played the album, I marvelled at how much they had further sharpened up the bass sound, making all the component parts even more extreme. 'Bitching' had the skull-scraping rhythm guitar and that fantastic bass run, as JJ bellowed out his homage to running with gangs. 'Dead Ringer' is another of those great lead bass lines with the weird kink in it …'duh duh duh kink', while Dave Greenfield does his Dracula on acid vocal, seething about a face on the scene that is not quite the person they remember. I read it was about Joe Strummer but maybe it's wrong, the band always had kind words for Joe.

'Nubiles' is so ridiculous, a paean to teenage sex, but stands the test of time; seedy but a great slice of bubble gum pop, they should have released it as a single! 'Something Better Change' is a definitive punk anthem – its chugging riffs and catchy chorus defining that long hot summer. The track 'No More Heroes' is the band's anthem – that bass intro is one of the greatest ever sounds recorded and the keyboard hook is mesmerising. Cornwell's singing style was also highly individual with his odd pronunciations and twisting of vowels out of shape.

'Peasant In The Big Shitty' was classic 'Punk Floyd', genuine weirdness over one of Jet's classic off kilter drum patterns. 'Burning Up Time' and 'English Towns' are perfectly punchy songs. Again they end an album with a climactic track, the pounding 'School Mam' driven by one of Burnel's greatest ever bass lines, Jet's thumping Tom Toms and Hugh leering out his dirty schoolteacher tale. A great finish'.

(Image courtesy of Duncan Round)

SAVAGERY

Prominent music journalist Jon Savage claimed in Sounds (24th September 1977) he had no axe to grind with the band and yet he practically made one for *the band* to grind in his review. 'The Stranglers offer nothing positive,' he moans, before adding 'No life-force, nothing vital. Not so that it's frightening, just dull and irritating ...'

25th September '77. Gig at the Canterbury Odeon, details from Chris Band:

> Set list: 'Ugly' (sung with plenty of venom by JJ), 'Straighten Out' (Hugh mentions, 'It's good you're standing up, you don't really need those seats'), 'Bring On The Nubiles', 'Sometimes' (launched into with some ferocity), 'Dagenham Dave' (it's heads down and going for it, scarce banter between the songs), 'Dead Ringer' (Dave Greenflew gets an outing as singer, and there's

no let-up even though it's a slightly slower tempo), 'Hanging Around', 'Something Better Change' (terse intro from Hugh with, 'ThisisSomethingBetterChange!' and straight into it, at the end a dedication from JJ to '... the arseholes who were at the gig last time...'), 'Bitching', 'I Feel Like A Wog' (before which Hugh says, 'Okay, it's very difficult to play if you keep spitting at us, cos we can't see where it's coming from. So just cut it out. This is called "I Feel Like A Wog"'), 'Five Minutes', 'Burning Up Time' (back into high gear, this is intense, rattling along like the proverbial express elevator to hell!).

28th September '77. The band play Ipswich Gaumont, a venue with lots of seats. They prefer playing to standing audiences and they usually let them know that. Afterwards, the venue's management ban all 'new wave' bands as seats have been ripped out during the gig.

October '77. Takes in most of the *No More Heroes* tour. In October 8th's *NME*, Tony Parsons adds a few more sneers to his Stranglers canon, for example: 'Just like gonorrhoea, The Stranglers' music is way too catchy for anyone to be certain they will not fall under its lethal spell...' suggesting too that Jean-Jacques Burnel was a 'Nazi' in his sixth form years and that the Finchley Boys were seen wearing swastikas. The Finchleys denied this, though one did draw one on his face for a Damned gig, apparently.

6th October '77. The 'No More Heroes' appearance is repeated on *Top Of The Pops* tonight.

8th October '77. Chas De Whalley is still a positive member of the press corps when it comes to The Stranglers. Reviewing their gig at Brunel University in Middlesex for *Sounds* (8th October), he says, "I couldn't care what anybody else says, The Stranglers are still one of the finest rock 'n' roll bands this country has spawned in years."

LIPPY

This month also sees a brilliant comment from a certain Mick Jagger in the NME (15th October 1977): 'Don't you think The Stranglers are the worst thing you've ever fuckin' heard? I do. They're hideous, rubbishy ... so bloody stupid. Fuckin' nauseatin', they are!' Could this be the same Michael Philip Jagger who in 1963 appeared in court for urinating on a petrol station forecourt having told one of the garage staff that 'We will piss anywhere, man'. It surely could. It caused a right fuss then, but now, of course, he has a knighthood. Funny old life 'eh?

On the No More Heroes tour, as well as Wire, Penetration, The Drones, The Saints, The Rezillos, Steel Pulse, Pop Group and Radio Stars all appear as support, while US band The Dictators - who Hugh Cornwell saw while in the States - join the latter stages. Opening act is a friend of Hugh's Called Johnny Rubbish, who may well be described as one of the first alternative comedians.

14th October '77. Liverpool University gig. The bootleg of this splendid concert contains the sound check too, with the band playing abridged versions of 'English Towns', 'Bring On The Nubiles' and 'No More Heroes'. Although it is just a sound check, it's their only known recital of 'English Towns'. Cornwell opens the show with a little dig about Liverpool Empire not allowing them to play, so they're here at the uni instead, and then 'I hope it's not all students else I'll get really depressed ... Just remember there's no more heroes, they're all dead so don't make any more!' and the gig opens with 'No More Heroes'. After, he politely tells the audience, 'Okay just stop the spitting Okay, cos we prefer to play without it'. A few minutes later, 'Sometimes' is abruptly stopped – it would appear there's trouble afoot ... Jet Black: 'Okay, it seems there's a couple of Gumbys in the audience'. There's a faint sound of an argument in the crowd, then Hugh says, 'I don't like being spat at alright ... Some people nowadays think that spitting at someone means something good, but we just think it's a fucking drag 'cos we can't play properly alright. If you want good music, cut out the fucking spitting alright!' Incidentally, 'Gumbys' are thicko characters from the supreme *Monty Python's Flying Circus*.

15th October '77. My own city. Leeds' main venue, the Queens Hall, hosts the band for the first time. Huge but only one floor, it used to be a bus depot, and a tram depot before that. And probably a horse and carriage depot before that, it was that old. Always a shithole, that's for sure, and lousy acoustics. Stranglers fan Chris Dalston attended:

> Before The Stranglers came on stage, one of the roadies gave the home crowd a hard time saying it was disgraceful how the city of Leeds had not supported Don Revie for what he'd achieved with the football club. He'd left the England job that year and was getting a lot of unjust stick for it. I was 17 at the time and it has always stuck with me, as has the memory of it being a great gig.

16th October '77. The Stranglers play Glasgow Apollo, the gig graced by the presence of some Glasgow councillors checking on the notorious band's behaviour. Aware of this, Hugh asks for the venue lights to be shone in the direction of the said 'suits' in the stalls, to whom he dedicates 'Ugly'.

19th October '77. Saliva rain still continues. 'Stop the fucking spitting, we can do without it alright,' snaps Hugh at the Sheffield Top Rank audience after 'Nubiles'. It appears he blames the US for most things though, with the 'Peaches' 'worse places to be' being the United States of America again.

29th October '77. 'What's been happening in Hastings then?' asks Hugh of the crowd early in the blistering gig at Hastings Pier Pavilion, before repeating their reply, 'Fuck all!' He then enquires, 'Don't no groups come down to play any more then?' and the answer is a resounding no.

More Mutations. A new Stranglers-linked release too this month, with Celia & The Mutations bringing out 'You Better Believe Me' b/w 'Round and Around'. JJ Burnel co-wrote the songs as well as playing bass, alongside ex-Dr Feelgood man Wilko Johnson on guitar. It sees no chart action.

6th November '77. Five consecutive nights at the London Roundhouse, and tonight, after performing 'Bitching', a spat on and pissed off Hugh snipes: 'Okay, it's good to know you've all been reading your News Of The World and you're spitting just like punks are supposed to do, that's REALLY good'. The gobbing decreases. Altered 'Peaches' line is '... like for instance in the United States of America ...' again. During one of the other Roundhouse gigs, just as the band commence 'Dead Ringer' someone shouts 'Wanker!' from the crowd. Hugh reacts by halting the song, 'Did someone say wanker? Where is he? ... Come on then, isn't he gonna own up?' It's a minor incident but will become part of Stranglers folklore.

Ireland 1978 (Image courtesy of John Shiels & Fran McCloskey)

NORTHERN IRELAND

Mully, a big Stranglers fan, born and bred in Belfast tells us:

Northern Ireland in the 1970s, at the height of The Troubles, was a commercial and entertainment no go area. Belfast was a virtual ghost town as security gates 'locked up' the city centre after 6p.m. and nightlife was virtually non-existent. Major music acts steered clear - not only could it be commercial suicide to tour here, it might also be life threatening. Dr Feelgood and Eddie & The Hot Rods put on concerts at Queens University in late 1976/early 1977, but the first real punk gig organised for Belfast was The Clash, set to play 20th October 1977. However, just hours before the doors of Ulster Hall were due to open, it was cancelled, the reason cited as 'insurance problems'. Just over a fortnight later on 9 November 1977, The Stranglers were also due to play the same venue, but then Belfast City Council announced this gig had been cancelled also, for insurance reasons again. The band did play on the next night, in Coleraine about 70 miles away, at the New University of Ulster, the first major punk act to perform in Northern Ireland.

Alan Simpson went and Donald Mackay asked him about it. Simpson, presenter of his own weekday BBC Radio Ulster programme, was a local punk and he turned promoter too around 1977, to bring bands to the Portrush/Coleraine area:

> There was an interview set up with Gloria Hunniford (local radio at the time) and it was supposed to be with Hugh Cornwell and Jean-Jacques Burnel, but JJ reckoned he didn't want to do a bloody radio interview! So it was decided that I would strangely morph and become him 'cos they reckoned Gloria wouldn't know! So I went in and pretended do all this (adopts dodgy London accent),'Yeah, right, lovin' it 'ere, Northern Ireland's great …' which was Okay and it seemed to go pretty well. But then she started to describe me, saying, 'Well here we are with Jean-Jacques Burnel with his purple hair and he's wearing a green rubber t-shirt with a zip …' and so on. Nobody else had sussed it apart from my mum!

10th November '77. The Stranglers at the New University of Ulster. Donald Mackay:

> I'm standing about ten rows back and over to the right hand side. On stride The Stranglers! There's no messing about, Hugh Cornwell and JJ Burnel strap on their guitars and then Hugh barks, 'There's no more heroes so don't make any more!' We roar back, I'm not sure why, but roar we do! JJ powers into the opening bass riff, followed by the rest of the band as they blast into 'No More Heroes'. It sounds so good, very loud but the music is clear and sounds just like the record, only better. Huge applause as the song finishes but no pleasantries from the band, it's straight into the next track. The band are ultra-confident, with JJ bouncing around all night at his side of the stage. There's quite a reaction in the audience over on that side, JJ is definitely creating a buzz. And Dave Greenfield, standing side on in his green boiler suit, attacking his keyboards, whizzing up and down. Hugh and JJ are looking lean and mean, in t-shirts and drainpipe jeans. JJ is using his green Fender Precision bass as a weapon of display – look at me but don't mess! Hugh is animated also with his head bobbing to the pounding beat. Jet solidly batters away in the background, with an electric fan blowing air at his stocky frame. Hugh: 'Our next single out in the New Year, it's called "Five Minutes"'. It has immediate impact, a great new song, but then it's all over as the lights come back on. I stand there smiling, ears ringing. My brother presents me with two rolled up posters, promos for Rattus Norvegicus and No More Heroes – brilliant!'

Tuesday 22nd November '77. A significant gig at the Hope & Anchor, with two tracks – 'Straighten Out' and 'Hanging Around' – chosen for the live compilation double album *Hope & Anchor Front Row Festival*. Also featuring The Wilko Johnson

Band, XTC, 999, Steel Pulse, Dire Straits and X-Ray Spex, and others. Ian Grant films The Stranglers' gig and fans of the band still harbour hopes the footage will one day see the light of day. Or the dark of cinema even.

Full set list: 'Tits', 'Choosey Susie', 'Goodbye Toulouse' (Hugh asks, 'Have you all got your Crackerjack pencils?' 'Yeah!' 'Well stick 'em up your arses'), 'Bitching' (JJ Burnel advises, 'Take acid, it really fucks your brain up real good. And helps you do crossword puzzles'), 'Mean To Me', 'School Mam', 'Peasant In The Big Shitty', 'In The Shadows', 'Walk On By' (Hugh introduces, 'Here's one for Dionne Warwick, God rest her soul.' Not that she was dead, then or now), 'Princess Of The Streets', 'Go Buddy Go' (smoothie Hugh invites any female to come up on stage and strip off, and then tells one woman to get her lipstick round his dipstick), 'No More Heroes', 'Straighten Out', 'Peaches' ('... like er ... being in the United States of America' again), 'Hanging Around', 'Dagenham Dave', 'Sometimes', 'Nubiles', 'London Lady'.

The band close November '77 with two performances in Stuttgart, Germany and two gigs at the Paradiso in Amsterdam. Fan and occasional scribe Eric Vonk remembers:

> The band's second visit to Amsterdam was combined with them miming to 'No More Heroes' at the TV studios in Hilversum for the music programme *Top Pop*, the Dutch equivalent of *Top Of The Pops*. After a couple of takes they made more fun for themselves by switching instruments. We see Dave on bass and pretending (badly) to sing lead vocals, Jet plays the guitar, at one time as if it were a violin, a leather clad chimp JJ goes wild on the drums and Hugh apparently plays the organ, his miming is actually worse than Dave's 'singing'. I vividly remember that this arsing around take was actually shown on the show!

27th November '77. It's their second night at the Paradiso Club, playing to a frenzied audience who seem to know all the tracks off by heart. However, for some, the occasion is marred by crowd trouble caused in part by 1,200 tickets being sold when the venue only held 800. Dutch publication *Hitkrant* reported that three arrests are made, one police officer is concussed and a few people injured by broken glass. The gig itself is electrifying, with Dave Greenfield's keyboards so original and futuristic, especially on 'Nubiles', sounding like a deranged on-acid R2D2 having a prolonged fit.

Dutch fans Chris Visser and Broodje Viergever attended the gig. Chris: 'We were very surprised to see a large group of Hells Angels on and around the stage with the band. We had seen them around town and knew of them but this was new. Apparently the band had befriended them ... Some Angels hit and intimidated young punks ... The band played their set and it sounded great but there was not much fun for us lot. I'd say most of us were between 14 and 17 years of age. Some even younger. And these guys were older, bigger, harder and meaner'.

Broodje says: 'I am not convinced that The Stranglers really were friends with the Angels but they were a bit older and were probably familiar with the happenings in Altamont in 1969, the Rolling Stones played that festival in the States and the Angels did the security. It ended horribly when a young black guy was murdered'.

DUTCH HELL'S ANGELS

That local chapter of the Hell's Angels bizarrely received funding from the Dutch government to build a clubhouse and the like. And you thought our politicians were bloody stupid! For the two Paradiso gigs, the Angels provide the security having taken the band to their hearts. Later, at the chapter's out of town clubhouse in the south of the city - complete with bar, garage, sleeping quarters and a makeshift shooting range - the Angels are getting up to 'some alarming pranks', as *No Mercy* put it. Guns, drugs, a gangbang and a game of Russian Roulette all happening. Possibly not all in the same room.

The band's publicist Alan Edwards, eager to keep as much Stranglers-news in the public eye as possible, has taken a few British tabloid journalists to Amsterdam, including *The Sun*'s Bob Hart, and during some high jinks both men have a pistol pointed to their heads. What a brilliant laugh eh? Eric Vonk asks Hugh Cornwell about the Paradiso events: 'When we played there we came into contact with the Hell's Angels in Amsterdam. They came on stage and we became friends, well they forced themselves a bit, but it was also more than fine because we had great fun together'.

Hitkrant also told of the band's visit to the Dutch offices of EMI. Up on the wall of the office of Karel Hille hangs a United States flag. JJ detests America, viewing them as aggressive, imperialists and warmongers, thus the flag does not meet his approval and so, unbeknownst to the other band members, he sets fire to it before making a sharp exit. The flag, unsurprisingly, is ruined, as well as Mr Hille's office curtains, his stereo and the carpet. Plus of course, The Stranglers' reputation within the walls of EMI Netherlands. Burnel tries to explain his actions: 'Which Dutchman in his right mind will put an American flag on display? You must have a screw loose to do so!' Asked if JJ is a pyromaniac, Dave Greenfield jokes, 'Give him a torch and he will burn down the whole city …'

December '77. The band are under orders from United Artists to take themselves away to Bear Shank Lodge, an old farmhouse in Oundle, Northamptonshire, to write. Despite their great successes so far, UA are pressuring The Stranglers to deliver more. The lodge (also known as 'Bearshanks') is owned by Dai Davies' former college mate and good friend, Ruan O'Lochlainn, a photographer who will be taking the photos for the album cover. The band have very little new material prepared so this third album can be viewed as a fresh start and with the band working 'to order' almost. With snow aplenty – and another white powder prominent too – they worked at various times throughout, day and night, causing feelings of disorientation, isolation and paranoia.

JJ Burnel, apparently, threatens to quit the band and his strong input on the album will be testament to his fragile frame of mind. This is also when The Stranglers begin to wear only black. They are not happy with having a Punk image foisted on them and so chose to wear black to rebel against such false imagery whilst creating a 'non image', black being a non-colour. A relatively original idea but their 'non image' simply creates a new image on its own, and they would often be called The Meninblack. A regular at Bear Shank Lodge already is Billy Bragg, together with his band Riff Raff. He gets on well with The Stranglers and his comments in Andrew Collins' biography *Still Suitable For Miners* show they had similar sense of humour — '... The Stranglers were proper pop stars, such twats.'

(Image courtesy of Duncan Round)

CHRISTMAS

As in any job when you work (and practically live) with the same group of people for long periods, pressures and strains increase within relationships. The Stranglers need a break, not only from work but from each other. So, while Dave, Jet and Hugh departed the lodge to spend Christmas with their families and friends, JJ and one of the Finchley Boys remain at Bear Shank Lodge. JJ's mood can't have been sweetened by the presence of crabs around his nether regions, but at least they inspire a certain song for a future solo project. Dennis Marks assists him by tapping out beats on Jet's drums while THE punk icon Burnel - as proclaimed by the music press - puts pen to paper.

UNITED ARTISTS

Two of the band's main allies within United Artists leave the company to form their own record label, Radar: managing director Martin Davis together with the main 'Stranglerphile' Andrew Lauder. As a result, the band's faith in UA begins to wane. They are feeling a little underappreciated by Albion, too. Like Dr Frankenstein getting bored with his unholy creations, Dai Davies and Derek Savage don't seem keen on The Stranglers any more, they are more interested in empire building with fresher-faced acts. And the agency moves to grander premises with an office in Oxford Street. Therefore Ian Grant is effectively in charge of The Stranglers now, while Davies and Savage concentrate their efforts on 999, The Jam, Generation X and The Vibrators, as well as forming a new label, Albion Records, and the publishing company Albion Music. The Stranglers believe Davies and Savage are succeeding and expanding thanks largely to *their* efforts, and are being overlooked themselves.

6 1978: BLACK & WHITE ... AND READ ALL OVER

Despite two hugely successful albums the previous year, some music critics doubt The Stranglers' ability to produce new records which are commercial yet original and still distinctly featuring The Stranglers' unique sound. A common prediction is that the band will fade into obscurity as their creative output inevitably dries up. The pressure is on them to produce the goods, and United Artists clearly haven't been averse to adding to that pressure either, demanding a new album in double quick time.

January 1978. The band spend most of the month finishing off *Black & White*, with a May release slated. A series of gigs has been scheduled too, but the GLC are still making life difficult for all the horrible spit 'n' swear bands ruining old London town. The Stranglers, of course, have cunning ways of deceiving the council ... which isn't difficult. Simply book a venue under a different name that Stranglers fans will be sure to figure out, while the slow witted jobsworths won't have a clue.

4th February '78. The 'Five Minutes' single is released. Another big hit which lurks around the charts for nine weeks, peaking at a healthy No. 11. Burnel wrote the lyrics, which concern his return home after a short break in Japan the previous summer. He was greeted with truly shocking news. He flatshares with Wilko Johnson, and occasionally Steve Strange and Billy Idol, while a girl called Suzie lives in the middle room. While JJ is away, Suzie is raped by five men. The flat is only five minutes away from Bishop's Avenue, one of London's most exclusive addresses. Burnel, rightly, isn't lambasted for writing about such a terrible scenario. However, if the journalists could translate his French remarks in the song in a superbly powerful song-ending, he might have been: 'Et si j'les trouve, Mon pauvre chouchou, enculés! J'les aurai! J'les aurai!' which loosely translates to, 'And if I find 'em, my poor darling, the motherfuckers I'll have' em, I'll have 'em!' Who can blame him?

9th February '78. Smiley DJ Peter Powell introduces the 'Five Minutes' video on *Top Of The Pops*.

Promo video for Stranglers singles 'Five Minutes'.
Various TV screens on stage on top of amps and speakers, while a digital timer in the corner of the screen counts up to, supposedly, five minutes (it's slightly fast). With frenzied 'light sabres' occasionally replacing the guitars, this is simple but superb, dramatic and exciting, just like the song.

10th February '78. In a 'secret' gig, The Skids support the band at Edinburgh's Clouds Disco; JJ Burnel is so impressed with Richard Jobson's group that he helps get them a London tour of their own in April.

14th February '78. As well as a thank you gesture to the proprietor, The Stranglers are testing new material in another secret gig as Johnny Sox. Tracks such as 'Tank', 'Toiler On The Sea', 'Threatened' and 'Sweden'. The venue is the Duke Of Lancaster pub and landlord Bill Phelan has been a long-time supporter. 150 lucky punters get in while another 1,000 unlucky sods have to make do with listening outside.

March '78. The band fly to America for a few dates. Waiting for them is a 32-year-old New Yorker by the name of Ed Kleinman, A&M Records had assigned him the role of tour manager. Ed Kleinman remembers:

I met The Stranglers at JFK airport for the first time. They knew I was picking them up. They got off the plane with small carry bags and I said let's get your luggage but was told they had it. Okay, a six week tour and they had very little with them. I learned later that they wore black pants and black t-shirts and washed them out after the shows. I believe they had two or three changes in their bags. At least I didn't have to worry about baggage then. I had Itineraries and knew where we were going and how we were getting there. They kept saying various things that at first I thought were rude, however I came to understand they were just testing people to see if they could deal with them. I had no problem, I thought I was dealing with a punk version of *Monty Python* so I just laughed and did my job.

They were set to do some recording prior to the tour at the Record Plant mid-town Manhattan. I guess it was my turn to get tested – they asked me to get a certain type of tea, all the past *Hustler* magazines and some Campbell's tomato soup. Okay, the *Hustlers* were easy, there were a lot of porno book stores around. The tea I got at an upscale market called Balducci's in Greenwich Village and, given I was unable to find the right kind of tomato soup they wanted, I brought back the phone number of the international Head of Sales who said the soup was only made for export to the UK and Europe. So I gain more credibility! The tour went well and, upon return to NYC, we found that the band hadn't had any of the $ tour support so I was able to get the record label to send the four of them back home on the S.S.T., the fastest passenger jet around at the time.

Unknown date in March '78. The band perform at the Old Waldorf, San Francisco. It's a fantastic gig with Hugh sounding as if he really dislikes the crowd. After 'Burning Up Time' is cheered vociferously, he snaps at them, 'Shut up, we don't need it, don't pose with your applause'. Next is 'Nubiles', with hardly any verse just the choruses, and then he starts jibing again – 'Well it's really nice to be in Los Angeles ... this is Los Angeles isn't it?' 'YEAH!' comes the reply. 'Yeah, so many posers in the audience I thought it must be the centre of the music business. Certainly lots of concrete ...' and after 'Hanging Around' he sneers, 'You're so laid back ... SHADDAP! – you're so laid back you'll even let K-SAN, your best radio station, take on a fucking playlist. You lot are pathetic!'

7th March '78. A gig at the Agora Ballroom in Cleveland Ohio. In a monotone drone, Hugh greets the audience: 'We ... are ... very ... excited ... to ... be ... here ... in ... America' and scant repartee arises all night. Nonetheless a superb performance, and it's more a case of him trying to get a reaction from the audience rather than actually hating them. Just before 'No More Heroes' he says, 'There's no more heroes, John Wayne is dying from a heart complaint', and by the half way mark it's possible that he's even warmed to the crowd. After enquiring if anyone there is in the American army, he asks, 'Do you know how to kill people? Good, this song is for you' and 'Tank' explodes into action.

21st March '78. They play the Act One Club in Philadelphia, Pennsylvania. 'Grip' is the opener again, before which Cornwell again drones a 'welcome' to the audience: 'Well we're really excited to be continuing playing in America, we can't describe how stimulated we feel ...'. Highlights, amongst many, are 'Bring On The Nubiles' and the relatively new 'Threatened'. On 'Nubiles', Dave's wonderfully ahead-of-the-times synth sounds like a computer powered fruit machine on jackpot loop, and 'Threatened' has a splendidly sinister vibe to it, perfectly complemented by Burnel's powerful singing and Cornwell's repeated 'malfunction, malfunctioning' backing vocals. The end of the gig is indicated by a tape loop of 'Thank you, goodnight' from Cornwell.

North America. The band play other American dates, before nipping over the border for two Canadian gigs, in Toronto and the High School of Commerce in Ottawa. Martin Rushent has received orders to fly out to meet the band so they can listen to tapes of the new album. Jet lagged, he meets them at Philadelphia airport to deliver the mixes of the new album, titled Black & White. He is hardly enamoured with the welcome, as they immediately take him to a recording studio to listen to the tapes, and even less so when they say they don't like them.

10th April '78. The band appear at Dooley's Tavern in East Lansing, Michigan. Hugh's altered 'Peaches' line is, 'I can think of a lot worse places to be, like for instance Los Angeles or even the Rotten Apple' but this visit will be remembered for more serious reasons. The Stranglers' sexist/chauvinist reputation has preceded them, and because it never takes certain members of the American public long to (over) react, dozens of vociferous placard-waving, leaflet-touting women are out in force before the gig, urging people to boycott it. The Housewives' Movement claims the whole of Punk Rock is to blame, not just The Stranglers, as well as capitalist venues like Dooley's who want to make money out of such exploitative concerts.

When fun is to be had, the band know few boundaries and so, instead of worrying about the consequences, and, as a prank, they attempt to bundle one of the protestors onto their tour bus. She however manages to struggle free while the band receive clouts to the head from various placards flapping down on them. At the start of the gig Cornwell tells the audience:

> Come and fill this space 'cos your arse is too big, 'cos you spend all day sitting down. Shut up! The next thing I've got here is a statement for your local female community who have been up in arms about us being here: In today's society cynicism is an ever present element of change. Through the use of cynicism we hope to draw attention to human situations which tend to be ignored. The appraisal … if we become the refusal [sic] to reappraise women's roles, then so be it. The Stranglers love women, have always loved women and they'll continue to love women at every possible opportunity.

And to add to the accusations of misogyny and sexism, JJ Burnel tells *The Sun* here in Blighty (and they seem to actually believe him): 'I only see women in bed. When chicks come up to me, they want something and they're never shy about it. They like the sense of fear. Because I'm a Strangler they think I'm either going to beat them or throw up all over them. I do neither. I like chicks that can talk to me, not ones that sit staring, unable to believe their luck. Anyway, they're not that lucky, I drop chicks as quickly as I pick them up. And if they irritate me, I hit them.'

May '78. A short European tour, but one which US tour boss Ed Kleinman initially isn't invited to work on because he has no relevant experience: 'There was talk about a European tour they were getting ready to do, but they were clear that even though I did a great job I had never been to Europe. Needless to say a week later I had a ticket to Glasgow and was now their world tour manager and I found myself throwing people off the stage (I had never seen a constant rush like that before). I got used to that and people in the audience spitting at the band'.

1st May '78. Promotional work for *Black & White*, their imminent third album, with a private plane hired by UA to take the band and specially invited journalists and record company execs to … Iceland. The agenda was three days of, essentially, partying, combined with a gig in the Reykjavik Exhibition Hall. That gig would be watched by 3% of the entire adult Iceland population.

The Stranglers are guilty of dastardly plotting too, to serve just deserts to a few of the press men who have upset them previously. Not that it takes much from the critics to actually do that – especially JJ who is probably guilty of being both too sensitive *and* volatile. Perhaps his hostile attitude is understandable, but it is a big concern for the band's management. Other than get extremely drunk though, his behaviour in Iceland is relatively mild and he cannot really be held accountable for journalists being publicly humiliated on the trip, or for one 'mysteriously' hurting himself in a fall whilst on a pony ride, or indeed for one falling into a geyser.

One unnamed scribe though, a real life 'upper class twit' from *The Times*, makes a grave error of judgement by challenging JJ to a drinking competition. At the start of the contest, JJ makes sure the reporter took the first drink, generously helping him do so by holding him down and pouring whisky galore down his throat. Eventually paralytic and covered in his own vomit, the journalist has to be left behind at Reykjavik airport and made to wait nearly three days for the next available flight to England. His troubles don't end there though, as he is apparently sacked due to his behaviour and is later spotted by Ian Grant and Alan Edwards on Brighton beach 'down and out'.

5th May '78. The Stranglers play at Club 4 in Oslo to a small, but keen, audience. The set list is almost identical to the March gigs; 'Tank' deserves a special mention as Greenfield's missile-effect at the song's climax sounds almost real. After 'Nubiles', Hugh mentions something about getting the mic back so they can sing what the audience wants them to sing — it seems some audience members are a bit too boisterous. And later he stops 'Hanging Around' to rant furiously at (presumably) the venue's management: 'Move those fucking tables … so we can play, you can dance and everyone can have a good time … This ain't no cabaret act'.

6th May '78. New single 'Nice 'n' Sleazy' is released, flipped with 'Shut Up', which clocks in at one minute six seconds, probably their shortest song ever. 'Nice 'n' Sleazy', although a hit, disappointingly only reaches No.18. The picture sleeve is a reproduced version of Kevin Sparrow's 1976 poster, depicting a murdered woman on a US sidewalk, with the caption 'Coming your way', which misleads some people in to thinking that is the song title.

7th May '78. The Stranglers play the Örebro Konserthus, Sweden; it's a fine performance but they get annoyed at apparent indifference from the crowd. Hugh opens by apologising for the cancellation there the previous year after their equipment was smashed up by the Ragarre.

Eventually some of the crowd get animated and invade the stage, quite a rarity for Swedes. Despite his earlier politeness, Hugh seems in a bad mood, a shame considering the quality and diversity of their set. 'Grip', 'Dagenham Dave', 'Nubiles', 'Dead Ringer', 'Hanging Around', 'Nice 'n' Sleazy', 'Something Better Change' (where he demands to know '…is there life in Sweden?' and then accuses the audience of being vegetables '…sitting on your fucking arses like this is a TV show'), 'No More Heroes', 'Tank'. 'Threatened', 'I Feel Like A Wog', 'Burning Up Time', 'Straighten Out', 'London Lady', 'Sewer', 'Five Minutes', 'Toiler'.

GRUB

```
Jet Black likes his food, it's hardly a revelation. And he can
get quite agitated when hungry, a bit like a bear. And if The
Stranglers are not well catered for or encounter poor hospitality
on their travels, he can be positively ogre-like. After a tough
night's gigging, one thing Jet Black wants, and needs, is food and
drink. Jet is later diagnosed with diabetes, which may explain
why he got a bit jumpy if he couldn't eat.
```

7th May (night) '78. At their Örebro hotel, after the gig, they are refused service. Jet responds by throwing a table across the bar before retiring to his room in a proper (and justified) old nark. He is nearly arrested for the crime, but the police officer knocking at his room door thinks better of it once he hears the drummer's side of the story, which is a straightforward but heartfelt 'Fuck off'.

12th May '78. The band play The Stadium in Paris. Fan Adam Burton was there:

After 'I Feel Like A Wog', Cornwell advises the audience, 'I was coming through Paris to this gig and I suddenly understood why you're all into snails ... because on all your roads nobody moves, they're just bumper to bumper fucking cars all over Paris ... Now I know why you've got this fetish about snails'. New tracks 'Curfew', 'Do You Wanna?' and 'Death And Night And Blood' get an airing, and after 'Threatened', he tells the crowd: 'We're gonna tell you about a country up north of here called Sweden, see if you're any better off ... if you don't think you are, you better go up there'. 'Sweden' follows, and then 'Tank', after which the crowd cheers and a few odd people shout 'God save the Queen', to which he responds, 'God save France more like, never mind God save the Queen, God save fucking France'.

15th May '78. The Stranglers' third album – *Black & White* – is released, a (hardly) limited edition coming with a free three track single too.

BLACK & WHITE
Released - 15th May 1978.
Label - United Artists Records.
Charted at No.2
Side One (White Side): 1 'Tank', 2 'Nice 'n' Sleazy',
3 'Outside Tokyo', 4 'Sweden (All Quiet On The Eastern Front)',
5 'Hey! (Rise Of The Robots)', 6 'Toiler On The Sea'.
Side Two (Black Side): 1 'Curfew', 2 'Threatened',
3 'Do You Wanna?', 4 'Death And Night And Blood (Yukio)',
5 'In The Shadows', 6 'Enough Time'.

In a few words – what the *Ford* are the songs about? Part 3

'Tank': Does what it says on the armour-plating, with reference to the grind of gigging and touring.

'Nice 'n' Sleazy': Is about the band's visit to America, plus their Amsterdam encounter with Hell's Angels. The title is much to the annoyance of Frank Sinatra's lawyers too, so that's a bonus!

Outside Tokyo: A Stranglers waltz about time, Hugh worships time 'more than anything'.

'Sweden (All Quiet On The Eastern Front)': Very interesting song about the band's not very interesting time in Sweden and scrapes with the Raggare.

'Hey! (Rise Of The Robots)': A 'filler' track, inspired in part by Isaac Asimov's *I, Robot* tale.

'Toiler On The Sea': Named after a book by Victor Hugo, Cornwell's lyrics recount memories of a bad holiday in Morocco with a girlfriend. The band name Flock Of Seagulls comes from this song too.

'Curfew': JJ Burnel's views of a politically oppressed land, a dystopia as opposed to utopia and possibly reference to East/West Germany of the era.

'Threatened': Is about fear and paranoia: there are so many ways one can die that in reality, we actually wish we were back in the womb.

'Do You Wanna?': Doesn't refer to anything much at all, it's 'blank verse'.

'Death And Night And Blood (Yukio)': JJ pays homage to renowned Japanese writer Yukio Mishima who committed ritual suicide (by seppuku) during a live broadcast in 1970, after a failed *coup d'etat*.

'In The Shadows': In Hugh's own words, this is him being Syd Barrett. Which probably means weird, experimental and 'out there'.

'Enough Time': Refers to the fallout from a nuclear explosion, the black rain. At the end of the song is a sequence of Morse code translating to 'SOS. This is planet earth. We are fucked. Please advise.'

Notable songs of the time not on the vinyl album:

'Old Codger': Cornwell's entirely fictional tale of a dirty old man hanging around churches looking for choirboys. The late George Melly sings as the eponymous codger.

'Rok It To The Moon': Various elements involved here: the future, the end of the world, Nostradamus, even cannibalism. Cocaine may well have been a contributing factor to this song.

✪

RESPONSE

Although *Black & White* reaches No.2 in the album charts and is received more positively by critics than *Rattus* and especially *NMH*, oddly enough it sells fewer copies. Nonetheless, it completes a hat-trick of gold selling Stranglers albums, some achievement for a 'new wave' band with allegedly limited originality and commercial appeal. Honoured with 5 stars in *Sounds* and a hardly shoddy 4 in *Record Mirror*, the *NME* praise it too, describing Side 1 (the white side) as the best work they had written, though Harry Doherty of *Melody Maker* was risking it with a generally only 'approving' review, the less than glowing remarks earning him a much unenvied place on JJ Burnel's 'Wanted' list.

John Robb reviews *Black & White*:

John Peel played the whole LP on his show before it was let loose ... This was a new soundscape and a record so daring and original that Peel let the whole album play without interruption.

Even the deceptively pop songs like 'Nice 'n' Sleazy', with its stunning lead bass, sounded like nothing before. Has there ever been a better bass sound than on this record? Few have managed to get near a bass as powerful and brutal, it really is one of the great recorded sounds in the pop canon. Not only was JJ on top form, Hugh's guitars were either splintered weirdness or skull-scraping Telecaster rhythm, splendid neo-Beefheart eccentricity that preceded The Fall and all the critical acclaim they got.

The songs were a new linear Stranglers, from the brutal opener 'Tank' which, in classic Stranglers style, was a slab of music that sounded like its subject matter down to the crashing missile of the track's fade out. 'Outside Tokyo' was the first appearance of Dave Greenfield's weird waltz timings; 'Sweden' was an infernally catchy classic rush, and 'Hey! (Rise Of The Robots)' was hard core Stranglers, a fast and thrashy surge of sound with a great sax too. 'Toiler On The Sea', the last track on side White, was a companion piece to 'Down In The Sewer', one of those classic twanging Stranglers workouts.

Side White was a new sound, Side Black was something else, a new music, a stark scenery of odd timings and strange atmospheres. A world as stark and different as the terrain of Iceland. I still love it and wallow in the bleak vision of the future of an invaded Britain ('Curfew') and then there's JJ's 'Threatened', a truly odd work about opinion built over stripped down strangeness that still managed to sound tough and menacing. There was also his homage to Japanese author, revolutionary, Yukio Mishima in 'Death And Night And Blood', such a great song, JJ's warrior fantasy coming to life, and the song segued effortlessly from the jagged 'Do You Wanna?'. 'Enough Time' should end the album as it's so menacing and heavy and end-of-time powerful that adding 'In The Shadows' seems out of place. Top song and all that but. *Black & White* was the band's finest hour, a blueprint for so much music that came afterwards, it just matched my mood intellectually and emotionally with the physicality of its music.

COLLECTABLES

75,000 copies of the album come with a free white vinyl 7-incher containing the splendid cover version of the Dionne Warwick classic 'Walk On By', plus on the reverse, 'Mean To Me' and 'Tits'. This version of 'Walk On By' is even better as it's extended. Interestingly, at least for collectors, other colours roll off the press: beige copies as well as less common shades of blue tint and vague pink versions. In a plain black sleeve, the freebie has a calling card with it and on the record's label,

1978: BLACK & WHITE AND READ ALL OVER

'This record has been given free. If offered for sale by a shop, write with details and they will be dealt with'.

BLACK & WHITE TOUR

The *Black & White* Tour spans May, June and July, taking in Britain and continental destinations such as Paris, Madrid, Brussels, Munich, Cologne and Zagreb. There should have been more but several European venues cancelled at short notice, scared of the band's apparently shocking reputation. Not only were the cancellations grossly inconvenient, they also cost the band much needed revenue too as, whether or not gigs are 'on', crew and entourage still need paying, in addition to accommodation and subsistence costs.

18th May '78. 'Nice 'n' Sleazy' is featured on *Top Of The Pops*. Jet stands to play the drums, Hugh looks stern throughout, practically snarling the lyrics. Classic Stranglers.

19th May '78. Spain is a very interesting place to be, with the fascist dictator General Franco's death in late 1975 helping the political and social climate to change radically, signifying an almost liberated mood for the previously 'shackled' youth of the nation. Punk/New Wave has arrived with perfect timing.

Madrid is the location for the band's last gig before embarking on the official album tour. This gig isn't perfect but it's still a belter. Set list: 'Dagenham Dave', 'Nubiles' (Hugh asks if anyone here speaks Spanish; hardly any response from the crowd so 'Obviously not' which is quite amusing considering the country he's in), 'Dead Ringer', 'Hanging Around', 'Sometimes', 'Ugly', 'London Lady', 'Sewer', 'Curfew', 'Tank', 'Nice 'n' Sleazy', 'Threatened', 'Sweden', 'Toiler', 'Five Minutes' and finally 'No More Heroes' (Hugh introduces with, 'There's no more heroes in Spain ... go out and be one in a riot, they're outside now waiting for you ...' and in the middle of the song, JJ Burnel shouts 'Freedom!).

26th May '78. At the first of two Glasgow Apollo gigs in three days, the band gets riled at the sight of security staff slapping the crap out of audience members without just cause. During the concert, Hugh orders the lights to be shone on the guilty bouncers to stop the fighting and show them up for what they are; bullies. JJ jumps into the crowd to rescue one kid and as the bouncers back off, some of the audience invade the stage. An alleged riot ensues, causing lots of expensive damage to the venue. And as if all that isn't bad enough, on their return to their digs at the Central Hotel, Jet is refused a meal even though the hotel has three restaurants. He causes a rumpus which results in he and Burnel being taken into police custody for a few hours until bailed by the band's management.

28th May '78. Before the second Apollo appearance takes place, the security men are asked by the band to lay off the audience. 'Lay off' in this context means 'leave alone' ,rather than that seemingly eternal government instruction to the industries they enjoy killing'

It seems to work, the gig passes relatively peacefully. Afterwards, though, said bouncers decide they want some violence for their supper and so wait for the band, hoping to have a crack at them instead. Not for the want of trying, they fail. And yet despite all these unappealing experiences The Stranglers have always counted Glasgow as a favourite tour destination.

(Image courtesy of Duncan Round)

30th May '78. At Stafford Bingley Hall, support band Steel Pulse are met with various missiles thrown from the audience. Enter Hugh Cornwell to the stage. Steel Pulse are a band The Stranglers like and respect, so after a reprimand from Cornwell and his threat that if the missiles don't stop then The Stranglers won't play, the gig goes smoothly from then on.

3rd June '78, issue of *Melody Maker*. In an interview with Chris Brazier, JJ explains a little of his antipathy towards the media, Harry Doherty in particular after his review of the last album: 'It was condescending, and I don't like being patronised by people with smaller brains than ourselves. He will go the same way as Jon Savage, tell him to stay out of town, keep out of my way. I cannot accept personal criticism because it's not valid, it's vindictive, some of these writers have personality problems'.

7th June '78. In aid of the Prisoners' Rights Association, the band play at Leeds University. The gig is cited in *No Mercy* as being the first to herald a female 'guest' stripper from the audience on stage during 'Nice 'n' Sleazy'. It's my home town, but I wasn't at the gig. I blame my parents for this neglect.

24th June '78. *Rock Pop*, a German TV show on channel ZDF, features The Stranglers mischievously miming through 'Nice 'n' Sleazy'. Jet, standing to play the drums, deserts his percussion duties to walk to the front of stage and join Hugh at the mic. He then pretends his drumsticks are a flute while Cornwell does a little bit of the neck masturbating routine with JJ laughing along. Other guests on the show are the Scorpions,

AC/DC and a virtually unknown Sting playing with Eberhard Schöner, a German 'rock meets classic' orchestra leader; sounds like a corker.

July '78. The band in front of television cameras (somewhere in the Midlands) once more, for the ATV show *Revolver*, a not very well known gem of a programme hosted by the late Peter Cook, an unlikely host for a music show. And yet it all worked very well, with some excellent performances by various artistes throughout the series. Know why it was called Revolver? Because the studio stage revolved! The Stranglers treat the audience to superb renditions of 'Curfew' and 'Tank'.

14th July '78. In Cascais' Sports Stadium, Portugal, through no fault of their own (which is contrary to media reports) the band cause a riot ... without actually playing. All tickets had been sold. Sizeable rock gigs being a rarity for the Portuguese and this becomes painfully obvious to the band's road crew (as well as support act 999's roadies) when they arrive at the venue at noon. The building of the stage has not been completed, the power supply is virtually non-existent, the German concert promoter isn't even there and communication with the venue workers was virtually impossible as they didn't understand English. Nevertheless, the band's roadies set up the gear on stage, only to be told late afternoon by Ian Grant to dismantle it all as the electricity supply is still AWOL.

Meanwhile, a few thousand increasingly edgy ticket holders wait to get in, and so when it seems that the gig is OFF and they could be rip-off victims, retribution becomes the name of the game for many of them. After a chase or two, thrown missiles and no police protection, a few injuries occur, as well as a few shades of Teutonic shit kicked out of the promoter when he turns up. Tour manager Ed Kleinman's account:

> A show in a sportatorium in Portugal, there was no power to the stage, the promoter couldn't get it to work. The crowd outside was getting angry and was getting very large. This was a 20,000 seat show and people had come from all over the country. We tried our best but then the riot started outside. We were able to pack up the gear and get the truck on the way. The tour bus left prior to it being smashed and the rest of us ran out the back of the arena and into the streets and surrounding area to find a safe haven. Myself and two of the crew burst into someone's house who were having a family dinner. I remember the rocks being thrown at the door once we got in. They called the police and we were taken back to our hotel.

Late July '78. Venue unconfirmed other than it's in New York and it's a superb gig, the lively locals enjoying it. Set list: 'Burning Up Time', 'Dagenham Dave', 'Nubiles' , 'Dead Ringer', 'Hanging Around' (Hugh shouts 'Shaddup' before this, no idea why, maybe just to get them warming to him). 'Sometimes' (before which he sneers, 'It's good to see that some of you haven't got stickers stuck to your fucking arses. What are you gonna do, sit in that all night? There's no television stuff tonight, Johnny Carson's just killed himself'), 'London Lady', an immense version of 'Sewer' ('New York is a grey city' – obviously people think he says 'great' ... 'I said grey not great, wash your ears out'), 'Curfew', 'Tank', 'Nice 'n' Sleazy', 'Threatened', 'Do You Wanna?' 'Sweden' (This is called Sweden, where most of you are from), 'Toiler', 'Five Minutes', 'Grip'.

12th August '78. Release of 'Walk On By' as the new single, complete with picture sleeve very like the *Black & White* cover except with Dionne Warwick's head stuck on Hugh's shoulders. Commercial stupidity or admirably 'punk' to bring out an abridged version of a song already given away with the album? The single, backed with 'Tank' and the ludicrous (and fabulous) 'Old Codger' still manages eight weeks in the chart and reaches No. 21.

17th August '78. The band perform to the single on *Top Of The Pops*. With the exception of Jet's white jumper and Hugh's white socks (Jesus, what was he thinking?) they're all clad in black.

September '78. *Rock On* magazine reports: '*Sounds* writer Jon Savage had cause to regret writing less than complimentary things about The Stranglers. Mr Savage was reported to be nursing a black eye and severe bruising courtesy of Jean-Jacques Burnel ... Seems Mr Burnel throws tantrums and punches with gay and frequent abandon'. The article also mentions that a certain *Record Mirror* writer is on JJ's 'to do' list as well, for accusing the band of ripping off fans, plus *Melody Maker*'s Harry Doherty for daring to dislike *Black & White*. Also in September, the band's sardonic tribute to Sweden is released as a single there, sung in Swedish and coming in a particularly boring picture cover. 'Sweden (All Quiet On The Eastern Front)' became 'Sverige (*Jag Ar Insnoad Pa Ostfronten*)'. It will be quite peaceful in the charts front too.

2nd September '78. Just because they could, and in the hope that it would really upset Greater London Council, the band play as The Shakespearos at the Red Cow in Hammersmith.

3rd September '78. This time as The Old Codgers, they play the Nashville. Just before the start, Hugh announces that at the Red Cow the previous night there had been a bloke who thought he was very clever for hitting girls. He left three with scars for life, apparently. 'We know he's here, he's in a blue shirt and we're giving him five minutes to get out of here, or else we won't be responsible for what happens to you. So just fuck off 'cos we can't stand people like you'.

Jet then changes the subject, '... this is the first gig of the Old Codgers and I hope you forgive us if we sound like another band.' Tonight the 'Peaches' 'worse places to be' line is '... like being stuck in the Red Cow playing disco for the rest of the time'. 'Straighten Out' features guest singer Fee Waybill of The Tubes and 'Bitching' possibly does too. At the end, the stage is invaded and the brilliant gig comes to a close.

4th & 5th September '78. The band's appointment diary lists The Ritz. This is nothing grand but simply Jet's witty code word for rehearsing in a certain insalubrious studio, presumably TW Studios in Fulham.

7th September '78. The Stranglers play Belfast's Ulster Hall. Fan Mully was there in a sell-out 2,200 crowd:

1978: BLACK & WHITE AND READ ALL OVER

Aged 16, The Stranglers was my first real, proper gig and two pounds for a ticket was well worth it. On the crowd's right, Hugh Cornwell in his obligatory long mac and leather choker, thrashing away on his Fender Telecaster, JJ Burnel left side, in biker jacket and Converse baseball boots, thumping away on his beloved Precision bass, pogoing and karate kicking his way throughout the set. Jet Black and Dave Greenfield situated behind: a pounding backbeat and keyboard runs perfectly complementing the two front men. People jumped from the balcony, easily a 20 foot drop, down to the floor to join the frenzied horde. By the final encore, about 100 audience members had scaled the stage to join the band, as a bare chested JJ continued with the closing number.' Set list (a piece of handwritten memorabilia proudly owned by Joe Donnelly): 'No More Heroes', 'Sometimes', 'Nubiles'. 'Peaches', 'Dagenham Dave', 'Burning Up Time', 'Hanging Around', 'Curfew', 'Nice 'n' Sleazy', 'Threatened'. 'Tank', 'Something Better Change', 'London Lady', 'Sewer', 'Five Minutes', 'Toiler'.

BOMB

Hugh, interviewed in *Strangled*, was asked how playing in Belfast had been, 'Great. Didn't enjoy eating there. We were staying in the Europa Hotel and they've got these huge plate glass windows and the restaurant is on the ground floor by the windows. They've got a space of about fifteen yards and then a fence with barbed wire on the top, and anybody could've lobbed anything over the top. So when you go in, everyone's sitting in the middle of the room'. The Europa was, reputedly, the most bombed hotel in Europe at the time.

8th September '78. Portrush Arcadia Ballroom (a.k.a. Chesters, a nightclub in the same building), The Stranglers are supported by The Undertones, one of their first ever gigs outside Londonderry. Gobbing aplenty with poor parka-wearing Feargal Sharkey ending up drenched in spit, but it's probably a compliment as the band go down very well. The Stranglers enter and the gobbing recommences, prompting JJ to threaten a walkout if it continues. Someone does indeed aim a phleg towards the stage so JJ jumps down into the crowd to whack him.

9th September '78. Across the border, a young, pre-ubiquitous U2 support the band, at Dublin's Top Hat Ballroom. The Stranglers reportedly take up two dressing rooms meaning that Bono and the boys have to get changed stage-side behind the speakers. In fact, the room next to The Stranglers is the hospitality room which is full of booze, so the non-drinking Bono nicks a bottle of wine from the rider and he and his bandmates get the bus home after their gig. Stranglers' fans are alleged to have thrown lit cigarettes at U2 while they played. To cap a perfect evening for the young band, The Edge broke a guitar string during the first number.

THICK AMERICANS

An *NME* article from Chris Salewicz (9th September 1978) features Hugh, in A&M's Madison Avenue office, being interviewed by an unnamed female New York reporter. As is his wont, he takes the mick, comments like 'You *have* all got smaller brains' annoying her, along with 'You may rule the Western hemisphere but you're pretty incompetent in any ruling of the cerebral hemispheres …'

However, it's The Stranglers' perceived sexism which really gets her goat, and she clearly didn't understand the irony in his droll statement of 'I *love* women!' by naively asking him 'How?' Thankfully he remained silent, moving on to quoting conspiracy theories about the C.I.A., the Mafia, Aristotle Onassis, the murder of J.F.K. and the recent assassination attempt on the life of *Hustler* magazine founder Larry Flynt. The band's apparent contempt of all things American brings death threats against them, received at A&M's US office.

12th & 13th September '78. At short notice, the gigs at Dunfermline and Aberdeen respectively are cancelled due to technical problems with Dave's keyboards.

16th September '78 – the Battersea Park furore. The infamous, controversial, disgraceful, sleazy, squeezy and altogether bloody great Battersea Park gig. Organised by their staunch supporters the Greater London Council, The Stranglers headline, with special guests Peter Gabriel, The Skids, Spizz Oil, The Edge, comedian Johnny Rubbish, and DJ Andy Dunkley. Considering all the grief the GLC had caused the band, and other similar pariahs, it's a surprise that any level of reconciliation had been reached at all. Much of the gig is filmed, with 'Grip', 'Go Buddy Go', 'Peaches', 'Hanging Around', 'Curfew', 'Death And Night And Blood' and 'Nice 'n' Sleazy' recorded.

A banner in the crowd says, 'Dave puts Rick Wakeman in the shade' and a barrage balloon in the sky emblazoned with 'Stranglers'. The 'war' connotations don't end there as during 'Go Buddy Go' a minor skirmish develops in the crowd near the stage. Also, there's manager Ian Grant's hiring of a Sherman tank to go on stage during the 'Tank' finale. But the major controversy of the day comes from friends of Jean-Jacques Burnel, 'friends' happening to be strippers, most of them anyway. They perform graphically for 'Nice 'n' Sleazy'. Whilst the media, the women's libbers and the morally outraged citizens cited such a stunt as more proof of the band's misogyny and sexism, the girls themselves had planned it, to show the world that The Stranglers were the exact opposite (eh?). A couple of the girls are seen later being interviewed by a not entirely disapproving or officious police inspector.

FILM

Hugh Cornwell owns a cine camera which is used to film the gig, and so the idea of a Stranglers full-length feature gains a little more strength. Film from within the crowd also exists. He tells *Strangled*: 'Me and a few friends have made films on Super 8 but we're still learning. The way the film industry is constructed is very similar to the music industry, but you have to multiply everything by ten. So if it takes a month to make an album, it takes ten months to make a film. So I don't expect to see anything for at least a year'.

28th September '78. Manchester Apollo gig. Fan Gareth Barber was there:

Before 'Burning Up Time', a clearly-delighted-to-be-there Hugh compares the audience to boring commuters waiting on a platform for a train ... 'It's alright, train'll be here any minute" before 'Nubiles'. Later he demands to know why they haven't found themselves a new venue since the Electric Ballroom [he means the Electric Circus] closed down, as the band hates venues like the Apollo: 'You should be watching films in places like this, not groups.' At the end of the gig, naturally being the considerate type, he tells the crowd to help security by filing out in a reasonable manner. Someone shouts 'Fuck off!' in response and Hugh just says, 'Yeah'.

19th October 1978 – The BBC 'Rock Goes To College' Controversy. The band are down to perform at Guildford University for the early evening BBC Two TV programme *Rock Goes To College*. The BBC are already pissed off with them after a certain pin up bassist kicks in a *Top Of The Pops* studio dressing room door belonging to a band called Child, some weeks earlier. It is rumoured that a fight ensued but JJ denied it, saying that yes he had smashed their door, but nothing more.

Strangled magazine is probably the only publication to print the truth of what really occurred at Guildford, which was that the band had an agreement with the BBC that they would only play the gig if half the tickets went to students and half went to kids from the town. That did not happen, and 700 tickets somehow 'disappeared', apparently to be sold later at a student cheese and wine party. Tracks performed were 'Ugly', 'I Feel Like A Wog', 'Bring On The Nubiles', 'Burning Up Time' and 'Hanging Around'. The first three tracks weren't for broadcast.

Hugh is feeling aggressive, that's clear enough, mocking the audience on a few occasions: '... this is fucking boring. You lot are a load of the most boring people I've seen in my fucking life', and likening them to snails who should be boiled alive accordingly. After 'Nubiles' he demands to know if any residents from two specific local estates are in the crowd – he counts two and then three people – before sneering that none of them have even heard of those places. Jet Black then asks if anyone there is from Guildford University (met with a big cheer). 'Fuck off!' he responds, to their amusement. Before 'Hanging Around', Hugh asks if they've all got their *Crackerjack* pencils; 'Yeah!' they cry, 'Well stick 'em up your arses!' he replies – again. After the song is finished, he declares, 'Guildford University never represented Guildford, we hate playing to elitist audiences so fuck off!' Jet then remarks, 'For the record, I think Guildford University sucks'.

Minutes pass before the near-revolting audience begin chanting, 'You're just a bunch of wankers' and 'What have we got? Fuck all'. Consequent BBC resentment towards the band is perhaps understandable, but anyone thinking the band intend ripping off fans or intentionally alienating the BBC is wide of the mark. It does however take the BBC a long, long time to insert the dummy back into Auntie Beeb's mouth after imposing an unofficial but barely secret Stranglers ban, while Guildford Uni write to other universities urging them not to stage their gigs. Interestingly, inspired by these events, a new Stranglers track is born –'Wasting Time'; it's good.

November '78. The Stranglers – well, Hugh in goal plus a few Finchley's outfield – take part in a charity five-a-side football competition at the Empire Pool, Wembley. And they win the rather grand trophy too, beating Capital Radio 3-1 in the final. Reports say they benefited from the help of Chelsea's Peter Bonetti too, but it's debatable whether he would have improved the team. Organised by *The Sun*, other participants included ELO, Darts, Elton John, Rod Stewart, Rubettes and Rich Kids.

1st December '78. The band are in a studio belonging to EMI, and the track inspired by the BBC/Guildford Uni controversy is recorded. What is initially named 'Social Secs' becomes 'Wasting Time'. Martin Rushent produce and Alan Winstanley engineers. Also emerging from this session are the first recorded versions of 'Fools Rush Out' and the beginnings of a track which will become the instrumental, 'Yellowcake UF6'.

GOODBYE A&M ⋯ AMERICA

The band are dissatisfied with their American label A&M Records because of their intention to release a sampler album containing selections from the first three albums; to the band this is disrespectful. It would have been wiser and less problematic to just let A&M get on with it but The Stranglers always knew better than everyone else!

As Christmas 1978 approached, they sent a telex to A&M's offices which read: 'Get fucked, love The Stranglers.' Not surprisingly, it was the end of a beautiful friendship. Though not before A&M sent a retaliatory telegram: 'Took your advice and found it to be a marvellous outlet for transparently contrived and ultimately tiresome hostility. Fondest best wishes for the holiday season'.

Here in the UK, the band's business relationships are also becoming increasingly fraught: Ian Grant will move out of Albion's office in Oxford Street into loaned (by a certain Harvey Goldsmith) premises on Welbeck Street. Grant has another friend, Paul Loasby (Goldsmith's assistant), and he offers free use of the tiny office for a few weeks which will stretch to nine months.

7 1979: FLYING NEAR STRAIGHT WITH PERFECTION

It's hardly outrageous to say that by 1979 The Stranglers are firmly established as a New Wave mainstay on the British rock scene. They sell more records than their contemporaries, they tour to, usually, sell-out crowds and they frequently make good news copy for hungry reporters too. It seems nothing can stop their quest for world domination other than their own unpredictable nature (individually or as a unit).

The fans will be treated to two new albums – albeit one being a live cut – as well as some singles and, adding fuel to the near constant 'Stranglers to split' rumour engine, two notable solo releases as well. The band are effectively under new management, with Ian Grant taking the reins from Davies and Savage, the duo having departed after suggesting to the band that they split up as they had 'lost direction'. The theory being they'd easily be able to reform and thus create a lucrative 'new' market for themselves as a result. Davies' and Savage's exit is quite acrimonious, as is their separation with Grant due to interminable legal wrangles. Such complications also caused long delays in The Stranglers getting their royalties too. At least Grant's own company emerge from the wreckage to look after the band's affairs: Black & White Management.

January 1979. The band are in the studio rehearsing and moulding new material.

20th January '79. Hugh Cornwell and Jet Black are guests on cult Saturday morning TV show *Tiswas* (along with the band Racey) and the videos for 'Grip' and 'Five Minutes' are screened. The two Stranglers have copies of the new live album to give away but reports of black Smarties and Jet holding brats in headlocks seem unfounded.

February '79. A short but important, and potentially lucrative, tour sees firsts for the band in Japan and Australia. However, a tour of New Zealand is cancelled once the authorities there hear how riotous the band's gigs in Oz (supposedly) are. The Japan tour is a big hit, The Stranglers being the first new wavers to make good there. The band fly to Tokyo to spend three days rehearsing, though their arrival is beset with problems as Japanese Customs Officers decide to dismantle most of Dave's keyboards for unconfirmed reasons. Like most customs officials the world over, they are incapable of returning objects to their original state, so the responsibility of adequately rebuilding the keyboards rests with Paul 'Sheds' Jackson and his road crew. Not an easy job, this is intricate equipment we're talking about. Also this month EMI take ownership of United Artists Records.

Typical set list for the Japanese gigs: 'Hanging Around', 'Burning Up Time', 'Straighten Out', 'Dead Ringer', 'Nubiles', 'Dagenham Dave', 'No More Heroes', 'Outside Tokyo', 'Curfew', 'Tank', 'Threatened', 'Nice 'n' Sleazy', 'Do You Wanna?', 'Death And Night And Blood', 'London Lady', 'Sewer', 'Five Minutes', 'Dead Loss Angeles', 'Toiler'.

Numerous bootlegs of Japanese appearances exist, including a televised Tokyo gig from 9th February, and proof of how popular The Stranglers are can be heard by the crowds' ecstatic reactions following every song and near constant clapping to every single beat, even the *erratic* 'Do You Wanna?'. Still, Cornwell and Burnel occasionally talking and singing to audiences in Japanese – for instance the intro to 'Straighten Out' is always going to go down well. Spoken in English though is 'Japan is a free country, so you're free to stand up' from Jet Black early in the February 9th gig, as well as Burnel encouraging the Japanese people to not fight each other but to fight Americans.

23rd February '79. Before the Australian tour commences, the live album *The Stranglers Live (X-Cert)* is released. It's criticised by the music press for being a bit of a 'cash in' by the band and UA, and for demonstrating that The Stranglers are lacking new ideas. Actually though, as live albums go, it's very good, with the sleeve artwork strikingly impressive too. And it reaches No.7 in the album charts.

AUSTRALIA

Up to now The Stranglers have been better known in Australia than in Japan; *No More Heroes* and *Black & White* have reached the Top 20 album chart there. But none of that means much when sections of the Australian media are looking for reasons to slag them off. Interviewed in their Sydney hotel, the band get asked a series of inane questions for the evening magazine show *Willesee At Seven* (named after its presenter Mark Willesee). One such probing enquiry is whether they like the 'things' punk rockers do, 'like the animal acts'. It seems the band are being set up, not dissimilar to Grundy's Pistols encounter in December 1977. The Stranglers are nowhere near as controversial as Rotten and co. that day but the bad seed has already been sown, the show's makers clearly do not like them and neither did the watching Ian Meldrum of *Countdown* (not the UK word show!). Meldrum, Australia's most popular rock show host, telephones Willesee's show to announce he's decided to cancel The Stranglers' scheduled appearance on his show, due to their 'appalling behaviour'. Not to worry, demand for gig tickets increases.

25th February '79. Sydney State Theatre is the venue for The Stranglers' first ever Australian performance, though JJ Burnel has already caused uproar by mooning to a journalist and photographer earlier. Controversy strikes when several strippers join the band on stage, while a local female journalist, said to have been pestering the band, is bound, gagged and lowered in to the audience as punishment. At least she'll have got her story out of it. Talking of stories, the band's publicist Alan Edwards busily feeds the UK tabloids with exaggerated or fictional accounts of the band's antics.

26th February '79. The first of two lively gigs at Brisbane Queens Hotel. Here, annoyed at being spat at by one particular local *phlegmy* punk, JJ manages to clout him around the head with his bass. Queensland's premier, the corrupt conservative Joh Bjelke-Petersen, disapproves of rock concerts and apparently instructs his henchmen to attend the two gigs to cause trouble and start fights so the 'culprits' can then be arrested. The Stranglers write 'Nuclear Device' in 'homage' to Petersen. For the completist fan, support act at the Queens Hotel is the grandly named Fuller Banks And The Debentures.

27th February '79. During this Queens Hotel gig, Hugh is hit on the head by a beer bottle, suffering a cut above his eyebrow which isn't serious, but which does bleed profusely. Like the trooper he is, he carries on without fuss. The audience is said to contain undercover policemen again, 'agitators' causing more aggro and thus enabling the authorities to revoke the venue's licence, as well as get the band into more hot water.

But Alan Edwards doesn't care as long as he has juicy content for his dispatches. This one from a cutting in a scrapbook I came across : 'Punk rock stars The Stranglers are up to their necks in trouble with Australian police. And LEAD SINGER AND GUITARIST Jean-Jacques Burnel was on the run last night. The controversial British group's stage performance in Brisbane ended in a punch up with the law. LEAD GUITARIST Hugh Cornwell was taken to hospital with head wounds. DRUMMER Jet Black and keyboard player Dave Greenfield fled for the safety of their hotel. And BASS GUITARIST JJB, who is believed to have knocked out two policemen, vanished.'

Jet Black said, 'We are terrified. We want to get out now but we don't even know if we will be allowed to leave Brisbane. And we don't know where Jean-Jacques is.' Their London agent Alan Edwards said, 'A group of men jumped on to the stage in the middle of the gig and started to drag the band off. The lads thought they were local yobs. They had no idea they were police.' Mr Edwards claimed all their equipment was smashed. He added, 'The band have 17 more gigs to go in Australia. But this could be the end now. The lads just want to get out. They have been in bother in the past, sure, but they are pretty mellow these days.'

'The Stranglers, who had a recent successful tour of Japan, ran into trouble as soon as they arrived in Australia. A Melbourne TV programme about them was cut short because of their language and opinions. Later, the TV station interrupted scheduled programmes to apologise for putting the band on the air. The band, which has had a history of rows, has been banned from giving concerts in Stockholm, Helsinki and London's Alexandra Palace. Their act was once axed by *Top Of The Pops* because the BBC found them too controversial. They have been involved in furniture smashing parties all over the world. In an Oslo shindig a cigarette machine was hurled through a window.'

2nd March '79. Interviewed on *Double J*, the band talk about Petersen and what happened in Brisbane. Jet does most of the talking and hammers Queensland, inviting listeners to call in to defend the government there. Most callers actually agree with Jet's appraisal of Petersen as a 'fascist' though.

Band at Ally Pally 1979. (Source *Unknown*)

10th March '79. The gig at the Adelaide Apollo Stadium draws an impressive crowd, but an oppressive number of police officers too, prompting Jet to ask them to leave. And they do, even though they hadn't seen Jet make the request as he'd crouched down to speak into one of his drum mics. The police nearly get their own back later at the band's hotel but eventually they leave empty handed, unsure who, if anyone, they can nick. Also in Adelaide come protests from a feminist group urging people to boycott and picket the band or, if they do go to see them play, to throw things at them. It's a fair dinkum guess that those 'things' won't have been women's underwear or flowers.

13th March '79. Bottles and cans fly towards the band as their Melbourne Monash Uni gig gets under way. Band and crew simply return the objects from whence they came, fortunately with no injuries reported.

1979: FLYING NEAR STRAIGHT WITH PERFECTION

18th March '79. At Bondi Lifesavers venue in Sydney, classic antagonism from the band, towards their 'hosts' and to Joh Bjelke-Petersen in particular, in the radically altered lines to 'No More Heroes'. Hugh introduces the song: 'There are no more Abo's in Australia, you killed the fucking lot of 'em' – then JJ's bass rumble arrives and Hugh's new lyrics: 'Whatever happened to … all of the Abo's? You kicked them out of their homes. And gave them three million dollars. Whatever happened to … dear old Fraser? And Bjelke Jerk off Petersen? You let him go … independent. Whatever happened to Australia? Whatever happened to Australia? Just look at Tasmania. Even that wants to fuck off and go independent. I dunno what's going on 'ere. I think I'm gonna go home very soon. Whatever happened to Australia? Whatever happened to Australia? No more Aussie Land anymore, No more Aussie Land anymore. Whatever happened to Channel Seven? It got taken over, by Kerry Packer. Whatever happened to Australia? Whatever happened to Australia? No more Aussie Land anymore, No more Aussie Land anymore, No more Aussie Land anymore, No more Aussie Land anymore'.

21st March '79. In spite of all the controversy and rough receptions, the tour is a profitable success. And while Hugh Cornwell catches a flight to LA from Sydney to continue a separate project with Robert Williams (drummer with Captain Beefheart), the band return to London. Hugh has to flit between various studios to work on a new album, whereas Burnel has managed to write all of his own solo effort in the space of a few weeks at Bear Shank Lodge.

6th April '79. Release of JJ's solo record *Euroman Cometh*, a concept album featuring Jean-Jacques as writer, vocalist and bassist. Brian James of the Damned plays guitar and Lew Lewis the harmonica. The sleeve shows JJ dwarfed by the pipes and vents of the Pompidou Centre in Paris. To help promote the album he embarks on the *Euroman Cometh* Tour but encounters problems, like the Theatre Royal in Drury Lane date being cancelled when the proprietors realise that JJ is a member of those horrible bastardsinblack. The LP will reach No. 40 in the charts with sales figures eventually approaching a hundred thousand.

EUROMAN COMETH

Side 1: 1 'Euroman', 2 'Jellyfish', 3 'Freddie Laker (Concorde & Eurobus)', 4 'Euromess', 5 'Deutschland Nicht Uber Alles'.
Side 2: 6 'Do The European', 7 'Tout Comprendre', 8 'Triumph (Of The Good City)', 9 'Pretty Face', 10 'Crabs', 11 'Eurospeed (Your Own Speed)'.
Guitar: Brian James, Harmonica: Lew Lewis, Drums: Carey Fortune. Drums on 3, 5, 6, Pete Howells: 8 Triumph Bonneville.

Robert Endeacott's review of *Euroman Cometh*:

Different from Stranglers' material, it came as a bit of a shock at first but I quickly grew to *really* like this album. 'Euroman' – a daunting intro track, bleak combined with weird 'In The Shadows' malevolence, it's brilliant, even if it is in French with deliberate monotone vocals. 'Jellyfish' is almost a trifling keyboard ditty, not unlike Devo, containing a superb but not loud enough bass flow throughout. So catchy, like a technopop hybrid of 'Go Buddy Go' and 'Nice 'n' Sleazy'.

'Freddie Laker (Concorde and Eurobus)' is JJ doing The Tornadoes-on-acid, a pulsating, driving bass thrust and eerie, distorted vocals. First class, the Beatles' 'Blue Jay Way' meets 'Rok It To The Moon' recorded in a dungeon. 'Euromess' – a fantastic Burnel bass lick as a foundation for another unusual track, robotic vocals bringing to mind the fab Fad Gadget. 'Deutschland Nicht Uber Alles' starts off like it will explode into a classic Stranglers anthem but then plummets into the dark and obscure. I don't care what they say, German lyrics delivered this way are disconcerting, which I bet is the aim.

'Do the European' – more 'nah nah' singing from JJ, yet more fantastic undulating bass combined with early Ultravox-like synth to add some zing. It's like a disco ditty left next to a throbbing radiator – warped and overheated. 'Tout Comprendre', with its moody keyboards and deadpan delivery, it's another 'In The Shadows' reminder. In French with yet more wonderful bass work to shudder the speakers, while a lovechild of R2D2 chirps away throughout. But overall, not a great track.

'Triumph (Of The Good City)' – JJ's Triumph Bonneville chugs away, over-layered with bass and synth. The bike provides an inept drumbeat and yet this all really does work well. 'Pretty Face' – like XTC armed with a mouth organ, JJ sings an 'Old Codger' type tune. Top class dirty new wave blues rock. 'Crabs' – incongruous but catchy, just like any self-respecting STD should be. 'Eurospeed (Your Own Speed)' – a decent track, more distorted Burnel vocals which could have suited *Black & White*, but not particularly an exciting a finale for this overall fabulous album. On the whole, *Euroman Cometh* is fresh, original and exciting, a creation that Burnel ought to feel very proud of.

(Image courtesy of Duncan Round)

13th April '79. Burnel releases the single 'Freddie Laker (Concorde & Eurobus)' which is flipped with the non-LP track 'Ozymandias', inspired by the Percy Shelley poem and in which JJ hams it up something grand, as the suitably weird melody provides the oddly appealingly backdrop.

16th April '79. The second date of JJ's 'Euroman' tour is Manchester's Apollo. A roadie on the tour — Keith Bowe — recalled that JJ enjoys plenty of opportunities to get in some karate-kick practice during the chaotic gig, despatching various invaders from the stage.

21st April '79. With the so-witty 'Euroman Boreth Something Awful' headline, Record Mirror's Ronnie Gurr 'reviews' Burnel's 15th April Glasgow Pavilion gig. Except there is no actual review at all, only a few lines about support act Blood Donor and a mention of the other support band REM. Not *that* REM, this is John Ellis' outfit. Gurr was clearly more interested in Thin Lizzy's gig in the nearby Apollo. He would soon wish he'd written about that concert ...

Stranglers fan Tony Stubley watched JJ's gig at the Ilford Odeon on Sunday 29th April, 1979 and relates how:

> I lost my gig virginity, final date of JJ's Eurotour. Small turn out, JJ surveyed the audience from a side door to the stalls and shook his head slowly. John Ellis doubled up as JJ's guitarist and during 'Triumph of the Good City', the two have a slight altercation which ends up with JJ in the audience right in front of me! Then the set continues with JJ giving icy stares at JE and warning the audience, after the umpteenth call for 'Burning Up Time', 'If you want to see that go and see The Stranglers, I'm only 25% of them so forget it if you are expecting that'.
>
> All of *Euroman Cometh* gets played except for 'Pretty Face'. One encore only — 'Euroman' — and my first ever gig is then finished'.

John Ellis admits: 'Yes I think JJ and I did have some kind of minor skirmish onstage, and, if I remember correctly, he ended up in the audience and lost his radio mic. Of course there were lots of drugs around at the time. Everything from glue to smack. It's always been like that in music for many reasons. And too many great musicians became casualties'.

25th April '79. The latest NME reports of a scandal involving Ronnie Gurr and JJ Burnel's associates on the night of a *Euroman* gig at Hemel Hempstead Pavilion. Via the band's publicist Alan Edwards, Burnel had invited Gurr to meet him at the White Lion pub in Covent Garden for an interview. When Gurr arrived however, he was met not by JJ but by a few of his 'fucking psycho' friends who proceeded to force him on to the coach for the gig. Gurr claims he was thrown against the coach window with such force that the window fell out. At the venue he was tied up and locked in a backstage room but managed to escape, running across the stage while Blood Donor played, his kidnappers in pursuit. Reaching the nearby police station, the local constabulary helped retrieve his belongings (tape recorder and scarf) from the Pavilion while half-heartedly investigating his claims of abduction. No arrests are made.

Interviewed on the supreme *Strangled* website, Burnel denies none of Gurr's story, admitting also to hiding in the women's toilets when the police went looking for him, but his memory of the entire tour is not particularly reliable due to the influence of heroin, a main item on his personal menu then. Ronnie Gurr, or more accurately, *Record Mirror*, get an iota of revenge by subsequently cutting JJ out of any Stranglers photos they publish.

7th May '79. A new Stranglers track, 'Two Sunspots', along with 'Meninblack', emerges from a session at Eden Studios, with Rushent and Winstanley again running the show. In fact, 'Two Sunspots' is the band's preferred choice of new single ... The track 'Meninblack' is actually the slowed down melody of 'Two Sunspots', with a few tweaks and the addition of Burnel's voice altered via a harmoniser. The band spend two weeks of May in Perugia, Italy, writing most of the material for the next album. Only two new tracks have been tried and tested so far though – 'Genetix' and 'Dead Loss Angeles' – so they have plenty of work to do to fill a whole LP. Not that they are feeling under pressure, because JJ Burnel's girlfriend's father owns a countryside property in Perugia, which the band has the run of. He is also a fine chef so they the Italian job works our nicely.

26th May '79. In between writing and recording the latest album, The Stranglers play the two day Loch Lomond Festival in Balloch, Dumbartonshire. Over 17,000 attend and the band are reportedly paid £20,000, the largest amount they've earned to date for gigging. The festival line up that first day includes Dr Feelgood, Third World, The Skids, UK Subs and The Dickies. Set list: 'Genetix', 'Burning Up Time', 'I Feel Like A Wog', 'Dead Loss Angeles', 'Peasant In The Big Shitty', 'No More Heroes', 'The Raven', 'Sewer', 'Nubiles', 'Dead Ringer', 'Do You Wanna?', 'Death And Night And Blood', 'Nice 'n' Sleazy', 'Tank', 'Sweden', 'Threatened', 'Five Minutes', 'Curfew', 'Hanging Around' and 'Toiler In The Sea'. The Stranglers present a spectacular firework display to mark the climax of the set, with numerous badges distributed as freebies.

14th June '79. The band fly to Paris to the EMI-owned Pathé Marconi Studios to begin recording their, as yet, unnamed new album. They need to find a new producer as Martin Rushent has abruptly withdrawn his services due to the band moving 'into an area musically which I couldn't relate to at all'. The band want 'Two Sunspots' as the next single but Rushent disapproves due to their 'over-keenness' to experiment when they already have a successful music making formula. Tracks are sped up, reversed or have harmonisers/voxes added, and this specific track eventually shape-shifts in to the bizarre 'Meninblack' track, which Rushent absolutely detests. He isn't too keen on the band either by now, considering them arrogant and difficult to work with, plus they are sampling drugs on a 'Hoover scale'.

10th July '79. The band are in the studio again, with 'Fools Rush Out' getting a reworking, soon to be the flipside to the imminent new single 'Duchess'. As well as a play on words on the old Rick Nelson single, the lyrics of 'Fools Rush Out' are a barely veiled dig at Derek Savage and Dai Davies. It's a decent tune too.

10th August '79. 'Duchess' is released, in a brilliant picture sleeve of the band dressed as choirboys.

Promo video for Stranglers singles – 'Duchess': Filmed in a church (with the vicarinblack's permission), this brilliant flick has, amongst other things, Hugh in the pulpit and over-the-top backing vocals from the band, all wearing sunglasses and dressed as choirboys. It would be even funnier if the reports of His Pureness Cliff Richard being offended enough to complain to the TOTP higher-ups are true.

15th August '79. Overseen by Steve Churchyard at Air London Studios, six different versions of 'Social Secs' are recorded – the variations are 'full with vox', 'full no vox', 'half-speed with vox', 'half-speed no vox', 'backwards with vox' and 'backwards no vox'. It is presumed by more-knowledgeable Stranglerphiles that the 'backwards no vox' recording would become the instrumental 'Yellowcake UF6', a B-side. Yellowcake is a form of uranium concentrate and UF6 is the chemical uranium hexafluoride, the basic material from which uranium is extracted. The Australian government has discovered huge deposits of uranium in the centre of sacred Aboriginal sites and decides to excavate whilst not giving a shit about the rights or cultural heritage of the Aboriginal people.

18th August '79. The band play Wembley Stadium as main support to The Who, with Nils Lofgren on first and AC/DC on the bill too. This is a huge event for The Stranglers, with well over 80,000 in attendance, so their choice of set list is surprising as it consists mainly of new material and none of the hits. The Stranglers and the Who are not on Christmas card terms thanks to Hugh slagging them off, and Pete Townshend slagging off The Stranglers in return (or Hugh at least), so to have the two bands on the same bill is some surprise. An audience member's Super 8 footage exists of some of the gig – including a glimpse of the large Raven-head insignia ignited at the side of the stage – and all the acts are well received by the huge crowd. Rumour has it too that AC/DC singer the late Bon Scott needs to have his stomach pumped before their slot.

During The Stranglers' set, presumably as a reference to mods and rockers and Brighton, Hugh comments, 'If there are any Brighton fans here, they lost four-nil today unfortunately'. He asks, 'Do you like our light show, it's pretty good innit? Cost a lot of money'. He introduces the first song – 'Are there any Australians here, anyone from Australia? We've just been there and we're gonna tell you a little story about this bloke there who runs a fascist state'. The majority of people at Wembley Stadium won't have noticed the electric scoreboard behind them showing each track as it features. Set list:

'Nuclear Device', 'Genetix', 'The Raven', 'Dead Loss Angeles', 'Baroque Bordello', 'Tank', 'Threatened', 'Shah Shah A Go Go', 'Ice', 'Sewer', 'Nubiles', 'Duchess', 'Toiler'.

Two new button badge ranges are produced to commemorate the event, with 'Who are the Meninblack' and 'Who are The Stranglers' printed above 'Wembley 1979'. Explosive controversy isn't far away, though the band are blameless. At the climax of their set, pyro-technician Martin Blake of Le Maitre Fireworks has arranged for a few mortar-like devices to be fired, and what an earth moving climax they make, literally. When they're set off, the stage is said to actually shift a few inches. As a result, The Who are banned from using their own pyrotechnics display – Le Maitre's again – to cap their own gig.

30th August '79. It's been a while but, introduced by David 'Kid' Jensen, the band appear on *Top Of The Pops* with 'Duchess', looking sombre yet cool as hell, especially Dave Greenfield, with his long floppy hair and sunglasses. The single reaches No. 14 and spends nine weeks in the charts.

September 1979. The new album *The Raven* is released, with a corresponding tour commencing too. 20,000 copies of the album come in a special 3D sleeve depicting a stunning image of a raven's head.

THE RAVEN
Released: 21st September 1979.
Label: United Artists Records.
Charted at No. 4
Side One: 1 'Longships', 2 'The Raven', 3 'Dead Loss Angeles', 4 'Ice', 5 'Baroque Bordello', 6 'Nuclear Device'.
Side Two: 1 'Shah Shah A Go Go', 2 'Don't Bring Harry', 3 'Duchess', 4 'Meninblack', 5 'Genetix'.

In a few words – what the *Ford* are the songs about? Part 4.
'Longships': A short instrumental written by Hugh who couldn't think of suitable lyrics. The band toured far and wide in '79 (not in longships) and possibly saw themselves as similar to the Vikings, unwanted visitors to distant shores and troubled times.
'The Raven': Burnel's fascination with the bird and its Nordic links shine through. Whilst at sea, if ever the Vikings were unsure of where they were and their sat nav was busted, they would use ravens to determine where the nearest land was as evidently they have an uncanny knack of knowing.
'Dead Loss Angeles': More evidence of the band's dislike of America, LA specifically, here though the first part refers to Chicago. JJ wrote the tune, Hugh the lyrics.
'Ice': More of JJ's interest in Japanese culture, this time seppuku, a form of ritual suicide ('chop sueycide' as Hugh called it).

'Baroque Bordello': Fictional lyrics, the band frequented no bordellos or brothels, of any architectural significance.

'Nuclear Device': A scathing, thinly veiled song about the disgraceful antics of Danish-descended and far right politician Joh Bjelke-Petersen, the premier of Queensland, Australia.

'Shah Shah A Go Go': Reference to the recently deposed Shah of Iran, the self-crowned monarch living in luxury and exploiting the people's adulation.

'Don't Bring Harry': 'Harry' being heroin, and 'Don't Bring' being Burnel's request to not see the stuff or be tempted by it again. Basically an anti-drugs song.

'Duchess': About a former girlfriend of Hugh's, a descendent of Henry VIII, who had a fair few aspiring suitors vying for her attentions.

'Meninblack': 'Sung' by an alien, it concerns mankind being a genetic experiment conducted by superior beings from another planet.

'Genetix': About genetic engineering and genetically modified foods, finishes with a quote from a leading figure in the science, Gregor Mendel ... though not in person as he died in 1884.

Notable songs of the time not on the vinyl album:

'Bear Cage': Recorded a few months after the album, the band's attempt at 'mechanical Germanic disco' with gloomy lyrics coming from a young East German's perspective, post-World War II. The closing bars contain a snippet of 'Three Blind Mice'.

'Who Wants The World?': Another 'sci-fi' track, this time about the experiences of aliens landing on earth and discovering that the human race has ruined it. Recorded after 'Bear Cage'.

✪

John Robb's review of *The Raven*:

The cover was a good start, that mean looking raven, like all four members of the band rolled into one feral foul fowl! *The Raven* is a great record, a sprawling work incorporating many different styles of music. Less jagged but with a richness and subtlety, even if that meant JJ's bass was toned down.

Opener 'Longships' had a swirling sea swept feel to it as Norsemen plunder foreign shores, perhaps an analogy for a rock 'n' roll band. The title track was a masterpiece, JJ utilising his 'new' confident voice discovered on his solo album to great effect, over a simple bass motif and keyboard sweeps that sound like the bird itself swooping down from the skies, and JJ gets personal in the words.

'Dead Loss Angeles' is Hugh's sardonic take on Los Angeles' sunshine culture. It even mentions the La Brea Tar Pits where thousands of early mammals died in the bubbling tar. Japanese ritual suicide raises its head again on "Ice", the most different style the band had traversed yet.

Side Two opens with 'Baroque Bordello' and it's perhaps one of their best intros that builds till Hugh's warm vocal comes in with lines of beat poetry. 'Nuclear Device' is a return to the punky Stranglers, with all the hallmarks of the great punk era: chugging bass, Hugh's phlegmatic vocals stirring controversy, lyrical content that saw him take a swipe at the governor of Brisbane. It also had one of those twangy sections like 'Sewer' and 'Toiler', a fantastic song. 'Shah Shah A Go Go' was yet another killer intro about the fall of the Shah of Iran, heralding a new era of tension in the Middle East.

'Don't Bring Harry' was JJ's lament to heroin that had crept into the band's life as they swerved into a very dark and destructive period. 'Duchess' is a pure pop rush, a short sharp shock of romantic yearning. 'Meninblack' was the band at their weirdest, the 'song' supposed to be an extra-terrestrial speaking. The slowed down track was added to with a weird high pitch vari-speeded vocal and a spaghetti western guitar. The final track was one of the last of the band's long album-ending pieces: 'Genetix' has become the holy grail of Strangler bass lines and is another fantastic piece of music. Dave Greenfield provides another one of his genuinely strange vocals as the band take a long look at DNA, genetic engineering and manufactured reproduction. And Jet Black's drumming on this track is stunningly brilliant.

✪

With sales probably helped by the Wembley gig, *The Raven* enters the charts at No. 4. It would almost certainly have hit the top had there not been another cock-up. Somehow, though not even in the shops yet, sales figures of The Police's *Regatta De Blanc* are mistakenly boosted by thousands of those belonging to *The Raven*. Sting in the lousy tale or what?!

12th October '79. A gig at Lancaster University. Nothing too unusual about this other than BBC TV's *Tomorrow's World* use footage of the remote controlled pyrotechnics at the programme's finale. Similar to the Wembley extravaganza but without the earth tremors, a large firework display is employed as 'Toiler' is played, rockets flying out horizontally above the audience.

20th October '79. The Australian politics-inspired 'Nuclear Device (The Wizard Of Aus)' single is out, it's about our old pal Joh Bjelke-Petersen. The B-side is the instrumental 'Yellowcake UF6'. The single only reaches No.36 in the charts.

Promo video for Stranglers singles - 'Nuclear Device': Filmed in Portugal, the band romp around dressed as stereotyped Aussies impersonating bouncy kangaroos and generally arsing about as a few explosions abound in the sand. Those Stranglers knees should be permanently kept from public view. Incidentally, journalist Deanne Pearson is in attendance and, not being particularly fond of reporters, the band have some 'fun' at her expense. They leave her stranded in deserted scrubland and she has to make her own way back to the airport.

20th October '79. The band play at London's Rainbow, the second of two nights there. Barry Cridland went:

> I'd just turned 15 and this was my first Stranglers gig. My first gig ever in fact. I had on my black Lewis leather biker jacket covered in punk badges and on the back a brilliant white silhouette of The Raven. And the huge Raven stage backdrop is fantastic. The lights go down. The stunning roar from the fans. Half way through the first song, the sweat is dripping off me. I have a good view: JJ looking menacing, Hugh cracking a few one liners to the audience, Jet with his head tilted to one side powering through the songs, and Dave ... Well I'm sure Dave was there but, surrounded by towers of keyboards, I could only see the top of his head. This gig was the start of a relationship spanning decades. The Stranglers, I fucking love 'em!

25th October '79. Hugh Cornwell's fine cover version of Cream's 'White Room' is released. It fails to reach the Top 40. The same night, The Stranglers play at Manchester Apollo. After playing the sexually themed 'Nubiles' and before the politically-edged 'Nuclear Device', Cornwell explains: 'While we're on the subject of pricks and cunts, we've got a little story about a prick – well we haven't made up our minds whether he's a prick or whether he's a cunt or maybe he's a hermaphrodite – in Queensland Australia. Once upon a time ...'

31st October '79. Cardiff Top Rank. Fan Paul Davies recalls:

> I remember them starting to play 'The Raven' but I noticed JJ staring at one member of the audience spitting at him. The look was 'if you don't stop, then you're in for some trouble'. Despite this the bloke carried on spitting so JJ stopped playing, took off his bass, threw it on the stage and leapt into the crowd. The audience just parted and left JJ and this bloke in the middle to scrap it out! No prizes for guessing who won. Once JJ was satisfied justice had been done, he climbed back up on stage, put his bass back on and the band carried on playing as if nothing had happened.

'Ello ello ello' Part One (English version) – 1st November '79: After the Cardiff gig, rather than stay overnight in the Bristol hotel booked for them, Hugh gets a lift in the hire car of Paul Loasby who had been promoting the tour, along with three French fans (two boys, one girl) who Hugh has arranged accommodation for at a friend's house in London.

From *Inside Information*, comes Hugh's version of events: 'We were stopped in a routine road block which was a complete Sweeney-type blockade, on main thoroughfares in the middle of the night, with arc lights and about 50 policemen and eight squad cars involved. We were stopped in Hammersmith Broadway which is about four lanes wide, with the squad cars diagonally across the road, cutting all the traffic down to one lane.

They were stopping every vehicle and checking every detail and, where anything looked a bit suspicious to them, they were searching the driver or the contents of the car…'

Loasby and Cornwell were arrested, the three (approximately) 16 year olds in the backseat of the car arousing suspicions that something illegal/immoral was going on (it wasn't). Officers seeing the presence of a small amount of Class A drugs in Loasby's shirt pocket obviously didn't help matters, nor did his having around £2,000 in cash even though it genuinely was concert takings. Also damning was the presence of a book on how to successfully sell (in bulk) cocaine! Cornwell was charged with illegal possession of cannabis, heroin and cocaine, while Loasby was charged with possession of cocaine. The drugs had been 'collected' by Cornwell from fans and the like as the tour had progressed, to be used personally, not sold.

9th November '79. The Stranglers release their first ever UK EP. Tracks are their 'Don't Bring Harry' plus 'Wired' from Cornwell & Williams, and on the flip are two live tracks, Burnel's 'Crabs' (from Hemel Hempstead in April) and 'In The Shadows' recorded by the band at the Hope & Anchor in 1977. Even with a snazzy Yuletide pic sleeve, it proves as popular as Christmas is with the turkey photographed on the cover.

12th November '79. French fan Philippe 'X' attends the Paris gig at Le Théâtre de l'Empire:

> An old movie theatre built in the 1920s, with big glass windows. Many TV shows were filmed here too, one of them being 'Chorus' who film this one. Tickets were cheap but in very limited quantities, just a few hundreds, so most gigs sold out pretty quickly. The bouncer took something out of his pocket and pointed it at me. It was a gun! POW, he fires it! Thank God, it wasn't a real gun but some kind of tear gas weapon. My eyes cried a little bit but I was Okay. 'You funny bastard!' I shout but because of the shot there is some confusion and I manage to get in.
>
> 'Down In The Sewer' is when things started to get wild. First, JJ jumped into the audience, still playing his bass. People began to get crazy … then Hugh went down into the audience as well. I couldn't see him but I could hear his guitar riff. 'Hanging Around' … 'The Raven' – good God, I don't know why but suddenly JJ showed his ass at the crowd and the camera! 'Dead Loss Angeles', 'Threatened', 'Baroque Bordello' … Things went out of control and around 20 guys, including me, hit the stage. A big bouncer tried to push one of us down but Hugh stopped playing and pushed him back! JJ then said in French something like 'Come on, we prefer people on stage with us, come on everybody …' The Stranglers played a stunning set, ending with 'Toiler' and then a sort of white noise effect.

16th November '79. The Stranglers are in Bordeaux. Whilst it's unclear actually when they started doing it, their arrival on stage tonight is preceded by one of their tracks, 'Meninblack', being played through the speakers. Set list: 'Five Minutes', 'Shah Shah A Go Go,' which smoothly blends into 'Ice', 'Sewer', 'Hanging Around', before which Hugh remarks, 'So this is Friday night in Bordeaux? But we're not in Bordeaux, this is sort of outside Bordeaux innit? It's like a huge housing estate, built for the future'.

'The Raven' on which Dave Greenfield's keyboards wondrously zoom and plummet like the wings of a soaring raven, and then JJ's bass segues brilliantly into 'Dead Loss

Angeles', then come 'Threatened', 'Baroque Bordello', 'Curfew'. 'Tank', 'Burning Up Time', 'Nubiles' and 'Nuclear Device' which marches straight into the wonderfully unworldly 'Genetix'. Then it's 'Duchess' and finally 'Toiler' to end a marvellous performance.

16th November '79. United Artists release the Hugh Cornwell & Robert Williams album *Nosferatu*.

27th November '79. Hamburg, Musikhalle gig. Apart from 'Hanging Around' replacing 'Curfew', this gig is the same set list as Bordeaux. After the dynamic 'Five Minutes' opener, Hugh mentions that the band always wondered what this place would look like full, their first appearance there three years ago had been watched by just six people, four of them being press, and still people had thrown things at them.

NOSFERATU
Side 1: 1 'Nosferatu', 2 'Losers In A Lost Land', 3 'White Room', 4 'Irate Caterpillar', 5 'Rhythmic Itch'.
Side 2: 1 'Wired', 2 'Big Bug', 3 'Mothra', 4 'Wrong Way Round', 5 'Puppets'.
R Williams - drums, percussion, tympanis, backing vocals, Moog synthesiser, Moog bass, syndrums.
HA Cornwell - guitars, slide guitar, basses, vocals, lyrics, Chamberlin mellotron, Prophet synthesiser. Ian Underwood - Yamaha synthesiser, Sonar Yamaha synthesiser, soprano sax.
David Walldroop - rhythm guitar.
Mark Mothersbaugh - Prophet synthesiser, vocals and lyrics.
Bob Mothersbaugh - guitar and backing vocal.
Duncan Poundcake - fairground barker.

Robert Endeacott's review of *Nosferatu*:
There's something coolly weird, weirdly cool, about listening to this album alone in a dark room. I was always massively in to the old horror films, so I was immediately drawn to this concept, but *Nosferatu* the vampire is actually not the sole reference here. Side One relates directly to *Nosferatu* but Side Two focuses on people's fears or phobias. 'Nosferatu' – great track, manic drumming, suitably manic vocals and strong bass, and some raking guitar and spine-chilling keyboard thrown in for a real edge.

'Losers In A Lost Land' – this could easily be a *Black & White* cast-off – very slow, Hugh's vocals are like he's singing to himself, deliberately out of key. Full on atmospheric, helped by fine bass work not unlike Mr Burnel's. 'White Room' – Cream's classic, this is a worthy cover version and Hugh's nihilistic delivery fits perfectly. 'Irate Caterpillar' – great tune, splendid drumming, daft song, reminds me of Wire on one of their more 'out there' jaunts. 'Rhythmic Itch' – sung by Devo's Bob Motherbaugh this definitely is heavily influenced by that underrated band, a cracking little number.

'Wired' – saxophone is just right, reminiscent of Bill's brother Ian Nelson, and this song does have a Bill Nelson's Red Noise feel to it but with even better use of guitar, synthesiser and edgy vocals. The whistling is a bit annoying though. 'Big Bug' is a bit of a tangled beauty, another one which wouldn't have been out of place on *Black & White* or even *The Raven*, it feels like a precursor to 'Bear Cage'. Avant-garde drumming adds to the whole skirmish, fighting with guitar and vocals for front of stage dominance. 'Mothra' – ace little tune that would have made a smart soundtrack for some weird short film like those *The Old Grey Whistle Test* used to show.

'Wrong Way Round' – the fairground barker is Ian Dury, listed here as Duncan Poundcake. This dark Cornwell ditty is fabulous, thanks to the deadpan vocals and grinding beat. Dury's presence actually spoils it as a tune. 'Puppets' – edgy, bizarre, freaky, scary. Pretty damned good. In summary, I don't care how poorly it sold or that its recording often took place at ungodly cocaine-fuelled hours, causing HC and RW to almost operate like vampires, this album is still pretty bloody hot and startlingly original.

✪

December 1979. The Stranglers play seven dates in Japan, the tour is hardly a flop but their appeal has worn off a little since last time. Financial disaster strikes anyway as the band get ripped off by the Japanese promoter: Paul Loasby takes payment in the form of a Japanese cheque – drawing English currency on foreign cheques is not allowed, so it's a dud and they were screwed.

6th December '79. Recorded in November, the band appear on *Top Of The Pops* with 'Don't Bring Harry'. They're all in black, with Dave sitting at a white grand piano while the barely involved Hugh sits statuesque on a stool, guitar in hand. Brilliantly understated and low key – the performance and the single – but it's a strange choice, arguably the least 'poppy' song on the entire album, even taking 'Meninblack' into account. Sales support the argument, it fails to reach the Top 40.

25th December '79. Flatmate of Chrissie Hynde and creator of The Stranglers' red logo, Kevin Sparrow, dies after taking a Mogadon pill and drinking a bottle of whisky.

8 1980: BLACK & BLACKER

A ground-breaking and truly memorable year coming up for the band. That is not to say it will be a *good* year though. No, 1980 will be remembered as a year doused in negativity and dark controversy, where even the highlights for the band are overshadowed by misfortune and regrets. On the music side of Stranglers' matters, there is to be plenty of action on the vinyl scene, plus in agreeing to a request from founder member of Polyphonic Size, Roger-Marc Vande Voorde, to produce their next single, a long relationship begins between JJ and the Belgian band. His production credit on that single, 'Nagasaki Mon Amour', is to be the first of many, and he will often guest on tracks for the Brussels new wave outfit too, as will Dave Greenfield to a lesser extent.

1st January '80. The France-only version of 'Don't Bring Harry' comes out, it's called *'N'emmenes Pas Harry'* and is sung in the vernacular. Backed with 'Livin' In A Bear Cage' it's issued with a unique picture cover too, not that it's anything special to look at.

6th January '80. Arrested last November, Hugh Cornwell and Paul Loasby appear in a west London magistrates' court on charges of possession of illegal drugs. In spite of their optimism that they would just receive warnings, fines or, at worst, suspended jail sentences (both are first time offenders), it all goes badly wrong. Loasby is sentenced to fourteen days in jail and Cornwell to eight weeks, with a £300 fine on top. Their incarcerations are suspended pending individual appeals at a later date, meaning they can't leave the country. It's a terrible result for the band too, as tour dates around the world have to be cancelled – lucrative gigs in barely-touched-before arenas such as Bangkok, Bangalore, Calcutta, Delhi and a stadium gig in Bombay, plus dates in Cairo and Athens. ALL have to be called off. A few months later and Sting, Andy Summers and Stewart Copeland tour the Far East to worldwide acclaim, and The Police's career consequently soars.

22nd January '80. The Stranglers are in Air Studios, London, working on the next album already intriguingly titled *The Gospel According To The Meninblack*.

(Image courtesy of Duncan Round)

1st February '80. At Saarbrucken University in West Germany, the band play a set that is, by turns, both splendid and shambolic. They open with a superb 'Shah Shah A Go Go' which almost spirals out of sonic control only to be reined back in line to the strains of the also fabulous 'Ice'. Then 'Down In The Sewer', a fantastic rendition, but the audience don't seem appreciative enough so Hugh, perversely, tells them to shut up. Then Jet says, 'Be quiet, can't you see we're trying to enjoy ourselves?' Next is 'Hanging Around' and then 'The Raven' which floats seamlessly and wonderfully in to 'Dead Loss Angeles'. Dave's keyboards work on 'Threatened' is the perfect ending to a unique song, but next up is 'Baroque Bordello' which starts off clumsily before properly getting in to the swing.

Jet chastises himself about a personally poor performance, chuntering, 'A load of bollocks, arsehole, cunt' at the end before slapping his drums around. 'Curfew' follows, connecting to 'Tank' with a fabulous pulsing 'alarm' effect from lead guitar. To close is 'Nubiles', Jet again showing he's not happy, ending another personal rant with, 'Bollocks, bollocks, cunt, arseholes, tit' tirade for some reason, and then he cocks up the end of the song too!

Late February '80. Paul Loasby wins his appeal in court and is reprieved. Hugh Cornwell's appeal is in a few weeks' time.

7th March '80. Recorded in January at Air Studios, the latest Stranglers single is out, it's a double A side with 'Bear Cage' and 'Shah Shah A Go Go'. It's also available as a limited edition picture-sleeved 12-incher with extended versions of the songs. A superb package but it only reaches No.36 in the charts.

Promo video for Stranglers singles – 'Bear Cage': This really suits the song, colourful yet bleak at the same time. JJ, Jet and Dave really go for it in their roles as *Bearlins* [a play on Butlin's Holiday Camp] staff; Jet and his beckoning finger is the stuff of nightmares.

19th March '80. The band record 'Who Wants The World?' at Air Studios.

21st March '80. Hugh Cornwell's appeal at Knightsbridge Crown Court is dismissed and he must now serve his eight-week sentence in HM Pentonville Prison, as prisoner F48444.

3rd & 4th April '80. Even with the enforced absence of their main frontman, the new 'trio' still fulfil the scheduled dates at the London Rainbow with a whole ensemble of personnel filling in for Hugh.

4th April '80. The wise Jet Black introduces the show. He should have been a politician, or a judge even: 'And then there were three ... You know the governments of this country have an uncanny knack of always getting it WRONG. You see, they thought Hugh Cornwell was a pop star so they gave him a big house in Pentonville Row. As it happens, Hugh doesn't like big houses, especially ones with bars on the windows and steel doors, and people walking around inside with chains and keys and fancy dress costumes. When Hugh was sent there I read in a newspaper that the judge said, "Let this be a lesson to The Stranglers' fans." I've been wondering whether you think that you need somebody to teach you a lesson ... "NO!" ... I'll do that again ... do you need anybody to teach you a lesson?'... "NO!!" The judge sleeps a lot so let's do that again ... do you need anyone to teach you a lesson?'... "NO!!!" 'That's great. Before we get on with this, and this is gonna be very unusual tonight and you understand why, it's gonna be an amazing gig. And we have been absolutely knocked out by the people who've come along and volunteered to help this thing to work tonight, so I want you to show your appreciation for that ... And also the crew who have been working their balls off so that this WASN'T a disaster. Thanks'.

Tracks are: '(Get A) Grip (On Yourself)' as well as 'Hanging Around' with Hazel O'Connor (Hugh's current paramour) and The Cure's Robert Smith. 'Tank' with Robert Fripp (King Crimson) and Peter Hammill (Van Der Graaf Generator) on vocals; 'Threatened' with Fripp too; 'Toiler On The Sea' with Fripp and Phil Daniels; 'The Raven' with Basil Gabbidon (Steel Pulse) and Peter Hammill again on vocals, closing it with: '... looking out forward over the prow of the longships' from his own song 'Viking'; 'Dead Loss Angeles' with Phil Daniels and Wilko Johnson; 'Nice 'n' Sleazy' with Gabbidon, Nicky Tesco (The Members) and Nik Turner; 'Bring On The Nubiles' with Richard Jobson (The Skids) and Wilko Johnson; 'Peaches' with Ian Dury and Matthieu Hartley of The Cure; plus Blockheads Davey Payne and John Turnbull and Toyah Wilcox.

Dury's amended 'worse places to be' line is '... I could be out in the street, I could be in hospital, I could be in Pentonville Prison!" 'Bear Cage' with Dury, Hartley, Payne, Turnbull and Wilko Johnson; 'Duchess' with Toyah; 'No More Heroes' with Jobson; 'Five Minutes' with Jobson and Larry Wallis of the Pink Fairies; 'Something Better Change' with Steve Hillage and Toyah; 'Down In The Sewer' with Jake Burns, Hillage and all guests. Before it, in his rich Irish twang, Jake Burns: 'For all the poxy pop stars who wouldn't do this gig, I hope every fucking one of you rots down in the sewer'. After 'Sewer' comes 'Do The European' from JJ's solo album, as well as a messy en masse attempt at 'Go Buddy Go'.

John Ellis plays lead guitar on all the songs, testament again to his great talent (and stamina). He relates how 'I enjoyed learning Hugh's parts and it was great to work with all the artists who did the show. That was the first time I worked with Peter Hammill, I subsequently did a lot of recording and touring with Peter. I also remember backstage being pretty crazy, I think there was a very large bowl containing some powdered goodies that we all dipped into. I seem to remember JJ and Toyah having some kind of physical encounter on stage while she was doing her song. I guess I was much more of a blues influenced player than Hugh. He's got a very individual style that I like very much. It's less influenced by the usual suspects and quite 'spikey'. I think Hugh's playing is brilliant. I realised how good he was when I had to learn his parts'. Support bands tonight include Section 25 and Joy Division whose singer Ian Curtis, thanks to the effects of strobe lighting, suffers an epileptic fit, collapsing back into Steve Morris's drum kit during their final song 'Atrocity Exhibition'.

25th April '80. Hugh Cornwell gets early release from prison, on grounds of good behaviour, having served five of the eight week sentence. He squeezes in a short break in Italy soon after with Hazel O'Connor. Despite the undoubted shock of being imprisoned, Hugh managed to 'enjoy' a settled time, and he seems to have learned an important lesson too. Asked afterwards on BBC *Breakfast Time* about run ins with drugs by all the members of the band, he replied dolefully – 'I think it's just me actually'. Is that behind him now? 'Oh totally. When you have problems with your personality, or you have problems fitting in with life, you resort to things like that. There's a lot of people with very good backgrounds involved in it, much more than you would imagine, and so it's nothing to do with how well off you are, it's to do with you having problems fitting in with life. Once you get over those problems then you have no need to resort to those things anymore'.

23rd to 30th May '80. The band are in Munich's Musicland Studios – with engineer Steve Churchyard – working on their next album. Two songs are recorded, 'Thrown Away' and 'Second Coming'. The studio was created by Giorgio Moroder around ten years before.

30th May '80. The new single 'Who Wants The World?' is released. Hopes are high of big chart success, thanks to positive press reviews and a good response from the fans (plus another 'gimmick' of two slightly different picture sleeves and the fact that it's commercial, catchy yet uniquely 'the Stranglers'). However, it only reaches No.39.

Promo video for Stranglers singles – 'Who Wants The World?': A great video for a fantastic song, the maninblack alien visitor complete with sandwich board wandering through proceedings is a fantastic image. Said alien is in fact Rik Kenton from Roxy Music and *not* Ian Grant, who is commonly believed to have played the part. With this video and the high quality of the song, it really is a mystery how the single flopped.

2nd - 9th June '80. The band are in Pathé Marconi Studios in Paris, adding material to the new album. The tracks 'Four Horsemen', 'Waltzinblack' and 'Hallow To Our Men' are recorded. For The Stranglers this new album is all a relatively long process, but nothing compared to the Rolling Stones in the same studio recording their *Emotional Rescue* LP. It has taken a year already.

12th June '80. Start of a short but eventful Euro tour. Ian Grant stays behind to concentrate on settling the band's tangled business issues and so Andy Dunkley is taken on as new tour manager. That's the Stranglers stalwart and same Andy Dunkley who DJ'd at Battersea Park. Grant's 'absence' is not popular with the band, they suspect he is losing interest in them. He wasn't.

14th June '80. The band perform at La Courneuve Festival in Paris. It's an outdoor affair organised by the *Parti Socialiste Unifié*. The Stranglers are scheduled to play on the main stage, but rain starts to fall and so the gig moves to a huge tent. Matters get rather boisterous in the audience. Set list: Introduction track 'Meninblack', 'Shah Shah A Go Go' (a superb rendition, the vocals are beautifully clear), 'Ice', 'Toiler' (after which Hugh remarks about not being able to see anything, so he therefore can't understand how the crowd can see to throw beer bottles and the like. JJ Burnel comments in French that it's *'tres méchant'* [roughly translates to "very nasty"] of them to be throwing stuff), 'Duchess', 'Hanging Around', Burnel asks the crowd if they're Socialist, to which a lot of booing ensues. 'Baroque Bordello' and then a new track 'Waiting For The Meninblack', which Cornwell on lead vocals struggles with, as if the notes are too deep for him tonight. 'Down In The Sewer' (the amount of graft Jet Black puts into the immaculate percussion of this epic track, especially the closing minute where he sounds more like a machine gun, is amazing), 'Who Wants The World?', 'Thrown Away', an extremely powerful 'I Feel Like A Wog', 'Tank', 'Nuclear Device', from which Jet's drumming seques like smooth machinery in to 'Genetix'. Finally, 'The Raven'.

20th June '80. The band have been lined up to play a gig in Cannes, but it's called off at a very late juncture. So a replacement is arranged, in Nice …

'Ello, ello, ello' (the French version) Part Two - The Nice, France, Incidents: The band are booked in at the Negresco hotel in Nice, the most luxurious they had ever stayed in, but, ironically, they will spend precious little time there though, instead having to make do with a Napoleonic shithole in the main. The whole affair is perfectly described in Jet's *Much Ado About Nothing*, but anyway …

On the afternoon of the gig, Andy Dunkley gets news to the band that the university's authorities, without explanation, are refusing access for the roadies' truck, thus meaning the crew have to lug the tons of equipment hundreds of yards to the stage. The crew are also denied a decent electricity supply for the gig, so their boss makes the decision to hire a generator. The university bosses then dictate that it can't be used, and, to add insult to injury, when the band arrive for the gig they have nowhere to change as the key for the dressing room was 'lost'.

Yet, in spite of being fucked around a treat, they take to the Nice University stage in determined mood for a gig which Hugh will later describe as one of the best they ever played. Unfortunately it lasts no more than half an hour, which is when the serious shit began to hit the (non-electrical) fan. After a third power failure, the band curtail the gig; they have no real option. As any good professional would do, Jet Black in English and then JJ Burnel in French, try to explain their decision to the audience. True, certain 'messages' within their statements might have been phrased with more tact, but the consequences of their explanation proved disproportionate to their 'crime'. As well as rightfully blaming the university for all the problems that day, both Jet and Jean-Jacques intimate to the audience that they should take out their own retribution – but not on the band's equipment – for the disgraceful situation. That is effectively what the disgruntled crowd do: hundreds riot, start fires, break numerous windows and trash as much of the place as possible. It will all rebound on the band disastrously.

21st June '80. Around 6 a.m., when Hugh and Dave return to the hotel after a dinner party, all four members of the band are arrested and taken to the central police station where they are held in squalid, stinking, hot, cockroach-infested cells. Although he doesn't feel unwell, Dave *looks* it due to an allergic reaction not to seafood but sea shells, just touching the things caused a harsh reaction to his lips and eyelids swell up, looking like those of a not very well protected boxer. Unfortunately for the band, in France you're guilty until proven innocent, and so they were charged under Article 314 of the criminal code, also known as the 'anti-smashers' law which came into being after serious student rioting in the sixties.

23rd June '80. Dave, as the only one not to address the gig's audience, is released. He catches a flight to Rome to work with Steve Churchyard on the next album. The remaining trio are moved from the shitty police cells to much less shitty prison cells. Their already stressed manager, Ian Grant, flies out to Paris to collect bail money amounting to around £30,000 from EMI France, and on to Nice to visit the band. Hugh Cornwell, not long out of jail as it is, takes this latest incarceration particularly badly.

27th June '80. The band are released from Nice nick this afternoon and have a low key party at the hotel to celebrate.

28th June '80. They leave for Rome to join Dave and Steve Churchyard.

July '80. The owners of United Artists, EMI, change the label's name to Liberty (oh the irony-in-black!) and relocate their offices to EMI's in Manchester Square, London. The band aren't happy about the changes and their concerns will be justified. Their alternative name for EMI – Every Mistake Imaginable – is also vindicated.

An early EMI *faux pas* concerns the label's intentions of releasing a JJ Burnel solo effort (from nearly two years earlier) called 'Girl From The Snow Country' as a single. However, as no one has deigned to inform The Stranglers camp – JJ doesn't actually want it released – a few thousand singles are pressed. JJ, at the offices one day, only learns of this by discovering boxes of the single ready for shipment. He confiscates and destroys as many copies as he can get his hands on, while the label promptly deletes the single. But, as fans advise *Strangled* mag, a few copies slip through the net and are on sale in Holland: they are now valuable collectors' items. EMI even advertises the single as 'Woman From The Snowlands'. Doh!

2nd July '80. Castel de St Angelo, Rome, Italy – the gig begins with 'Shah Shah A Go Go' and 'Ice' after which Hugh asks the talkative audience to 'lend us your ears for one hour', his polite way of telling them to shut up while they're playing. Then comes 'Toiler' and some more repartee from the eager to please Cornwell, apologising for his poor attempt at Italian, saying it's very good they're in Rome and that he saw Pope John Paul II at the Vatican, which was good. He mentions that they would have visited earlier but they were jailed in France; this earning a big cheer from the crowd.

They play 'Duchess', 'Hanging Around', 'Baroque Bordello', 'Waiting For The Meninblack', 'Sewer', 'Who Wants The World?', 'Thrown Away'. Continuing with the charm offensive, Cornwell introduces 'I Feel Like A Wog' with 'This is one of the first towns we've come to in the whole of the world where people haven't treated us like foreigners'. 'Tank', 'Nuclear Device', 'Hallow To Our Men', 'The Raven' and 'Threatened' follow before a rather messed up version of 'Peaches', Cornwell missing out the skewer line completely, possibly because he'd already had his absolute fill of 'worse places to be' this year!

The short European tour has been scheduled to end in Milan but the road crew are informed beforehand that there is an inadequate power supply at the venue. The band decide they'd taken enough risks for one summertime, or even one lifetime, and cancel.

7th July '80. London's Rainbow sees the start of the band's Who Wants The World? Tour. Around this time comes Ian Grant's 'Who Wants To Manage The Band?' announcement, as he submits his resignation with a few weeks' official notice. He feels frustrated with the direction the band is taking and believes they no longer value his judgement or advice. They don't even seem to take his resignation seriously. It isn't the most acrimonious of splits but nonetheless it is a sad end to the relationship; he has grown to love the band like they are family.

17th July '80. The band play at Sunderland's Locarno. In the audience is an ambitious 16-year-old with high musical aspirations of his own. His name is Baz Warne.

23rd July '80. In Corby, Northants, the band play a Benefit For Steel Workers event at the Festival Hall, where tickets are reduced to 35p, less than the price of a vinyl single. The set list is reduced too, to thirteen tracks, though there would have been more had there not been so much saliva flying around. Having taken the trouble to help out, the band aren't too impressed by the gallons of gob spat at them during the concert and so they refuse to do an encore. Fan Phil Coxon reckons it's the worst spitting at any Stranglers gig he's ever seen. The Stranglers, of course, do not do requests and so after the ninth track, 'Who Wants The World?', Hugh cryptically responds to specific shouts from the crowd. 'That's right, there aren't any more heroes. There aren't any more jobs either'.

August '80. The first week of the month sees the band resuming work on the next album, at Ringo Starr's Startling Studios in Berkshire (Beatles aficionados will know that John Lennon and Yoko had lived there previously). It has a 70 foot fibreglass Tyrannosaurus Rex in the grounds and a big plastic rhino which had been a gift from Keith Moon.

17th August '80. The Stranglers appear at the Bilzen Festival, Belgium. The Ramones play the previous night, but Hugh is unimpressed with them. The third track of the night, 'Toiler On The Sea', begins with excellent drum and bass lines only for it all to go to pot when the keyboards and guitar enter the fray. One, or possibly both, are out of tune. The band stop playing ... Hugh, 'Okay, er we're not The Ramones that's why we stopped cos we're out of tune, Okay? We're The Stranglers, so we're just gonna tune up properly'. The restart is a big improvement but the gig is far from one of their better performances.

18th August '80. The gig at Bath Pavilion is nearly spoiled by the aggression of Nazi fuckwits causing trouble. 'Sewer' is interrupted by skinheads attempting to start fights in the audience. One skin gets on to the stage and starts Seig Heiling. JJ lands his own form of right hander on him and the skinhead falls back in the audience. He and his mates soon exit to cheers from most of the crowd.

19th August '80. The gig at Nottingham Theatre Royal is filmed for TV's *Rockstage*; it's a superb display. And it's packed to the rafters, especially near the stage where the pogoing is almost constant throughout. When the lighting strikes it, The Raven backdrop seems sinisterly animated. Not much is different about the set list, but it's obvious that The Stranglers are intent on putting on a great show whilst trying to avoid causing too much offence to anyone.

The opener is 'Shah Shah A Go Go', brilliant and weird as always, segueing into 'Ice', where JJ's vocals are among the best he's contributed live. Dave Greenfield's timing seems a little out during the refrain, however. Hugh says hello to the fans: 'Wotcha Nottingham ... how you getting on, alright?. What do you think this is, a request show or summink? We don't know "My Old Man's A Dustman" and even if we did, we wouldn't play it'. Next comes the fine 'Who Wants The World?', which isn't as classy as normal due to some imperfect guitar work, and then, with possibly the best filmed example of JJ's martial arts walk/dance/poise, together with the stampede of his bass, 'Toiler' arrives, accompanied by Cornwell's searing lead riff, which sometimes is a toil but not tonight.

Then it's 'Thrown Away' with JJ singing his near-monotone, near-perfect vocal, while Hugh harmonises impressively. 'Tank' follows, storming in with military precision, then 'Nuclear Device' which is as explosive as ever. This flows into the unique 'Genetix', via Jet Black's supreme drumming and complemented by Dave's, frankly, odd but spectacular vocal and the eeriest of choruses, closing with Hugh's Gregor Mendel quotation. It all adds up to a classic finale for a fantastic show.

22nd August '80. The band are in London's Air Studios again, finishing the new album.

September '80. By the close of the month, The Stranglers have a new manager, Ed Kleinman, who recalls: 'As for taking over their management, that happened in 1980. By now I had my own management company and I had stayed in touch with the band. I got a call from them saying was I interested in managing them? Smart ass me asked them if they still could play. I went to the UK for a week and travelled with them for a few shows. I came back a few weeks later with my lawyer and we got them new lawyers, accountants and the release of a couple hundred thousand dollars that EMI had been holding up based on complications with their old management, Dai Davis and Ian Grant. Ian was a good guy'.

24th September '80. The Stranglers IV LP is released in America on Miles Copeland's I.R.S. label. It's a compilation but one with a difference. Tracks are 'The Raven', 'Baroque Bordello', 'Duchess', 'Nuclear Device', Meninblack, 'Five Minutes', 'Rok It To The Moon', 'Vietnamerica', 'GmbH' and 'Who Wants The World?'. 'Vietnamerica' is previously unreleased while 'GmbH' is a remix of 'Bear Cage'. The album comes with a bonus EP containing JJ's 'Do The European', 'Choosey Susie', Hugh's 'White Room' and 'Straighten Out'. The album sleeve is virtually the same as the wonderful picture cover for the 'Who Wants The World?' single. 'Vietnamerica' was written and recorded during the band's making of The Raven.

October '80. The band are embarking on their second American tour. There are some memorable gigs and events, even if the general reception is rather modest: the shock of the new (wave and punk) lost momentum some time ago. The band's dislike for the US is well-known – and if any further ammo is needed, they will soon find it – but was it actually genuine? Their American manager Ed Kleinman doubts it: 'I was never sure how real this was. They would never answer the question with a real straight answer. I think that they were just trying to "take the piss" out of everyone. The more reactions they got as people tried to protest or get angry at their comments, the more the band laughed and realised that they could have some fun. They were pretty straightforward with the American press, given my now wife was helping them stay straight with the press and not screw around as they had for so long in the UK. And they did a decent job'.

5th October '80. The band and entourage fly from Heathrow Airport to NYC in the US of A.

7th to 9th October '80. Rehearsing in New York and testing their equipment.

North American Tour. Details of this tour have always been vague, accurate records a rarity it seems. But not with manager Ed Kleinman, who still possesses much of the itinerary and paperwork thanks in large part to sharing the work with very well organised partner and wife Susan Erlichman. In addition to the gigs featured below, other intriguingly named venues were visited, like Williamantic, Connecticut, the Ontario Theatre in Washington DC, the 688 Club in Atlanta, My Father's Place in Roslyn, Long Island (where the local paper advertised 'Reggae with The Strangers!'), The Spit in Houston, Club Foot in Austin, the Hot Klub in Dallas, the Boomer Theatre in Norman, Oklahoma, Bacchanal in Tempe, Arizona (4th November, the US presidential election day), the famous Whisky A Go Go in Los Angeles (four consecutive nights in fact), the Coconut Grove in Santa Cruz, the New Faces Roadhouse in Salt Lake City, the Rainbow Music Hall in Denver, Merlyn's in Madison, Bogart's in Wisconsin, and Detroit's Harpo's on 25th November, the penultimate night of the tour. In other words, they get to see a lot of the country they professed not to like.

Above and right: Dave and Jet at Aldo's Hideaway, Lyndhurst, New Jersey, 16th October, 1980. (*Bob Leafe/Frank White Photo Agency*)

10th October '80. The band's first gig is at Cherry Hill, Emerald City in New Jersey. It goes pretty well, though Dave Greenfield's sensitive keyboards are a constant concern. After the gig, Jet discovers a theft has been made, of a rubber-backed carpet used to ensure the drums stay in place during performances. The mysteries don't end there …

12th October '80. Following their gig in Albany, NY, Jet's spare bass drum pedal goes missing.

14th October '80. The band play in Boston at The Channel. After 'Toiler', Hugh shows he knows his stuff by asking the audience if this is Beantown (Boston's nickname) adding that he hopes they haven't been eating beans today 'otherwise you're all gonna be farting all over the place'. 'Duchess' next, then he mentions that they were late coming on due to BBC Radio recording the gig, but only bringing a 1918 tape recorder to do it with and not being able to get a gas supply to run it. One audience member comments on that being a pisser, Hugh twists it in to him wanting to be pissed on – 'I'm sorry I don't know you well enough'. 'Hanging Around' and 'Baroque Bordello' and Hugh asking for space to dance as there are some people on the stage now. Jet responds to some nonentity's twattishness with, 'Fuck you too, buddy'.

16th October '80. Aldo's Hideaway in Lyndhurst, New Jersey. Hugh greets the audience with 'I think this is possibly one of the smallest places we've ever played in our lives. Apart from ... hang on, apart from my mummy's womb, I played in there, that was a pretty small place'. Another superior gig and, again, there seems to be mutual respect between the band and the American crowd.

21st October '80. The Ritz Ballroom, New York, host to another fine gig. Some pretty raucous New Yoiker voices in the crowd too, which is probably what The Stranglers prefer from an audience so they can antagonise them that little bit more. Notable tracks in the set list ... 'I Feel Like A Wog' which Hugh intro's with 'I feel like an English wog' before delivering a pulsating and intense rendition with JJ's bass perfectly frenetic accompaniment. 'This one's for Marylou' Hugh says before 'Toiler', following that with, 'Well I see we got some arseholes tonight sitting down, because if they stood up we'd be able to see they're arseholes.' Before 'Sewer', someone with a very queenly tone tells the band to 'Take some clothes off!'. Hugh's fully clothed performance of the song is suitably theatrical and he dedicates 'Who Wants The World?' to one of his favourite Americans, 'This one's for Ronnie, Ronnie boy, Ronnie Reagan of the Whitehouse soon to be elected' and from the crowd comes an equally keen-on-ole-Raygun remark – 'Fucking cunt!'. Then there's some delay so Hugh impatiently fills the gap, telling the audience to '... just amuse yourselves for a few minutes, you've been doing it for two hundred years.'

THIEVING SEPTIC TANKS

In the small hours of the following morning, serious misfortune strikes in an incident which has near catastrophic financial consequences for the band. Ed Kleinman remembers: 'Their equipment got ripped off after the show in NYC. The truck was stolen when the two crew members were taking showers to get ready to drive to the next gig. It was about 2 a.m. The record company, I.R.S., would not help with support, I asked the band if they wanted to do the entire tour, they said yes and we bankrolled all the equipment that had to be rented along the way. When we arrived in LA, my partner came down from San Francisco and we gave everyone on the crew and the band one hundred dollars each to spend any way they felt. It was a thank you for busting their balls to keep the show on the road and running ... We were glad that the group wanted to continue the tour. We spent a lot of time on the phone talking to promoters so they could help direct the crew when they arrived to where they could rent some of the gear, and if the promoter had access to some for use by The Stranglers.

'I.R.S. and Miles Copeland refused to help. Ian Copeland [Miles' brother], the booking agent, helped though, by trying to find the replacement gear we needed or as close as we could get. The tour went off well, or, as best, as it could given not all the gear was what was what they were used to; they always get much respect for continuing the tour'. Due to the theft, the Ontario Theatre in Washington DC gig is postponed, while in Atlanta on the 22nd October, the band's minibus is broken in to and more belongings stolen, by a pistol-toting varmint undeterred by the presence of a bouncer guarding the area of the 688 Club.

26th October '80. Ole Man River's in New Orleans might well be just a moderate size venue and it's not exactly rammed tonight, but this is a significant occasion for the band, for obvious reasons. They could justifiably be depressed and pissed off with the States, but they don't show it, instead putting on a solid show. Hugh's new rented guitar seems pretty normal but JJ's bass sounds like a barrel full of softballs; Jet's drums appear to be substandard clones and Dave's keyboards – the hardest to adequately replace due to modifications over the years – sound weedy, and yet it all works pretty well. After 'Toiler', Hugh asks, 'So this is New Orleans. In fact I've no idea, this is Gretna innit?' Before 'I Feel Like A Wog', he comments: 'You realise that we suffered from the New York Syndrome earlier this week, we had all our gear stolen. Those people up there, you can't even shake hands with them, they'll take your hands off. So we're surviving on borrowed and hired gear, so it's probably not gonna sound anything like you'd expect The Stranglers to sound, it's a complete disaster'.

But it isn't, no way. 'Nubiles' follows, then 'Duchess' and 'Hanging Around' which seems to just peter out with Jet and Dave plugging away hopelessly with some strange noises coming from the keyboards, until it's just Jet clattering about on his own! And it still isn't too bad! Prior to 'Baroque Bordello', Hugh remarks, 'Well it looks as though everything is not totally fucked, well that's a miracle for you …' JJ's bass pummels the air in a faster version of 'Sewer', making it not quite as epic but still the unorthodox masterpiece. 'Who Wants The World?' follows, dedicated to Ron and not The Two Ronnies. The song practically jumps out at the audience; it's an assault and it is excellent.

Their version of the traditional Lord's Prayer, 'Hallow To Our Men', is extremely odd, but well received anyway by the audience who are then treated to 'Threatened', 'Tank' and 'Nuclear Device' on which Dave's opening notes sound like they're from an inebriated bee in a kazoo! The drum link into 'Genetix' is, as ever, inspiring, and the song is sheer weird and unworldly class as always, thanks in large to Dave's horror story vocals. Finally 'The Raven' floats and veers above the audience, a fantastic closing song to cap a surprisingly fabulous gig.

13th November '80. Keystone, Berkeley in California. 'Peaches are out of season' responds Hugh to audience song demands. They get, amongst others, 'Toiler', 'Duchess', 'Baroque Bordello', 'Hanging Around' and then 'Sewer', after which he remarks that he's never met such a noisy audience before, especially as Berkeley is known as a quiet place. 'So quiet' he says, 'I was walking on the sidewalk and heard a cockroach sneeze'. He could probably hear the response to the joke too, that of rolling tumbleweed. But he's on a roll now … 'If you watch Channel Nine on Saturday you're in for a big treat, you've got seven-and-a-half hours, a full seven-and-a-half hours, of your favourite president, Mr Raygun, in some of his best movies … As it's his birthday, 69 again, this year, this is for him, it's called 'Who Wants The World?'. Happy birthday, Ronnie'.

15th November '80. Ed Kleinman tells of a strange happening during the gig at The Stone in San Francisco: 'A stripper who came up on the stage was a guy working on getting a sex change op. We all thought he was a female to begin with until his clothes came off. He still had his penis along with big breasts. JJ and Hugh invited him back to the hotel after the show and they spent some time playing and goofing on him'.

23rd November '80. At Stages in Chicago, prior to delivering 'I Feel Like A Wog', Hugh tells the crowd to stop throwing beer or else he's gonna get fucking electrocuted. 'Who Wants The World?' is the focal point for some more Hugh anti-American diatribe (anti one American in particular) telling the audience that the president elect – a certain Ronald Wilson Reagan, count the letters in each name – will be in power in a few months and is going to get them into another World War.

26th November '80. The Stranglers are scheduled to close the tour at the Masonic Temple in Toronto, Canada, the gig set to be broadcast on local FM radio. One problem though, Canadian immigration authorities refuse entry to Hugh due to his drugs conviction. As the gig has been sold out for weeks, 'another Nice' is a worrying possibility. The band proceed to Toronto without Hugh, hoping he'll meet up with them a little later. Their management hire two lawyers to resolve the issue and he finally gets to the venue with a few minutes to spare.

It is a marvellous gig and further proof that Hugh is a superb vocalist. After the fourth song 'Sewer', he comments on coins being thrown at the band, 'Great, money, amazing! A Canadian one cent, that'll get me a long way ... I can go for a piss now.' 'Who Wants The World?' is dedicated to the audience's 'neighbour', Reagan, who the crowd clearly don't like either. Someone asks them to play JJ Burnel's infamous solo song, Hugh responds 'You got crabs? I should see a doctor about that immediately'. 'We're quite fond of Australia so we're gonna do another ... for those lovely boys down under. They got lovely rippling muscles and big surfboards, I love em' – 'Nuclear Device'. Disappointingly there is no more dazzling repartee, not even before 'Dead Loss Angeles', though the crowd are treated to a classic rendition of 'I Feel Like A Wog,' with JJ's bass shuddering the night, lead guitar slicing through the ether, Jet's drumming an adrenaline-filled pulse and Dave's scintillating keys sounding straight from a spine-chiller movie; this masterpiece of menace complemented perfectly by Hugh's vocals.

BALLSUPINBLACK

Due to lack of communication and organisation, together with the departure of manager Ian Grant, insurance payments on the band's equipment had lapsed. Instalments were due twice a year but the second was unpaid and so, after the truck-load of gear was swiped in New York, the band's chances of an insurance pay out vanish like the stolen gear. The theft costs them well over 40 grand and could easily have done for their careers too. Perhaps surprisingly, Hugh is the most resolute of the quartet here, refusing to surrender to the latest disaster.

Such a shitty year, but this latest twist has actually galvanised them and they vow to carry on. All that said, such strength and unity doesn't pay the bills or satisfy their employers, they need new chart success and sooner rather than later. The bad news isn't finished either alas, with the death from cancer of friend and former tour manager Charlie Pile.

PARANOIA CAN EXIST
Regarded by sceptics as possible proof positive that The Stranglers are insane, is the band's theory that bad luck derives from the malevolent influence of the Meninblack, UFOs and the like. Various things have gone badly wrong for them or for close associates ever since the 'Meninblack' track off *The Raven* album. The band believe everything happens for a reason, someone/something is intent on harming them.

9 1981: THE GOSPELINBLACK AND BEYOND

Another frenetic year in store, but thankfully one that would be considerably less chaotic than the last, even though a planned tour of Poland in the summer gets cancelled due to the social unrest there. Away from commitments to the band, French new wave group Taxi Girl take on JJ as producer of what will become their most successful album, *Seppuku*. Jet provides percussion too, stepping in after the death of their drummer Pierre Wolfsohn.

13th January '81. Not Nice. The band are informed that they have received suspended sentences, but they must pay near £2,000 towards the damage made to Nice University. Shameful on the Nice authorities' part but nonetheless a relief for The Stranglers.

29th January '81. 'Thrown Away' is on *Top Of The Pops*. Tommy Vance is tonight's presenter, he introduces the song as 'Blown Away'. And effectively it is, reaching just No. 42 in the charts.

9th February '81. Release of the band's fifth studio album, *The Gospel According To The Meninblack*. It comes in a gatefold sleeve with a quite stunning new version of Da Vinci's *Last Supper* painting, together with more striking Stranglers iconography and font. Unfortunately, to listen to the album is not such a pleasurable task, according to critics. It enters the charts on a deceptively high notch at No.8, only to descend at an alarming rate. Selling around 50,000 copies, it's an unimpressive return given the high cost of making it. Having said that, it fares better in Europe than any of their previous albums, a probable side effect from all the publicity garnered from the Nice scandal.

1981: THE GOSPELINBLACK AND BEYOND

THE GOSPEL ACCORDING TO THE MENINBLACK
Released: 9th February, 1981.
Label: Liberty.
Charted at No. 8
Side One: 1 'Waltzinblack', 2 'Just Like Nothing On Earth',
3 'Second Coming', 4 'Waiting For The Meninblack',
5 'Turn, The Centuries Turn'.
Side Two: 1 'Two Sunspots', 2 'Four Horsemen', 3 'Thrown Away',
4 'Manna Machine', 5 'Hallow To Our Men'.

The Stranglers are billed as: Hughinblack - guitars & vocals,
JJinblack - bass & vocals, Daveinblack - keyboards & vocals,
Jetinblack - percussion and vocals.

In a few words – what the *Ford* are the songs about? Part 5.

'*Waltzinblack*': The band's most famous instrumental grew from a basic beat from JJinblack enhanced by Daveinblack's Wasp keyboard mastery and all embellished by the sped-up laughter from the band and Steve Churchyard.

'*Just Like Nothing On Earth*': A real team effort of original sounds, the lyrics are about various witness accounts of alleged encounters with alien beings, including Jet's own sighting of a UFO.

'*Second Coming*': About the second coming of Christ and how, if it happened, no one would believe him and he would end up being rejected, imprisoned, institutionalised or assassinated.

'*Waiting For The Meninblack*': Many people who claim to have encountered UFOs also claim to have been visited by sinister men dressed in all black; these figures could be aliens or indeed government agents; either way they're not a force for good.

'*Turn, The Centuries Turn*': Another instrumental, this time using tape loops of Jet's drumming over and over, just like the years keeping passing but nothing really changes.

'*Two Sunspots*': Yes it's in part about sunspots but mainly it is about breasts and nipples.

'*Four Horsemen*': Sung by Daveinblack, it's a reference to the Four Horsemen Of The Apocalypse of the Bible, plus some of Nostradamus' ideas again.

'*Thrown Away*': JJinblack singing, from the perspective of an alien visitor to earth.

'*Manna Machine*': From a book called *The Manna Machine* referring to a contraption which created manna, food tasting of honey, which saved the

Israelites from starvation in the desert as described in the Old Testament books of *Exodus* and *Numbers*.

'Hallow To Our Men': More 'jazz' according to Hugh, the lyrics his alternative to the Lord's Prayer, here they're pleading to superior alien beings as if they're gods or rulers of the planet.

Notable songs of the time not on the vinyl album:

'Top Secret': About Nostradamus who, apparently, was a doctor during the day and writer of his predictions at night.

'Man In White': This mildly irreverent song is about the Pope and the hysteria of his followers.

'Vietnamerica': Hugh had watched *Apocalypse Now*, which inspired him to write about the United States' shameful involvement in Vietnam.

✪

Fan Guy Westoby's review of
The Gospel According To The Meninblack:

Creative genius in full flourish or the death throes of a once great 'punk' band lost in a drug-addled haze of stunted potential? For me it's definitely a case of the former, a science fiction concept LP, each track containing beautifully unworldly keyboard effects from the musical wizard Dave, or Daveinblack, I should say. The scene is set with the delightfully sinister 'Waltzinblack'. Part of the thrill of this album is its unpredictable nature, and the next track 'Just

Like Nothing On Earth' with its alliterative lyrics and slowly spoken, distorted repetition of the title, played against JJ's strummed bass and Hugh's guitar riffs, is as astonishing as 'Waltzinblack'. 'Second Coming' follows, an intriguing track about how we'd (over)react if Jesus Christ returned to earth. Drums and keyboards then come to the fore in 'Waiting For the Meninblack', about the existence of these black-suited aliens of the album title. It's mesmerising, echoing the uneasy feeling a visitation by such figures would cause. The instrumental 'Turn, The Centuries Turn' unsettles the listener further with a slow, persistent and claustrophobic beat.

Side Two kicks off with 'Two Sunspots', a fast, catchy and commercial tune which isn't science fiction at all ... Next, 'Four Horsemen', for me the weakest track, with an overly repetitive stop-start beat. The album's first single, 'Thrown Away', follows. It's a captivating keyboard riff coupled with near spoken vocals, chugging bass and ridiculously appealing disco beat; the album's most accessible track. And 'Manna Machine', its variety of seemingly unrelated keyboard sounds set against spoken vocals and minimalist guitar making it the least accessible. To finish, we have the latest Stranglers epic, 'Hallow To Our Men'; a fitting closer, pulling listeners in with hypnotic keys and drums that take us through Hugh's mantra-like prayers to the Meninblack. A disturbing, alluring album, amongst their best, a superb record which for me sits comfortably amongst the most creative ever made.

Left and above: Acetates of 'Sunspots' and 'Men In Black' which never saw the light of day as singles. (*Images courtesy of Dean Bourne*)

9th February '81. The night the new album is released the band play at Bristol's Locarno ... it's an unusual gig. In between songs, Hugh (Hughinblack in fact) addresses the audience as an alien/Maninblack, using a vocorder to distort his voice, so he sounds a tad like the mice from *The Chipmunks*. Let that take nothing away from the sky high standard of music.

After the theatre of wickedness intro 'Waltzinblack' we're then treated to 'Threatened' with the dynamic duo of Burnel and Cornwell simultaneously vocalising so powerfully. Next 'The Raven', thunderous JJ bass to start with, Hugh's guitar striving to soar and the majestic Greenfield keys helping it swirl into the atmosphere. But then Hugh addresses the audience in his altered, alter ego voice, like he's had a helium overdose, the first comprehensible words being, 'We normally feel very honoured to be your first concert of the tour but ...' and the rest is briefly lost in translation and a tangle of squeaks, until 'I'll tell you a little story, it's about science fiction' and then comes one of his exceptional deliveries perhaps only the fans really appreciate: 'Just Like Nothing On Earth'. It's a unique tongue twister, a real achievement just to sing it fault free, which he manages while weaving guitar chords at the same time.

'Thrown Away', 'Who Wants The World?' and 'Don't Bring Harry' follow, the latter not working well live, as Jet's bass drum is too heavy, Hugh's guitar solo is at the edge of being plain poor, while the mellow vocals of the single aren't easy for JJ to replicate. Then it's 'Waiting For The Meninblack', followed by the eerie, unsettling and strange 'Meninblack' and on to the demonic singing of Dave on 'Four Horsemen'.

After that, Hughinblack: 'You've all not heard some of these before' met by silence from the crowd. 'Dave collects wasps and spiders, well one of the wasps is dead ... Awww', as one of the keyboards plays up, prompting annoying tuning from Mr Greenfield. 'Second Coming' and 'Hallow To Our Men', a futuristic knotty mass here, before Hughinblack dryly observes, 'As you can see, we've remained a professional band... lots of pregnant pauses as they say ...' in readiness for 'Nuclear Device' and 'Genetix'.

Then he warns, still in alien guise, 'I hear there's a bit of a bus strike in Bristol, that's why we were so late opening the doors'... so just remember there's a strike tonight, because the bus crews don't want you to pay the extra fares ... fucking great!'.

12th February '81. Tony Stubley is at the Canterbury Odeon to see The Stranglers:

> ... personally memorable as I was invited to watch the sound check where they played 'Turn, The Centuries Turn', a track which they never performed in concert, and 'Tank' and 'Just Like Nothing On Earth'. Plus the fact that it was the first time I met JJ, Hugh and Dave. I had met Jet before. Even more exciting was Hugh dedicating 'Duchess', the first encore of this gig, to me with, 'Right, now there's a bloke here tonight who has come all the way from the Isle of Sheppey, he's called Stubsinblack and he's an interesting character and we'd like to play this for him.'

16th February '81. Mark Ray's account of the Birmingham Odeon gig:

A dreary February evening, my first Stranglers gig. My first gig full stop. The Stranglers are my teenage heroes. The lights go down and 'Waltzinblack' booms from the sound system to regale them. There they are: Black/Burnel/Cornwell/Greenfield, and then we get 'Threatened', 'The Raven' and 'Toiler'. Hugh: 'Hello Birmingham. Can you understand me now?' in bad Brummie accent, 'I think we better miss Birmingham out next year – we're coming here too often … A bit of sci-fi for you..' and 'Just Like Nothing On Earth' then 'Thrown Away'. One for Reagan, 'Who Wants The World?' with 'Baroque Bordello' after Hugh tells us, 'No point shouting out for songs, this ain't the Jimmy Young Show', so we get 'Second Coming' and 'Meninblack'.

Hugh: 'Did you know Iran's got 49 spies and three hostages?' and 'Shah Shah A Go Go' arrives, then 'Hallow To Our Men' before he asks, 'Is anyone here in the army?' Crowd: 'No!' Hugh: 'Good!' and 'Tank' thunders in. 'What is this spitting lark? It's 1981, you know'. 'Nuclear Device', 'Genetix', 'Duchess'. Hugh says, 'Open your hymn books at page 276 and we'll sing "Hanging Around"'. And then it's, 'Goodnight Birmingham'. My first Stranglers gig … better than losing my virginity.

24th February '81. Edinburgh Playhouse, identical set list to Birmingham. Before 'Toiler', Hugh welcomes the audience, 'Hello Edinburgh … twice in eight months I think it is. You're getting spoilt!' and following it, 'Well it's facking freezing here tonight!' adding that the floor has caved in '… so I hope you've brought your own ambulances'. 'You know the bloke Ted that runs this place? I'm surprised he's managed to keep this venue going actually, he deserves a bit of applause for that'. Now we're gonna take you down to Devon, this story starts in Devon' and it's 'Just Like Nothing On Earth'. A few minutes later he talks about Prince Charles' very recent announcement of the date of his forthcoming wedding to Diana Spencer, '… he said she couldn't ride, but he'd put it right. I don't know what he meant by that but anyway, this one's for him, it's called "Second Coming"'.

25th February '81. Misfortune strikes road crew boss Alan McStravich after tonight's Glasgow Apollo gig, suffering a heart attack brought on by snorting angel dust mistaking it for coke.

March '81. 'It was pretty simple, Stiff US wanted to promote *The Gospel According To The Meninblack*. They were helpful and great people to work with. I don't remember it being anything other than an easy contact in New York and off we went. Never any hassles and we never expected any great things nor did they promise anything. It just was that the album was there and why not get it out? And their slogan was great: "If it ain't Stiff it ain't worth a fuck!"' explains Ed Kleinman on his acquisition of a Stranglers deal with Stiff US for the release of *The Gospel* … Simultaneous sensible decision making from The Stranglers camp too, with an American and Canadian tour from late March to late June. Commencing in New York on the 26th, the band need a positive reception and sales, EMI aren't happy with the new album despite its obvious originality. The Stranglers are feeling confident, and ahead of their travels, JJ declares, 'America is going blackwards'.

North American Tour. Typical set list is intro 'Waltzinblack', then 'Threatened', 'The Raven', 'Toiler', 'Just Like Nothing On Earth', 'Thrown Away', 'Who Wants The World?', 'Second Coming', 'Meninblack', 'Shah Shah A Go Go', 'Hallow To Our Men', 'Tank', 'Nuclear Device', 'Genetix', with occasional gems such as 'Baroque Bordello', 'Tank' and 'Sewer' thrown in.

30th March '81. Completely unrelated (probably) is the news that in Washington DC, an assassination attempt is made on new president Ronald Reagan; The Stranglers are miles away in Pennsylvania at the time.

11th April '81. At the Emerald City in Cherry Hill, New Jersey, Hugh is positively sociable with the crowd, 'We were in Virginia the other day and all the people were going woowoowoo, they were mimicking police cars ...' Someone in the audience makes the same sound ... Hugh responds, 'Hey you're good at that!' Later, 'Short commercial break ... I'd like to explain the virtues of drinking cider to you people, I'm sure you're all very thirsty. In England we have cider, which is very rough alcohol made out of apple wine ... two pints of that and you're really sluicing the gates at both ends. And you end up having hallucinations, you remember hallucinations. They were big in the sixties remember?'

20th April '81. At Ole Man River's in New Orleans, Hugh greets the audience, 'I've got some good news and some bad news for ya ... I'll give you the good news first: this time we've come back with our own equipment ... and the bad news is that some people over here have got Superglue on their arses ...' (the crowd isn't showing enough enthusiasm). 'Well, it's three weeks to the day that Alexander Haig committed political suicide', a quip in reference to the assassination attempt on Reagan: while the president was hospitalised, Secretary of State Haig said, 'I am in control here'. He wasn't. 'So this one's for Alexander the Small, not Alexander the Great'. After, JJ fronts 'Meninblack' using a vocorder, Hugh asks if anyone has been mugged today, then tells of a very enterprising mugging team going around jumping out of a Cadillac and mugging someone at one end of town, jumping back in, driving off and jumping out to mug someone else at the other end. They keep doing this, it's a plan and so the police are looking for a Cadillac full of kangaroos. Overall the gig sways from brilliance like 'Shah Shah A Go Go' to the awkward and unappetising 'Second Coming', which just doesn't work well enough when played live.

9th May '81. Chris Band's Palo Alto, California, gig review:

Hugh: 'Allo, allo, Palo Alto! Does anyone know what Palo Alto means? I'm going to test your general knowledge now ... who knows what Palo Alto means? I'll tell you what it means – the skinny tree with no leaves on it'. 'Toiler On The Sea', a good version, full of pace and energy, he gets the guitar note perfect. 'Does anyone here like drinking? I tell you we like drinking in England more than you do in America. And I'll tell you why, we've got one good reason for that, it's that you don't drink scrumpy which is made out of apples, it's rough cider. Anyone experienced that stuff? I've never seen an American drink a pint of that and remain on his feet, they unleash the hallucinations. You remember you used to have them out here in about 1967? California ... hallucinations ... you know?'

'Once upon a time ...' and 'Just Like Nothing On Earth' sounds great. Barely time to breathe before 'Thrown Away' on which JJ's vocal delivery is interesting with odd emphasis on certain words which reminds me of a Cyberman. Hugh: 'Does anyone know what year it is? Last year was the year of the child, Jimmy Carter was president, right? This year, the year of the paraplegic, Ronald Reagan in the White House, Margaret Thatcher at Number Ten, makes sense. Oh, and Alexander Haig, Secretary of State. You know that man, you know "You are in my control"? I thought they were going to send him up in the Space Shuttle and leave him up there'. 'Who Wants The World?' and 'Baroque Bordello'. Hugh responds to an audience comment: 'It's pretty limp? Then you should rub it harder. Actually, you're probably the man this song's all about. Do you suffer from premature ejaculation? Whoever it is that says it's pretty limp down there, maybe has problems ... This is a consolation prize, "Second Coming", just for you'. It sounds suitably otherworldly, with a lot of interesting keyboard stuff going on, setting the stage nicely for 'Meninblack' which I would love to have seen the audience's reaction to!

'Tank', 'Shah Shah A Go Go', on which Hugh's guitar playing is really impressive, fluid and yet angular at the same time. Straight into 'Hallow To Our Men'. Here it's urgent, taking on a more in-your-face feel than in the studio version. Hugh: 'Any Australians here? No? Does anybody like Australians? I tell you, they're very good at standing on their heads. While they're lying down' ... 'Nuclear Device' into 'Genetix' and finally 'Down In The Sewer', classic finale for a sassy, classy gig.

19th/20th June '81. Bond's Casino, Broadway, New York earned recent notoriety thanks to gig promoters grossly selling too many tickets for a series of Clash gigs. With New York's Fire Department insisting on new, more stringent arrangements (to which the Clash honourably adhered to) all scheduled gigs there are delayed. This included The Stranglers' shows and so their stay in America is extended by a week.

July '81. The band spend six weeks writing and rehearsing new material for the crucial next album, much of it at Jet Black's home. The North American tour was not a flop but the record sales weren't massive, they need to improve or it will probably be a case of the band being 'let go' as their label, considers them too different and too difficult. All this despite The Stranglers' opinion that *The Gospel* ... is their best work to date. So, EMI increase the pressure to create a new album to outsell their last offering, while costing much less to make.

August 16th '81. Recording of a new album, *La Folie*, begins at the Manor Studios in Oxfordshire, owned by Richard Branson (the studio, not the county of Oxfordshire ... probably). Steve Churchyard engineering and the band producing, with Tony Visconti controlling the final mixes. They stay in the idyllic surroundings of the Manor until September 6th, and a further week is taken to mix the album at Visconti's Good Earth Studio in Soho, London.

9th November '81. The Stranglers release their sixth studio album, the title, *La Folie*, is French, loosely translated as 'the madness of love'. Although the band don't officially admit it, it is also a concept album, concerning the perception of love, and matters of the heart. The song titles alone are fascinating, and their content shows some very insightful observations on 'love'. Without pretention, JJ Burnel remarked in *Strangled* magazine that 'The only possible love is the love of oneself'. What an old romantic!

(Bob Leafe/Frank White Photo Agency)

LA FOLIE
Released: 9th November, 1981.
Label: Liberty United Records.
Charted at No. 11.
Side One: 1 'Non Stop', 2 'Everybody Loves You When You're Dead', 3 'Tramp', 4 'Let Me Introduce You To The Family', 5 'Ain't Nothin' To It', 6 'The Man They Love To Hate'.
Side Two: 1 'Pin Up', 2 'It Only Takes Two To Tango', 3 'Golden Brown', 4 'How To Find True Love And Happiness In The Present Day', 5 'La Folie'.

In a few words – what the *Ford* are the songs about? Part 6.
'Non Stop': Title changed from 'Non Stop Nun', it's about the intense devotion of nuns to God.

Hugh, plus friend, in New York's Bond's Casino, June 1981.
(Bob Leafe/Frank White Photo Agency)

'Everybody Loves You When You're Dead': Written by Hugh after the murder of John Lennon, how fickle people are, changing their opinions of someone just because the person has died.

'Tramp': Self-explanatory title, though Hugh later professed to it being part autobiographical too, about searching for love.

'Let Me Introduce You To The Family': About a tight-knit family situation, but not Mafia related. The family of a friend of Hugh's enjoyed a very close relationship, something which he hadn't experienced in his own childhood.

'Ain't Nothin' To It: A tribute to Milton 'Mezz' Mezzrow, a white American musician from Louis Armstrong's era who created 'jive talk' and who started the first two-tone band with black and white musicians. The lyrics are extracts from Mezzrow's autobiography.

'The Man They Love To Hate': The title comes from the *Dallas* character J.R. Ewing, the lyrics from Jean-Jacques, which are at times autobiographical. Do you remember who shot J.R.?

'Pin Up': Sailors' fantasies of pin-up girls.

'It Only Takes Two To Tango': Inspired by the USA/USSR Cold War, with reference to Adam and Eve too, plus observations of people not making do with what they've got and starting wars to get more.

'Golden Brown': Refers to the skin tone of a girlfriend of Hugh's and, more importantly, to heroin. The melody derives from a sequence Dave had worked on for inclusion in the track 'Second Coming'.
'How To Find True Love And Happiness In The Present Day': a complex title but surprisingly it's almost a 'filler' track, the lyrics reference people who Hugh knew but has since forgotten the identity of.
'La Folie': Sung in French, much of this concerns the case of a Japanese student loving a girl so much that he killed her and ate her, the ultimate crime of passion, the ultimate madness/folly of love.

Notable songs of the time not on the vinyl album:
'You Hold The Key To My Love In Your Hands': A Tune worthy of better lyrical content, a cheap joke about a woman holding a fella's you know what.
'Love 30': An instrumental combining clips of a tennis umpire's calls during a match. If the BBC had used it as a theme tune for their Wimbledon coverage, The Stranglers would have been quids in. However, the Beeb prefer to use the tune 'Sporting Occasion' by Arnold Steck (real name, Leslie Statham). He departed this life in 1974, so can't enjoy the royalties.

✪

Jim Radley's review of *La Folie*:
Perhaps I'm in the minority, but I rate this as the best Stranglers album of all. Nothing against the rest of them but I find it less crazy-ape-shit out-there as the others. It's the closest to a commercial sounding album from a very un-commercial band. Bowie producer Tony Visconti does a sterling job on production, really making each track sound like a single in its own right. The opener 'Non Stop' has a gorgeous approaching keyboard intro combined with a rich yet deadpan delivery. 'Everybody Loves You When You're Dead' is typical of the *La Folie* vibe, a sardonic ditty about the darker side of love, with a delightful keyboard run forming the basis of the surprisingly light and melodic song.

Similar in context is 'The Man They Love To Hate' with Jet's pounding drums forming the spine, layered with JJ's perfectly timed vocals, all stitched together with guitar and keyboard riffs making it a heavyweight track. Rolling tug-of-war drums and guitar weave through the mega catchy 'It Only Takes Two To Tango' with ridiculously high pitched backing vocals that shouldn't work but actually do. There is the jazzy 'Ain't Nothing To It' too, the majestic 'How To Find True Love And Happiness In The Present Day' and also 'Tramp', which is the most orthodox track on the album and should have been a single, according to many.

The sleeve art also deserves a mention as it complements the album wonderfully, a stylish front cover image and on the back a cool live shot of the band. It's an early '80s take on '60s French hip iconography and it works rather well. It has a lavish inner sleeve too, decked out in a non-garish pink background, full lyrics and iconic imagery for each track.

This album is not for everyone – even Hugh later said it was his least favourite Stranglers album and sounds like 'two dogs barking in a shed', but listeners should make up their own mind; many have fallen in love with the madness of *La Folie*, and rightly so.

11th November '81. At The Granary, Bristol, this Stranglers gig is filmed by BBC West. The tracks televised on the show *RPM* will be 'Tramp', 'Golden Brown', 'Let Me Introduce You To The Family' and 'Duchess', but the whole gig is brimming with eclectic brilliance. JJ wears a red big-collared shirt and the boys have trendy, floppy, foppy hairstyles, demonstrating that the punk image has all but gone, as well as the Meninblack persona.

They enter to the strains of 'Waltzinblack' and the gig opener is 'Just Like Nothing On Earth', then 'Who Wants The World?' and Hugh commenting: 'Well it's taken us seven years and we've finally made it to The Granary. We really feel like we've got somewhere, we really feel that we've got somewhere in the music business 'cos we've made it to The Granary, this is a really big night for us. We were really nervous, you know. But we're not really a local band, half of us don't really live here so I feel like a bit of a wog really'. That's the intro to the song, of course – lead guitar prominent, good to hear, and Hugh really going for it on the vocals. They then play 'Tramp' 'for any tramps present', the tempo really hammering along, Jet drumming brilliantly and the whole thing *so lively.*

Hugh surprises no one with his premature ejaculation intro for 'Second Coming', the song much better than the joke of course. 'Baroque Bordello' and 'Golden Brown' with Dave's keyboards both majestic and uplifting. 'Pin Up' – a false start on the vocals initially but soon corrected. It seems like they were unsure how to end it as it just kind of falls away ... Jet's drums then pound the intro to 'Thrown Away' and the guitar is greatly abrasive and aggressive. 'Tank' – the audience very vocal here, which adds to it all. 'The Man They Love To Hate' – this works well live. After it, Hugh says, 'Who loves their mum and dad? I really love my mum and dad. Awfully much', and the thrashing brilliance of 'Let Me Introduce You ...' arrives. 'Nubiles' next, the 'cocktail' version and then the proper one, though it's sanitised. At the end, the band go off and so the audience starts shouting 'Stranglers! Stranglers!' in a very definite Bristol accent. On the band's return we get 'Duchess' and then 'Nuclear Device' which melds into 'Genetix' with a seamless, faultless transition. A superb concert.

14th November '81. 'Let Me Introduce You To The Family' single is released, but it only reaches No. 42 in the charts, a real downer for the band again, as they had high hopes for it; a 'pastiche disco' song which is excitingly original and commercial at the same time. Obviously not commercial enough, DJs seem keener on playing a certain other track from *La Folie*. No cigar for guessing which one.

JJ in Coventry, 1981.
(*Unknown*)

17th November '81. Early on in this gig at the late lamented Hammersmith Palais, it proper kicks off when the second song of the night, 'Threatened', encounters technical problems. Tony Stubley remembers JJ's amplifier not working correctly, and is taking a minute for his bass to accompany Jet's opening percussion for the track. And then the amp cut out again, prompting JJ to assault it with a kick and a guitar-butt, damaging the bass head at the same time. He furiously exits the stage, Hugh soon following. All the while, Jet and Dave continue playing. Hugh seems to have persuaded JJ to return and we then get a seven minute version of 'Threatened'.

The concert proceeds undaunted and after 'Golden Brown' comes an interesting comment from Hugh, in a French accent, 'This madness they call love, it makes people do strange things'. Next song is 'Tramp' but the gig finale, the night's best – and most appropriate given what happened – is 'The Raven' which of course contains Burnel's most introspective lyrics.

4th December '81. The last date of the *La Folie* tour, at London's Rainbow, which enables Hugh to treat the packed audience to a brief rendition of Judy Garland's 'Over The Rainbow' from *The Wizard Of Oz*. Even weirder is the appearance of Mr Sprat's 21st Century Popular Motets replacing the band on stage as the recorded version of 'La Folie' brings an end to the gig. The troupe are dressed up in sheet-like costumes and they shape shift to form the letters of 'La Folie'.

10 1982: RECOVERY

Although 1981 provided grateful Stranglers fans with a rich harvestinblack, the cold facts gleaned from the record charts showed that the band's popularity was declining. Critics in the media hadn't helped; the reviews of *La Folie* had generally been moderate. And the majority of those reviews actually overlooked the outstandingly original track 'Golden Brown' as if it was a trivial novelty song, almost. To (inadvertently) redress the balance a little, there were certain radio shows who really pushed the track, even if it was seemingly at the expense of all the other terrific tracks on the album.

The second half of the coming year was comparatively quiet for the band with no tour, no new material and not even any incarcerations. Naturally, serious artists rarely switch off completely though, even when copious amounts of heroin are involved: Burnel and Cornwell will work together preparing their next assault on the album charts, while JJ will also work on a film soundtrack album with Dave Greenfield, commissioned by the film's maker, Vincent Coudanne. It's a semi-animated feature titled *Ecoutez Vos Murs* (translated as 'Listen To Your Walls') and scheduled to be shown at the Cannes Film Festival in 1984.

9th January '82. The harpsichord-strong, waltz-led wonder that is 'Golden Brown' is officially out as a single. It's hardly a surprise, given their nickname of Every Mistake Imaginable, that EMI cocked up again, somehow allowing a supply of copies to be made available early for purchase in December. The song was getting radio play and good reviews, and so those few initial copies sold quickly and enabled the premature release (if only it had been 'Second Coming' eh?) to actually figure in the outer regions of the charts. Thus, when it is correctly released, its chart impact is dissipated somewhat. The single reaches No.2 but probably would have topped the charts had its release been carried out correctly. Instead, the Jam's 'Town Called Malice' and Tight bloody Fit's 'The Lion Sleeps Tonight' obstruct it over a spell of twelve weeks, despite it selling more copies than both of those put together.

14th January '82. 'Golden Brown' on *Top Of The Pops* sees Jet and Dave accordingly in all black, but JJ sporting a nice cream jacket and Hugh wearing a blue shirt. Sacrilege?! The sleepy audience sways along smoothly to the band miming to the sumptuous song but thankfully there are no lit lighters or matches being waved around.

Promo video for Stranglers singles – 'Golden Brown': Using stock footage of Egypt, this sees the band as a grubby 1930s cocktail lounge quartet. Jet in particular is brilliant as the almost vicar-esque figure, but they all look magnificently seedy and it's interesting that this video is aimed at diverting attention from what the song is *really* about.

TEXTURE LIKE SUN ... OR TOAST.

With a single's success usually comes increased interest in the lyrical content. 'Golden Brown' is as poetic as it is melodic, and just like much poetry it possesses a wondrous air of mystique about it. Many Stranglers fans know what the song was about, having read band commentary in *Strangled*, or simply by using a bit of the old grey matter, but *publicly* the band try to preserve an air of mystery. And all is going well until JJ reveals in interview that it is about heroin. Consequent media melodramatics declared that the song **promoted** the usage of heroin. It doesn't. What harm this furore did to sales is uncertain, though it is irrefutable that radio airplay decreases once the 'news' has broken.

STRIKING WHILE THE IRON IS HOT

A hastily arranged tour gets underway to feed on the success of 'Golden Brown', with the near chart toppers playing to sell out gigs all over the country. Starting with ...

25th January '82. At the Brighton Top Rank. 'Waltzinblack' intro, then 'Sewer', 'Just Like Nothing On Earth', 'Second Coming', 'Non Stop', 'The Man They Love To Hate', 'Who Wants The World?', 'Baroque Bordello', 'Golden Brown', 'How To Find True Love ...', 'Thrown Away', 'Tank', 'Let Me Introduce You ...' which here has the backing vocals of 'I love the family' from JJ adding a brilliant extra layer to a unique song. 'Tramp' is greeted like an old friend. More class with 'The Raven' and JJ at his breathiest, and 'Nuclear Device' jogging along into the fabulous finale 'Genetix'. After 'The Raven', Hugh tries to promote a CND compilation LP, though at one point he says 'Campaign Against Nuclear Disarmament' before getting it right with '... for Nuclear Disarmament'. As someone throws a CND badge at him, he remarks, 'It's probably one of the most important albums you could buy in your life.'

26th January '82. At the Guildford Civic Hall the band is again on top form, a marvellous concert even with the age old 'technical problems' occasionally hindering them. Second track is 'Just Like Nothing On Earth' after which Dave's keyboards are playing up, so Hugh has a chat with the audience, while a screeching sound emanates from the maestro's machines. Hugh asks if anyone knows the Jackpot off licence in Farnham Road, because Jet used to live there and they're thinking of putting a plaque on the wall, saying 'Jet Black drank three thousand gallons of gin on this spot, between 1972 and 1974'.

He mentions too that one of their first ever gigs was in Guildford, in the Star pub, so they'd like to meet anyone who went to it. 'I was there!' someone shouts. 'You're lying' says Hugh, and a lot of people laugh. Moving on … 'I tell ya, if you're gonna buy a synthesiser don't buy it from Marks and Spencer's cos they don't fucking work!' before taking the mick out of Michael Appleton, the *Rock Goes To College* producer, who lives 'round here' and who had an epileptic fit whilst eating his cornflakes after someone mentioned The Stranglers to him.

Up next is the great and weird 'Second Coming'. And on the excellent 'Non Stop', Hugh's delivery is at times sung, other times relayed like an actor reciting his lines. On 'The Man They Love To Hate' Jet's drumming comes to the fore with more class skin-pounding; Greenfield's keyboards seem to be behaving again, judging by his amazing work on 'How To Find True Love …', a beautiful track. And Hugh loves to twist 'happiness' in to 'a penis'. We're treated to 'Let Me Introduce You …' – a song ahead of its time and one that would make for an epic mosh pit monster nowadays.

A downturn soon though with 'Tramp' which is rather a mess, lead and bass guitars conflicting instead of combining. And 'The Raven' is spoiled too as keyboard problems return. Before 'Nuclear Device', Hugh promotes the CND album again, 'Go out and hear it, you might like it enough to wanna steal one, though it would be better if you bought it, cos, you know …' 'Nuclear Device' is brilliantly done, its smooth but exciting transition into 'Genetix' a real piece of audial art complemented by Dave's mad scientist singing.

27th January '82. Another storming gig, this time at the St Austell Coliseum. An almost identical set list, begins with the immaculate 'Sewer', which Hugh follows up with comments about the place being really out of the way, he then asks where's the furthest anyone has come from today, adding 'We know someone's come from Belgium … A couple of us saw a UFO last week, the first time we've ever seen one, so we're celebrating now'. A sign of the soppy times when 'Golden Brown' arrives, met by (too) many in the audience clapping along and giving it the loudest cheer of the night.

Following a perfect rendition of 'The Raven', Hugh finally responds to shouted requests 'Play that, play that, play that, play that … Well none of you are gonna get what you want … You'll get what you're given' and that is 'Nuclear Device'. The event's close is signalled by the strains of 'La Folie' over the venue speakers as the band exits.

30th January '82. At the Swindon Oasis, a person in the audience spitting at the band receives a 'spanking' as Hugh calls it, from he and JJ. Local press later reports that there were a few spitters so the ringleader was apprehended and dragged on to the stage to have his trousers removed so that his bare buttocks could be used as tom-toms during 'Golden Brown'.

1st February '82. The nauseating issue of gobbing returns at the Bristol Locarno tonight, after just the first track ('Sewer'), with a Hugh rant: 'If you see anyone gobbing, thump 'em 'cos we can't see who's doing it, alright. If you want good music we can't do it for being fucking spat at all the time ... You do that you're gonna get a lousy performance, you want a good performance you don't do it. Does everyone understand English?' The gig proceeds smoothly from then on, and his mood is much improved too, plugging the CND album again and saying 'hello mum and dad' as well as praising BBC Bristol men as 'the nicest bastards he's ever worked with'.

5th February '82. Hugh is in witty form at the Ipswich Gaumont, endearing himself to one lucky individual he spots in the crowd very early on. Once the supreme 'Sewer' is completed, his tirade commences – 'Evenin' all ... What have you done to your hair?! There's a bloke down here who's really got the blues. Look at this boy. No, no, I didn't say you could come up here. Look at his hair. What's he done to it? Well, once upon a time, we'll get back to what we were doing ... completely threw me off seeing that blue head. I've seen black heads, I've never seen blue heads though. It's horrible!' Mercifully, Hugh leaves him alone for the remainder of the gig. He hasn't finished digging though: 'You ain't half got a lot of rabbit up here in Ipswich, haven't you? More rabbit than Sainsbury's, I think. Yabba yabba yabba. Gabba gabba gabba. "Peaches", "Peaches", "Hanging Around". Fucking do this, do that. Well, as you probably know, The Stranglers have never gone crawling to their audience so I don't care what the fuck you call out, you're not gonna get it ...

'I wanna tell you about something. I wanna tell you about a record, alright? Look, just pipe down for a second would ya? Just shut up for a second, give your lungs a rest. I want to plug a record for the Campaign For Nuclear Disarmament – CND ...' The crowd cheers. 'You're all cheering but none of you have bought this record that came out, right? Who bought this record? Honestly? You actually bought that record, yeah? *Life In The European Theatre*, a collection of tracks. That's great. Well, that's about the best on this tour. I've got about six people in the audience who bought it. That's amazing. Out of 1,500 people, six people have bought it. Fucking great, ain't it? You're obviously very much into CND up here.

'Actually, up here they're gonna build the bases up here, ain't they? They're building a lot of bases up here. Great. Well, do you want them up here?' Crowd: 'No!' Hugh: 'Well why don't you go out and buy the fucking record then and get some money spent on the bloody CND? That's all I'm gonna say. Just go out and buy the record, if you want to have a safe Britain and Europe'.

19th February '82. Germaine Greer hosts the BBC TV programme *Friday Night, Saturday Morning*, The Stranglers play two tracks, 'La Folie' and 'Tramp'. Artistically shot, the beginning of 'La Folie' has them sitting amidst dry ice, JJ miming and the three others looking sombre and philosophical, Hugh in particular looking likely to smirk at any moment.

10th March '82. A fascinating BBC 2 documentary called *The Colour Black*. Written by Hugh and Jet, narrated by Jet too, it studies the nature and presence of black in society and culture, featuring amongst other things the Meninblack phenomena and the frequent connection between black and evil. A few ace clips from the Bristol Granary gig last November too.

Goodbye, EMI. March 1982 is when the band tell EMI they will be leaving. Prompted by their advisors' observation that EMI had failed to renew their contract, The Stranglers need little encouragement to move on.

AND CHEERS, ED.

March also sees Ed Kleinman and his partner Susan Erlichman curtail their management of the band, in an amicable agreement. Their final contribution is to help find them a new label; it's achieved quickly with CBS offering a generous contract, which 'gazumps' Richard Branson's Virgin Records offer. From Kleinman's perspective, EMI were not the buffoons often portrayed in historyinblack, while he declines any credit for the move to CBS. Nonetheless, he got some; The Stranglers liked, trusted and most importantly respected him and were grateful for his input.

Ed Kleinman: 'I had no problems with EMI including a new publishing deal with them that I closed for the band. EMI was on track with me and doing what they had said they would do. As for the publishing deal, I had a goal of a $250k. This was for the publishing and administration of all The Stranglers' music, not only the past (which EMI needed to renew), but all future music for the next five years. 15% went for the Admin side, 10% went to EMI and 75% went to The Stranglers. Also, the band earn 100% of writer royalties, as does publishing royalties on the music. Every recorded song - whether a hit or not - earns publishing and writer royalties. It was a good deal. I believe we got close to the $250k.'

19th March '82. After lengthy negotiations, The Stranglers are signed by CBS subsidiary Epic at 1.30 a.m. in a deal worth £850k.

4th April, '82: Hugh Cornwell to appear in the play *Charlie's Last Round* with Bob Hoskins and Stephen Rea at the Almeida Theatre, Islington, London.

9th April '82. The No Nukes Festival at Utrecht in Holland is filmed for Dutch TV. The Stranglers appear, along with acts such as Dave Edmunds, Bad Manners and Steel Pulse. Splendid gig, with opener 'Down In The Sewer' going down like a bomb. Bad pun intended. Hugh tells the audience that The Stranglers don't want nukes ANYWHERE, not just the US, Russia, England or here. 'Who Wants The World?' is excellent, very appropriate for this event, and 'Baroque Bordello' adds majestic finesse to the proceedings. 'Golden Brown' clearly flutters the heart strings of many Orangefolk, followed by the thrashtastic 'Let Me Introduce You …'.

There is then the curiosity classic of the JJ-sung 'How To Find True Love …' containing more fantastic work from Jet and guest percussionists from Steel Pulse. 'Tank' is rapturously received too. After an exemplary 'The Raven', Hugh and JJ skulk off the stage, still playing their guitars. The encore 'Genetix' is the finisher, featuring the third lead vocalist of the set in Dave, in itself a remarkable aspect of a remarkable band. Following the gig, the sage Jet Black is interviewed about No Nukes … 'I think the idea is exciting because through music one can reach a lot of people with a lot of new ideas. And although it's easy to be fooled into believing that you're really achieving something, in real terms it IS important in that expressing ideas through music does definitely reach people and make them think. I think it's a bit of a pipedream to expect the Russians or the Americans to scrap all their nuclear weapons simply because we played a gig in Utrecht, but nevertheless, the idea of spreading the message that nuclear weapons are no good to anybody is a valid one'.

20th April '82: the band appear on Granada TV's *Late Night From Two* miming to 'La Folie' and Jet giving possibly the best 'death stare' by anyone living ever to a television camera! Maybe it's that stare that's deterring people from buying the single though.

24th April '82. The band's follow up to the hugely popular 'Golden Brown' is … 'La Folie', the lovely, the atmospheric and the spoken and sung in French song. If its arrival was eagerly awaited, then its departure seems just as eagerly awaited too, it doesn't even make the Top 40. Merde!

Promo video for Stranglers singles – 'La Folie': Great opening shot of the band wandering down from Sacre Coeur, very atmospheric and cinematic. This gives the feeling of a deeply thoughtful French art house film that looks grand, but provides absolutely no clue as to what is actually going on.

27th April '82. According to *Strangled*, the band are due to appear on German TV programme *Bananas* in Cologne today.

22nd July '82. Irrespective of the failure of the 'La Folie' single, the *Top Of The Pops*' producers clearly expect strong sales for The Stranglers' next one, 'Strange Little Girl' as they're on the show before its release. An impressed and cheesy Simon Bates introduces them, telling the viewers cheesefully that The Stranglers have changed their style. Still, mock him as I do, at least he wasn't indecently assaulting anyone or having a very sly, very wrong fondle of underage innocents nearby, like some BBC colleagues were in those days.

24th July '82. 'Strange Little Girl' is released, their last single on EMI and, whilst the separation is not the most amicable, the single's sales – nine weeks in the charts, peaking at No. 7 – certainly sweetens the pill. Indeed, the band savour the irony of it being a huge seller, because the track is not radically different to the original demo of it which EMI rejected in 1975.

Promo video for Stranglers singles – 'Strange Little Girl': Nice story video with Hugh seeming to be a guardian angel or the girl's conscience even. The tale has an upbeat ending too, with the girl finding her place in a good crowd despite initially being a lost soul.

September 1982. The Stranglers are in Brussels, Belgium, working on their next album.

13th September '82. The final stipulation from EMI is a Stranglers compilation album. And so, *The Collection 1977-1982* is released, containing fourteen tracks, including 'Strange Little Girl' and 'Waltzinblack' but not 'Five Minutes'. In an era when the charts weren't saturated with greatest hits by artists too young to vote and without any actual hits to their name, this 'best of' is a notable success, reaching No.12 in the chart, sales hitting silver.

And that is despite it having one of the worst sleeve designs ever created, by anyone. Yes, EMI loused up there too, though the initial suggestion had been to use an image of the band's usual logo pressed through cellophane, giving it an embossed effect illusion. It looked good, but the band disagreed so the label unilaterally decided on a black leotard-clad model standing next to the normal red logo set in a black diamond. Coined as the 'keep fit' cover, it is, artistically, aesthetically, technically and objectively speaking, absolute fucking shite.

16th October '82. The Stranglers are filmed in concert by TVS for ITV's *Off The Record* programme to be broadcast on the 18th. Lucky lad Tony Stubley attended:

> Three days after my eighteenth birthday, I find myself waiting by the stage door outside the TVS studios in Duncan Road, Gillingham, Kent trying to obtain entry to a gig for which there were only a 100 tickets given out and is for the recording of a new TV show. I'm only there for twenty minutes when JJ appears and upon learning that I don't have a ticket says he will sort it for me. Half an hour later a woman appears and asks for 'Stubs', she then presents me with a ticket for the gig. We hear the sound check from outside and a brand new song 'European Female' is rehearsed. The gig itself is an hour long and the band kicks off with the best version of 'Sewer' that I have ever heard. Although nothing is played from Heroes or *Black & White* we still get a great set with the band closing with 'Nuclear Device'/'Genetix' and an encore of 'The Raven'. Also played were 'Just Like Nothing On Earth', 'Hanging Around', 'Golden Brown', 'Duchess' and 'Let Me Introduce You'.

21st December '82. The single 'European Female' is released as a standard black vinyl seven-incher in a picture sleeve as well as later in picture disc format, the band's first such limited edition. The delightful single will fare well too, making No.9 in the charts.

30th December '82. The *Top Of The Pops* Christmas special has a studio appearance from The Stranglers for 'Golden Brown', easily one of the year's top selling singles. The band, all in black, look customarily unimpressed with all the gloss and schmaltz of the show, whenever it was recorded, probably in the autumn.

16.10.82 TVS Theatre, Gillingham - Broadcast on ITV *Off The Record*.
(*Image courtesy of the author*)

11 1983: FRESH START?

This will prove to be an interesting year in terms of creative output from the band. Even with the spectacular flop of 'La Folie' after the equally spectacular success of 'Golden Brown', 1982 had been a good year. Oddly enough, the three noteworthy singles of '82, as well as showing the unpredictable nature of the band and of the record buying public, were all gentle songs, implying that the band were mellowing. 'Golden Brown', 'La Folie' and 'Strange Little Girl' are all effectively smooth, soothing ballads, yet the tracks on the *La Folie* album contradict such suggestion, they're hard-hitting and acerbic in comparison, showing again that the band can change and progress their music without detracting from the quality. It is hard to think of any other single concept album to match the intelligence and commerciality of The Stranglers' latest offering, but would the move from EMI to CBS, from the outset a far less demanding 'employer', indicate even more change in musical direction? It will certainly signify a change in their working routines.

BELGIUM RATFIGHT

During the making of the new album, the band spend less time together than they had before. The increased physical distance between JJ and Hugh, and JJ's inclination to spend summer weeks in Grasse, France, with his mother are relevant factors also. While it's clear that the bulk of the song writing workload has been edging towards Hugh anyway, more creative constraints come with Jet and Hugh living in the West Country and JJ and Dave residing in Cambridgeshire. So, whenever the foursome do actually manage to meet up, the chances of arguments and even a band fall out aren't unlikely.

Finalising the album over in Brussels, Hugh and Jet - with Steve Churchyard - have been working into the early hours on a rough version of one (unidentified) track. JJ and Dave are out socialising and when they return – after Jet and Hugh had gone back to the hotel – they played the tape of the track and apparently dislike it so much they scrunch it into an envelope which they then stick to the studio door; derogatory comments being added to the envelope too. When Jet and Hugh find out, they are unsurprisingly furious, but Hugh reacts further by booking a flight back to London. He has, effectively, quit the band, but profuse apologies from JJ prompt him to reverse his decision. The damage however has been done. Hugh was deeply upset about the incident and it probably signifies the first serious crack in the relationship, especially between him and JJ.

6th January '83. Introduced by squeaky clean BBC Radio DJ Mike Smith, the new single 'European Female' is mimed to by the band on *Top Of The Pops*.

21st January '83. Channel 4's irreverent rock/pop music show *The Tube* has The Stranglers performing 'Midnight Summer Dream', 'European Female' and 'Who Wants The World?' in one of their best ever TV appearances. Paula Yates and Jools Holland host the show.

22nd January '83. The new album, *Feline*, is out today. Considered by some as almost an 'unplugged' Stranglers album, most of it was written at Jet's house and whilst CBS had exerted minimal pressure on them, tensions still arose during its making. The album has taken longer than usual to write, much of that because Hugh and JJ, when actually together, spend too much time 'lying around semi-comatose' from the effects of heroin, 'the most dangerous and wonderful drug' according to Hugh. The release from EMI's shackles probably influences matters too, the more comfortable working arrangement with CBS allowing the band to relax and focus more on their personal lives. Possibly too much so, in fact, to the point of complacency.

FELINE
Released: 22nd January, 1983.
Label: Epic.
Charted at No. 4.
Side One: 1 'Midnight Summer Dream', 2 'It's A Small World', 3 'Ships That Pass In The Night', 4 'The European Female'.
Side Two: 1 'Let's Tango In Paris', 2 'Paradise', 3 'All Roads Lead To Rome', 4 'Blue Sister', 5 'Never Say Goodbye'.
Backing vocals on 'Paradise': Anna Von Stern – France Lhermitte.

In a few words – what the *Ford* are the songs about? Part 7.
'Midnight Summer Dream': Burnel's melody, Cornwell's lyrics, about Hugh's late night chat with George the charming old timer who used to live at Jet's home.

'It's A Small World': The 'six degrees of separation' theory, that everyone on the planet knows everyone else. The song also possibly touches on the instability of the band.

'Ships That Pass In The Night': The first line refers to Hugh's US girlfriend Judy and his becoming weary of travelling to see her, but it's generally about things you can cling on to for reassurance, like religion, politics, doctors ...

'The European Female': JJ's song about his French girlfriend Anna, and about Europe and Paris.

'Let's Tango In Paris': A prime example of Hugh bastardising well known titles, the lyrics are straightforward.

'Paradise': About a luxurious holiday JJ spent in the Seychelles, where so much poverty existed close by. Thus, paradise is really an illusion. His girlfriend Anna sings backing vocals here, quite ironic as the lyrics also allude to an unsettled relationship.

'All Roads Lead To Rome': More Hugh lyrics about travelling between London and New York, and using cocaine. Written after the rest of the album, it's the first Stranglers song to feature Jet using solely a drum machine.

'Blue Sister': About problems Dave was having with a girlfriend, the band were worried about him.

'Never Say Goodbye': The first line refers to Dagenham Dave and Charlie Pile and the whole song refers to the dear departed and with meeting up with them after death.

Notable songs of the time not on the vinyl album:

'Aural Sculpture Manifesto': Not a song, more a death knell for songwriting soaked in sarcasm against contemporary music. A free one-sided single that disappointed fans as it's not new music, and met with scorn by reviewers who don't understand its intention.

'Cruel Garden': Almost a swing sister track to 'Old Codger', Hugh describes this hastily arranged gem as a new slant on 'Down In The Sewer' but without the 'relevance'. What is relevant is that his use of acoustic guitar helped him decide to go acoustic on all of *Feline*.

'Savage Breast': A good song, but apparently referring to nothing in particular.

'Pawsher': (recorded in New York a few months later) A one word lyric repeated over and over, so the lyrical content is vague other than Pawsher is an old Greek name, usually spelled 'Portia'.

'Permission': (recorded in London a few months later) Meaty reggae bass, about the CRS riot police in France loitering with intent, waiting for permission to dive in and do some damage.

'Vladimir And Olga': A Stranglers curio, like a modernised Russian folk song, a humorous tale about fictional characters in Russia. Here, Vladimir eats some bread laced with LSD. JJ and Dave created the music and sent the tapes for Hugh and Jet to add lyrics to and finish the recordings in Bath.

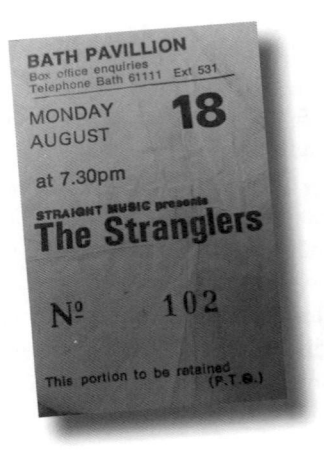

(Image courtesy of Duncan Round)

✪

Bernie Nessbaum's review of *Feline*:

Dark, moody and secretly threatening ... that's just the sleeve, a black panther on a black background. The band have moved boldly, drastically changing their powerful melodic new wave to a smart mix of acoustic and electric tunes. Their usual intelligent, thought provoking lyrics continue, as does the unique sound and ability of breaking down genre-specific barriers. *Feline* is a fine balance of soft and hard textures fused with drum and bass-heavy melodies, sometimes startling in intensity, sometimes soft as a kitten's paw. The listener is in for an aural treat.

Opening track is 'Midnight Summer Dream', a gentle song with a melodic synthesiser intro and powerful bass and drums, accompanied by Hugh's almost poetry recital delivery, which gives it a timeless appeal. 'It's A Small World' features a beautiful acoustic guitar intro joined by an almost electro dance groove; great vocal harmonies AND JJ's growling bass! 'Ships That Pass In The Night', another interesting keyboard intro leading into a near tango rhythm section from Hugh's acoustic guitar and Jet's Symonds electric drum rim shots. 'The European Female' is pure beautiful pop, a vocal delivery by JJ that almost melts on the mind, complemented by a sweet, haunting acoustic melody. 'Let's Tango In Paris' starts with Hugh's vocals matching Dave's bass keyboards in a rather sombre style before exploding with uptempo almost summery harmonies.

'Paradise' has sultry, sexy female harmonies building into effectively a soft pop tune, very different to the normal aggression we're used to. 'All Roads Lead To Rome" – a timeless dance rhythm with repetitive electro style drums, underlined by brooding lyrics and atmospheric swathes of Dave's synthesisers. 'Blue Sister' features classic Burnel bass heavy rhythms and great drumming from Jet, accompanied by Hugh's crooning vocal delivery. 'Never Say Goodbye' is another almost tango style beat and tempo, before JJ's throbbing bass lines confirm its deeper substance; a very distinctive piano signature too.

Don't waste time reading these words, just put the album on and enjoy it for what it is, a 'different' yet still superb album!

FELINE FINE

Although sales of *Feline* are lower than *La Folie*, it still gets to No.4 in the charts, a pretty damned fine start to their CBS career. It's more popular in Europe and is often cited as the one that 'broke' the band there. The Spanish and acoustic guitars, together with the perceived romance of the album, probably helped it, and, aside from a bizarre comment in *Melody Maker* referring to Richard Clayderman, it is well received by the music press too. The band had wanted to strip the sound down – and although it isn't a concept album, while they were making it all four Stranglers were romantically entwined with various partners and the softer sounds and words do suggest such a glow.

Record Mirror summarised the album with, 'Lap it up but don't be fooled, the purr is really a soft growl' yet it does lack a customary edgeinblack. The band's new usage of acoustic guitars and electronic drums works well at times but not all the time, there is a distinct feeling that *Feline* would have benefited from the input of an "outsider" producer.'

28th January '83. The commencement of the *Feline* tour, beginning with Chippenham Goldiggers. Chris Band experienced it, likening Jet Black's 'new' drum sound at times to that of a biscuit tin. This tour's intro is the 'Aural Sculpture Manifesto', the set list typically involving 'Nuclear Device', 'Toiler', 'Ships That Pass In The Night', 'It's A Small World', 'Just Like Nothing On Earth', 'No More Heroes', 'Who Wants The World?', 'Never Say Goodbye', 'Baroque Bordello', 'Golden Brown', 'Princess Of The Streets', 'Midnight Summer Dream', 'European Female', 'Tramp', 'The Raven', 'Duchess', 'London Lady', 'Strange Little Girl' and 'Genetix'. 'Blue Sister' also features tonight, a true live performance rarity.

30th January '83. The venue is Poole Arts Centre. Once he's finished singing 'Ships That Pass In The Night' Hugh chastises the audience for their treatment of the night's warm up act: 'Well I'm surprised that we've got a load of cheapskates here, throwing money at our support act, but no 50p pieces. What a bunch of cheapskates eh. Anyway his name's Nick Malham and we think he's great, but obviously some of you didn't agree with us. Free country innit?'

A few tracks later is 'Never Say Goodbye', a lovely, touching song perhaps incongruous for a live set; after it he pretends to blame the crowd for technical problems with Jet's drums, 'Okay, we've busted one of the drums. You're breathing too heavily, you've busted one of the drums. Great.' Someone from the audience shouts an apology, Hugh replies pleasantly, 'Don't say sorry, chum'.

31st January '83. Tonight at Bristol's Colston Hall is one of THE gigs of the band's lifespan even though there are still those delays thanks to Dave's keyboards going wonky. Again Mr Cornwell waits until after the fourth track 'Ships ...' to properly greet the gathered hordes. Describing Bristol as 'oo-ar land' ('I should know, I live here') the support act is the topic of conversation again: 'Did you like Nick, that friend of ours Nick? The erm tap dancer ... I don't care if you didn't like him, I don't give a fart whether you liked him or not. He made six quid tonight, it's not bad is it? You threw six quid at him which is pretty damn good. But we're cheapskates, we take 10%. He only made three quid last night in Poole, so you're obviously flush up here'. He later accuses the crowd as being as quiet as the grave but there is no question that the audience enjoys the gig immensely, with superb renditions of 'Golden Brown', 'Princess Of The Streets' and 'Baroque Bordello' particularly popular, culminating in the sublime 'Genetix'; monumental, acid jazz new wave at its best!

2nd February '83. The tour moves to Birmingham Odeon, the first of two nights there. Fan Mark Ray attended, he even watched the support act:

It was the bloke who wore a tux and mimed to 'Putting on the Ritz' ... no mathematician could count the sputum in the air that cascaded like a waterfall in his direction'. Nice. 'Ships ...' is stopped early as Hugh and JJ pull out a girl from the front of the audience who has passed out. Hugh asks us, 'What did you think of our support artist?' and someone shouts 'Wanker!' to which Hugh replies, 'A gentlemen there says he didn't like him. He takes ages to tune his acoustic guitar for 'Never Say Goodbye' while JJ chats to the crowd and hands out drinks. 'Duchess' ends abruptly as something goes wrong; JJ and Hugh point at each other accusingly and then laugh. In 'London Lady', JJ mumbles the lyric 'Plastic's real when you're real sick.' but then stops and says, 'Ah, you know the rest'.

Hugh starts jumping up and down on something. It's a plastic rat, 'Right, has anybody else got any pets? Bring 'em up here, now ... come on! Any rubber ravens or rubber cats?' 'Tramp' is, fittingly, messy and sort of unapproachable, I was never as confident as some that it would have been better as the follow up single to 'Golden Brown' than 'La Folie'. During the encore, Hugh pokes more fun at us: 'Look you bunch of morons, we just went for a drink and you start shouting for more after we slogged our guts out for an hour and a half. We were just trying to have a quiet bevy in the back and you want more, you ungrateful lot. Has anyone ever got out of Birmingham alive, eh? And your women keep passing out everywhere. No backbone, all lily livered'. 'Genetix' is the closer, prompting an audience stage invasion. 'Waltzinblack' eventually floats over from the speakers as the outro to a brilliant concert.

15th February '83. Surprise surprise, The Sun misreports tonight's gig at Hammersmith Odeon as 'a riot'. True, some seats are smashed, the reasons for the damage though are clearer when *genuine* accounts are taken into account. Once the second track 'Toiler' is over, fans in the front rows begin to revolt due to not being able to see the band due to bouncers standing in front of and facing the audience. The band announce that they will not play on until the bouncers are out of the way, demanding that the house lights be switched on so everyone can see who is responsible. After a few minutes, Jet explains: 'What's happened here, as very often, we find we're playing to a dozen people with their backs to us and they're standing right in front of people who have paid to see us. We think this is an insult to us, and that it's an insult to you. The management here have taken them out to explain to them, and we believe they understand the situation, and they have told us that these people with their backs to us are no longer going to be standing with their backs to us. And we've told them that our audience haven't come here to wreck this lovely theatre, they've come here purely and simply to enjoy themselves, and to watch us'.

Cue much cheering from the audience. Hugh then says, 'Okay, so like basically you guys out in the audience you don't need any security, cos you aren't going to damage anything, Okay?' The concert restarts and proceeds without any more real to do, though their next night's show there is cancelled. Hugh has a whinge tonight before 'Nubiles' about the seemingly new trend of lobbing odd stuff on stage. 'Has someone lost 20 French centimes? I have here a ... is there a one legged man here with a big cock? Oh there he is ... And is there a one legged man with the right leg missing? Is that the wrong bloke? I mean, who wants it? I don't fucking want it. You seem to think that you can bring all your shit along that you don't want and just throw it on stage. Thanks very much!'

20th February '83. More sophisticated repartee from Mr Cornwell at the Markethalle in Hamburg, Germany. Throughout the concert, amongst all the cheers and song requests, one female voice is prominent. Late on in the gig Hugh has had enough of her screeching. Remarking that the audience is too far away, he says, 'We played here in '79 and we couldn't keep people off the stage and it's complete now, you know. We've been talking about you back in there and we want to know this girl that's screaming. We want to know ... oh there she is ... we just wondered if you've got something up your arse or something. Why are you making all this noise? Is someone molesting you? D'you want to go to the toilet? If you want to go to the toilet there's plenty of public toilets ... *oooh I like shouting.* Can you have a look and see if there's something up her dress because it's very embarrassing seeing someone screaming ya know, very embarrassing.'

Dave pictured in 1983.
(Image courtesy of *Phil Coxon*)

20th February '83. Excellent German concert TV programme *Rockpalast* is screened, with highlights from the two Markethalle gigs. Mercifully, the young lady does not feature, and the show is about perfect. Not that the band seem happy, it looks as if they want to get it all over and done with quickly. The only chat comes from Hugh by way of criticising the packed but generally lifeless audience for requesting 'Grip' as it's 'from about eight years ago'.

21st February '83. The band travel to Nijmegen in the east of the Netherlands to play at De Vereeniging. Recorded for broadcast on Dutch *Radio 3*, selected songs are 'No More Heroes', 'Baroque Bordello', 'Golden Brown', 'Princess Of The Streets', 'Midnight Summer Dream', 'European Female' and 'Tramp'.

26th February '83. 'Midnight Summer Dream' single released, in 7" and 12" formats but still only manages to hit No. 35 in the charts.

Promo video for Stranglers singles - 'Midnight Summer Dream': a really effective atmospheric feel, reminiscent of a 'Ghost story for Christmas whatever' type of affair. There's also an intriguing cyclical aspect, the 'horror film' house in the video is the same one used for the *Rattus* cover photo shoot.

28th February '83. The band play at Palais de la Mutualité in Paris, the audience loving the gig, especially the finale 'La Folie', which is performed beautifully and, as it's in French, gains the special ingredient of audience participation. Such is its popularity here, it seems its release as a single isn't such a commercially bad choice after all.

March '83. Derived from an idea of Antoine de Caunes, better known for *Rapido*, the French TV show, *Houba Houba* features fantastic footage of the band's Mutualite concert: 'No More Heroes', 'Midnight Summer Dream', 'La Folie', 'Tramp', 'The Raven' and 'London Lady'. Also during this month, clips of March's Newcastle gig appear on local television show 'Live At Newcastle', tracks being 'European Female' and 'Midnight Summer Dream'.

7th April '83. BBC studio appearance for the band, filmed 'before a live studio audience' miming to 'Midnight Summer Dream' for *The Kenny Everett Television Show*. It wasn't filmed on this day; The Stranglers are starting a North American tour at The Paradise in Boston, Massachusetts.

3rd May '83. The band play the Masonic Hall in Toronto, Canada. The gig will be broadcast on FM radio again too, the sound is beautifully clear and the vocals from both Hugh and JJ are faultless. People may find fault with Cornwell's less than PC witticisms but not his singing. After first track 'Ships That Pass In The Night' he mentions that they would have been there earlier but someone is getting a golden handshake from the Masons, and then he asks if there are lots of Italians in Toronto because the audience is only throwing five cents coins as they're so tight. And then he comments on Italian cars which have five reverse gears and no forward ones. Rest of the set list: 'It's A Small World'; 'Just Like Nothing On Earth'; 'No More Heroes'; 'Never Say Goodbye'; 'Baroque Bordello'; 'Golden Brown'; 'Midnight Summer Dream'; 'European Female'; 'Tramp'; 'Duchess'; 'London Lady'; 'Nubiles' (Cocktail version) and 'Genetix'.

5th May '83. At the Kabuki Club in San Francisco, the band aren't particularly talkative, Hugh seems bored as hell, unfriendly in fact, slightly detracting from a very good gig. After 'Never Say Goodbye' and while Dave Greenfield warms his keyboards up, audience members shout out their song requests, including one chap who keeps asking for 'She's A Lady'. Eh?

After 'London Lady', Hugh targets a nuisance drunk Aussie in the crowd, telling him to fucking stick to 7Up. He then pitches *Strangled* magazine, 'the most important document to come out of Europe, since the Bayeux Tapestry ... or the Magna Carta ... This is called *Strangled*, it's got nothing to do with The Stranglers whatsoever, it's a non-profit making organisation. You don't believe it, do you?' as an object lands nearby. 'Take your fucking beer bottles home with you. Don't litter this stage please ... If I can sell this magazine to some very intelligent person for $50 you will help The Stranglers' tour break even. You don't believe me, do you? You think we're playing here for thousands and thousands of dollars and you're all being ripped off and we travel around in limousines and all this ... Well y'know you've fucking completely got the wrong end of the stick. We've got a Lear fucking jet'.

Another bottle smashes on the stage. 'Honestly, can't you take a bit of humour? Anyway look, what am I offered for this piece of literature? This is the greatest thing to come out of England since erm ... sliced bread'. A coin lands nearby, 'Okay, that's five cents ... well look, we've wiped our arses on this, we just all wiped our arses, this has got genuine excrement from The Stranglers on, I tell you it has'. Cheers from the crowd. 'Someone appreciates that, you're weirder than I thought ... I thought they were weird in LA, they're even weirder up here. Come on, bring out the green backs! We'll even sign it.' Final song from the band is 'Genetix', which feels even better than normal due to Burnel's bass sound distorting somehow, making even more fantastic growling noises than usual.

AIMLESS VIDEO

During that first week in May a LA based friend of JJ's films a promo video for 'All Roads Lead To Rome', even though the song is not intended for release as a single. In spite of Dave and JJ collaborating on their *Fire & Water* album together, it is a generally quiet summer for the band, with intermittent gigs and the release of just one single which doesn't even make the Top 40. The 'Stranglers star' though is definitely rising in Europe, France especially, where album sales are strong and the public avid for the band like they're a new sensation.

15th June '83. The Stranglers play at the Eindexamen Festival in s-Hertogenbosch, Holland...

16th July '83. ... and the Elixir Festival in Brest, France.

29th July '83. 'Paradise' single released, it reaches No.48.

13th August '83. During the De Panne Seaside Festival at Ostend, Belgium, strong winds and major technical problems cause the gig to be described as one of the band's worst recorded performances ever. Not that it was just the equipment issues to blame for occasional poor musicianship, the band were possibly under the influence too, or maybe just 'rusty', and JJ's bass has fallen out with its owner by the looks of it. Second track of the set, 'Nuclear Device', sounds like Dave's playing with gloves on, while Hugh's guitar has possibly been tuned by a tone-deaf chimp. His vocals are good though, Hugh's – not the imaginary chimp's. The substandard sound continues until, ironically, 'Golden Brown', which is built around graceful keyboard and intricate lead guitar. Twelfth song 'The Raven' arrives but the crowd gets just an instrumental version as JJ has had enough of his guitar cutting out and walks off. He returns for 'London Lady' which goes well enough until the end (a mess), and 'Sewer' commences in a mess and doesn't improve, finishing in chaos.

26th August '83. The Reading Festival or, to give it its full title, 'The 23rd National Jazz, Blues & Rock Festival'. It occasionally enjoys unusual guest slots, The Stranglers being one such unusual choice today. And Hugh naturally has a few things to say about it. 'Well someone must have had a very sick sense of humour putting The

Stranglers on at Reading, don't you think? I like that, I like someone with a sick sense of humour'. Tonight they're headlining, above re-formed psychedelic rockers Man; fine purveyors of reggae, Steel Pulse, and special guests Big Country, amongst others. Steel Pulse are bottled off after 'one and a bit' songs, so clearly there are some thick bastards in the crowd who prefer watching an empty stage.

The Stranglers have never been easily deterred by such crapness, Hugh informs the 30,000-strong audience that the band want to play at the Marquee tonight but the bloke there said to him, 'I'm sorry but you played here about six years ago, you broke a window so you'll have to play at Reading instead'. The festival crowd, far from hostile, is treated to a memorable display. 'There now follows a special request for all heavy metal fans ...' announces Hugh, as Jet and Dave bring the refined sweetness of 'Golden Brown' to the generally smelly masses. Apart from the occasional 'fuck off' from a few rockers, it all goes well, and maybe even a few more fans are gained. To add to the occasion, The Stranglers put on blond wigs for their encore.

Gentlemen prefer blondes - unless it's Hugh and JJ at Reading Festival in 1983. (*Barry Plummer*)

EUROPE AGAIN

Another European tour starts September 21st, kicking off in Spain at Studio 54 in Barcelona and taking in Madrid and San Sebastian. France next, with gigs in Toulouse and Bordeaux and then Paris at the Espace Ballard. Prior to that, rehearsals were in preparation for the French TV show *l'Echo Des Bananes*, with the band effectively completing a full gig even though only two tracks get broadcast, 'Midnight Summer Dream' and 'Tank', together with an interview with Jean-Jacques.

19th September '83. The *l'Echo Des Bananes* rehearsals, FR3 Studio, Paris, consisting of: 'Bring On The Nubiles' (twice), 'Thrown Away', 'Tank' (twice), 'Hanging Around', 'Midnight Summer Dream', 'Never Say Goodbye' (thrice), 'Let Me Introduce You …' (thrice), 'Non Stop' and 'Tits', which JJ sings in French and which in reality is just a piss around, the band laughing about it at the end, especially when they're applauded by the fortunate few spectators. There are 'improvisations' (also known as arsing about with their instruments) as well as an unidentified instrumental which is very waltz-like and actually pretty nifty too.

Then comes Vincent Lamy's interview with Jet Black for the French Stranglers fanzine *Black & White*. A few extracts:

> Lamy: What does Jet think about the album/film soundtrack that JJ and Dave have done? Jet: 'I'll tell you about the music when I hear it, I haven't heard it yet. The fact that they're doing it is fine, they're expressing something outside of The Stranglers and I'm sure I will find a lot of admirable qualities when I hear it'. Lamy: With the next Stranglers album, will there be something new, new style, new visions? Jet: 'Well everything we do is new isn't it? Lamy: 'Yes of course … is it a new concept? Jet: 'We've never been more advanced in our concept for the next album. We have the concept, all the artwork is completed, the album sleeve, the idea of promoting it, and we've got a lot of funny gimmicks internationally to make attention for the album. Erm, the only thing we don't have is music!' he laughs'.
>
> He is asked about his best and his worst memory with the group; he doesn't provide a best, however: 'The worst memory was probably being given a week's free accommodation in the south of France …" Does he mean Nice? 'Affirmative. The strange thing was, we never received an invitation … Going through it at the time, we had really mixed emotions because when you get arrested and thrown into prison you think "Oh God, The Guillotine!" then you think "This is ridiculous, we're just trying to play some music!" and then the next minute you think, "Well hang on, I've been in here three days", and then it's four days and then it's five days and you're beginning to wonder, and it does psychological damage to the brain unless one is able to think sensibly. Does Jet respect the 'old' fans like the Finchley boys or the 'Golden Brown' brigade'? Jet: 'Well let me tell you, our philosophy is possibly unique because we regard what we do as being done for us, we do what we do for us – we write our music for us, we don't care about you, we don't care about the English, the Japanese, the Americans , we write for four people, The Stranglers. What we do we do for us, and if people like it then it's nice'.
>
> And are The Stranglers satisfied with their new label CBS? Jet: 'We've never been so happy with a company for the simple reason that they sat down and decided to have us on their label, and it's been a long time since that's happened. They've really taken an interest and, within the limitations of big business, they're really trying their very best, as far as we can see, to do what we want them to do. It won't always be possible but when you're with a large multinational company, we think we're doing very well. Sometimes we say "Don't do that" and to them it's crazy, this is uncommercial, but they do it and we respect that, so, by and large, we're very pleased with our relationship so far'.
>
> And what's Jet's opinion of Margaret Thatcher? Jet: 'I think Margaret Thatcher is the most astonishing embarrassment to the British people, she really is. I mean, she doesn't hold the respect of anybody other than the middle class conservative majority and it's a disastrous situation, but it's the norm in so many western countries where that kind of figurehead is respected, but they're always leading people down the wrong avenues'.

1983: FRESH START?

30th September '83. The day after the Espace Ballard gig in Paris is this Parc Des Expositions concert in Lille. Tonight, in Lille, it seems the British have invaded by coach [this was pre-Channel Tunnel, of course] and Hugh alludes to this fact: 'If there are any French here, you may want to give a welcome to all these Brits …' It's a good enough gig to send the punters home happy, though the lead guitar on 'Toiler' is patchy again, the bass not powerful enough and the wait for the keyboards to sort themselves out after the track is as frustrating as ever, especially as no one on stage says a word. And then the keys on the next track 'Ships That Pass In The Night' sound all at sea anyway.

Later, Cornwell stops 'Hanging Around' before it has properly started: 'Hang on hang on, what's the hurry?' He wants to take the piss out of the locals first: 'We know that Lille isn't … doesn't look, y'know … If it's anyone's first visit to France, **don't** judge France by Lille …', which is greeted with a fair few French whistles. 'We must give Lille its due, Lille is the centre of western civilization today …' Ironic cheers … 'It's not quite the centre but it's close.'

2nd October '83. Woe betide anyone incurring the withering wit of Hugh Cornwell! This gig at the Europa in Metz, east France, is a good one, peaking with an electrifying rendition of 'London Lady', following which: 'Well someone has just proved some of my suspicions… because someone's just shouted "London Lady", and we've just played it. Now obviously the guy's either deaf or asleep. And someone said to me earlier, that the people from Rouen – well … "don't expect much". This was a French guy. He said they listen, but they don't do much'.

5th October '83. Most of August's Reading Festival gig is broadcast tonight on the David 'Kid' Jensen Radio One show.

10th October '83. Although The Stranglers speak minimal Italian, the Rolling Stone Club, Milan, sees them producing a *bellisimo* gig watched by an impressive, impressed crowd. And a translator is on hand between songs to help Hugh communicate with the locals. Early in the set, he tells them about a gig the band were supposed to play at a park somewhere north in Milan city, near a big industrial estate about four years ago: 'The road crew said "Nice place but where's the electricity?" A few minutes later one of the venue men returned carrying an electric shaver plug'. And later he asks: 'This is the home of La Scala right? What, you've never heard of it? Well it's not a shop … La Scala is the seat of Italian opera. Open your ears for a bit of sculpture … and all gays can meet upstairs on the balcony, just like La Scala, as usual'. 'Hanging Around' closes the gig, rapturously received.

11th October '83. Back in France, at the Maison Des Sports in Clermont Ferrand, another fabulous gig takes place. Fabulous, but imperfect. The opener, 'Down In The Sewer', is cocked up early on as their timing is all to pot. After a short delay, they restart and get it right. Before the fourth song, 'It's A Small World', with JJ translating, Hugh teases the audience about being unresponsive, beginning with 'You facking silly bit of crumpet!' just to test their understanding, then, 'You might have noticed, well you thought we had a slight technical problem at the beginning ... well there wasn't any problem, you just looked so asleep we thought you should be woken up', adding with mock sympathy, 'Listen, it's not your fault that Giscard d'Estaing comes from this area of the country'.

Following 'London Lady', he has another gentle swipe: 'For some reason, you might think this very presumptuous of us ... but none of us find you very exciting. Maybe it's Clermont Ferrand. We asked someone, "What's the biggest industry in Clermont Ferrand?" And we were very surprised with the answer: "The biggest occupation is trying to escape from Clermont Ferrand." Maybe they should have a television series *Escape From Clermont Ferrand.*? Do you agree with this, that Clermont Ferrand is the most fucking boring place in France?' Judging by crowd cheers and laughter, they certainly do agree. Last song is 'Hanging Around', again received by the audience with great gusto.

27th October '83. *The Kenny Everett Show* is repeated on BBC2 and the edition with The Stranglers performing 'Midnight Summer Dream' is broadcast again.

11th November '83. Official release date of Dave Greenfield & JJ Burnel's *Fire & Water* album. Scant promotion for it, and scant chart action too, as it only nudges the charts at No. 94 by December. It was recorded at Spaceward Studios, a Cambridge studio converted from an old schoolhouse. The album's most commercial (and most un-Stranglers track imaginable) 'Rain And Dole And Tea' was originally intended for JJ's girlfriend Anna to sing but her vocal range couldn't cover it, so her friend Maggie Reilly (of Mike Oldfield fame) was invited to help out. Anna does have a spoken part on the song, however. It will be the only single release from the album but does not impact on the singles charts, despite the bizarre promotional photo shots of Burnel and Greenfield gallivanting and pouting in 60s style black dresses, make up and wigs.

FIRE & WATER
Side 1: 'Liberation'; 'Rain And Dole And Tea'; 'Vladimir And Sergei'; 'Le Soir'.
Side 2: 'Trois Pedophiles Pour Eric Sabyr'; 'Dino Rap'; 'Nuclear Power (Yes Please)'; 'Detective Privee'; 'Consequences'.
This album forms the musical basis for the film 'Ecoutez Vos Murs' by Vincent Coudanne.

Robert Endeacott's review of *Fire & Water*:
I'd hoped for an experimental but darkly commercial, synthesiser-driven album propped up by masses of the legendary bone-thudding bass, like an early Human League opus but edgier, grittier and braver. My hopes weren't realised but I do recommend this album nonetheless, it's a good LP and way above the average pap of the day proffered by so many artistes.

First track is 'Liberation', it wouldn't have been out of place on *The Gospel* ... LP, a pleasant tune enhanced by JJ's recital of Einstein's 1949 statement shown on the sleeve. Keyboards are reminiscent of Tubeway Army work, this tune has a poppier drum beat. A very promising album opener. Then it's 'Rain And Dole And Tea', a lovely Shangri-Las-like song with matching vocal from Maggie Reilly making it a fine pop song. Even with a catchy bass hook and majestic keys sweeping throughout, it certainly is not something I expected from a Greenfield and Burnel album. 'Vladimir And Sergei' is very easy on the ear, more Stranglers lampooning the Soviet Union again, set against a waltz. 'Le Soir' is almost jazz funk, containing typically brilliant shuddering Burnel bass, which sadly is a little let down by rambling and too-soft keyboards; it would make a decent film noir score.

Side Two starts with 'Trois Pedophiles Pour Eric Sabyr' which is a powerful, dramatic instrumental with strong electric drums. 'Dino Rap' is like Alexi Sayle on Valium, annoying and a waste of track space! 'Nuclear Power (Yes Please)' is sardonic and good, very like *Euroman Cometh* in terms of style and attitude, complete with a thunderous synthesiser spine. JJ is being very clever in delivering the vocals in a manner suggesting he wants to conceal that wit and intelligence, almost like an alter ego, a thug with a brainy persona. 'Detective Privee' is JJ 'acting' again, in French, a pleasant Gallic ditty feel to it. Echoes of Human League complemented by JJ's vocals which are gentle but just right. Finally, 'Consequences', occasionally exquisite, almost like Kraftwerk meets Vangelis, and a perfect way to close the album.

✪

12 1984: ALL QUIET ON THE STRANGLERS FRONT

Even though *Strangled* magazine consistently denies there is a possibility The Stranglers are splitting up, the band's relative inactivity in the forthcoming year fuels followers' fears that they *will*. Any solo or collaborative releases only add more fuel to those fears, and further 'evidence' comes with the fact that Hugh has hired himself a stylist, Jackie Castellano. Jackie's involvement with Hugh's affairs, and indeed with the band's, will gradually increase over time, but it will be autumn before any actual new Stranglers material emerges. The crucial hope for the band (and the label) is that fans think the wait is worth it.

January 1984. Greenfield and Burnel's 'Rain And Dole And Tea' – with Maggie Reilly's vocals – is released. What little media attention there is focuses on the two Stranglers-in-drag rather than the (very good) music.

February '84. Recording for the next planned Stranglers album, *Aural Sculpture*, takes place as well as a photo shoot for the cover, in Trafalgar Square, London. A thirteen-foot polystyrene model sculpture of a human ear is erected in the Square (as it supposedly fits in with the other sculptures there) and the band are in fancy dress to mark the occasion: Hugh is Admiral Lord Nelson, Dave is Biggles, JJ is Joseph Chamberlain and Jet is dressed as a traditional country vicar. Unfortunately, using bird seed to tempt pigeons to shit on the ear – created by artist John King, brother-in-law of Hugh – to increase authenticity prove ineffectual. Perverse little buggers pigeons, 'cos they shit everywhere else.

March '84. The band is in Brussels continuing work on the new album. At first envisaging it would be ready for release in June, the realisation that they have too much material for it means a delay is inevitable.

1984: ALL QUIET ON THE STRANGLERS FRONT

12th March '84. 'Golden Brown' and 'Strange Little Girl' are re-released as a double-A side on Golden 45's, a subsidiary of Liberty. In a bland picture sleeve and with minimal exposure, it sees no chart action.

July '84. The band are again in the studio in Brussels, recording a few new tracks different to those chosen earlier in the year. In *Strangled*, Hugh tells Chris Twomey, '... I'm really pleased with it, it's so refreshing. People are going to be saying "Thank God for The Stranglers"'. But then, from somewhere across the studio, comes the voice of Jet Black, 'That'll be the day'. Laurie Latham is producing the album, he is best known for his work on Paul Young's *No Parlez* LP. He didn't like some of the band's 'pretty shoddy' production on *Feline*, so it will be interesting to hear his input and influence on the next release. News that Latham has the idea of having brass/horns on some of the new songs as well as backing singers will probably perturb sections of the fanbase.

4th October '84. From the forthcoming album comes the single 'Skin Deep' and the band appear on *Top Of The Pops*. It's a lovely melody, soft but instantly catchy, and it will be a success, lasting seven weeks in the charts and eventually reaching No.15. The signs are good and this release is aided by cunning CBS marketing, available as it is in 7" and 12" format, with a limited edition 'skin texture' sleeve plus some copies coming with a 'Skin Deep' tattoo as well.

Promo video for Stranglers singles – 'Skin Deep': Studio footage of the band playing, with a huge ear in the background and Jet on bongos giving a magnificent glare to camera, then film of a huge snake slithering across a man's tattooed flesh. Finally, face masks are torn off the band, uncomfortable and interesting at the same time. All in all quite a classy video.

17th November '84. *Aural Sculpture* is released. Despite favourable reviews, it fares less well commercially than the previous albums. Following on from the softer, poppier impression left by *Feline*, *Aural Sculpture* does indeed contain the first appearance of the brass/horn section. Full of 'proper' pop songs and thus no epics or customary Strangler idiosyncrasies, it's their most pretentiously titled album, conversely containing their most basic music.

29th November '84. The single 'Do They Know It's Christmas?' is released by charity 'supergroup' Band Aid, as founded and led by Bob Geldof and Midge Ure. The Stranglers have no involvement with the record whatsoever.

AURAL SCULPTURE
Released: 17th November, 1984.
Label: Epic.
Charted at No. 14.
Side One: 1 'Ice Queen', 2 'Skin Deep'*, 3 'Let Me Down Easy',
4 'No Mercy', 5 'North Winds'*.

Side Two: 1 'Uptown', 2 'Punch And Judy'*, 3 'Spain', 4 'Laughing', 5 'Souls'*, 6 'Mad Hatter'.
Hugh Cornwell: Vocals & Guitar.
JJ Burnel: Bass & vocals.
Jet Black: Percussion.
Dave Greenfield: Keyboards.
Horn section on 'Ice Queen', 'Punch And Judy' & 'Mad Hatter': Paul Nieman (Trombone), Paul Spong (Trumpet), Tim Whitehead (Sax).
Backing vocals on 'Let Me Down Easy', 'No Mercy' & 'Mad Hatter': Jimmy Chambers, George Chandler, Tony Jackson. Female voice on 'Spain' taken from a speech by Carmen Franco.

In a few words – what the *Ford* are the songs about? Part 8.

'Ice Queen': Hugh had just split up with his American girlfriend (fiancée, in fact) when he wrote this about her.

'Skin Deep': From a JJ riff, the lyrics concern Hugh's ice queen again as well as beauty being superficial.

'Let Me Down Easy': JJ's dad had recently died and so this is a tribute to him, with another fine JJ riff and with Hugh's words.

'No Mercy': The title and lyrics are self-explanatory, but this is non-specific, referring to life in general.

'North Winds': Profound lyrics from JJ, dealing with the two World Wars, modern day weaponry and also the birth of Israel.

'Uptown': In New York, 'uptown' can mean a person is high on cocaine and Hugh was still using it at the time of writing the song. He would often say it's about horse racing (the recorded version does indeed contain a snippet of racing commentary) but it isn't.

'Punch And Judy': Hugh referring to his American ex again, plus mention of his band commitments too.

'Spain': Concerns the post-Franco development of the nation and includes a short speech – recited by an actress – from Franco's daughter Carmen when she was 8 years old.

'Laughing': A tribute to Marvin Gaye, shot dead by his father. The band had considered asking Marvin to produce this album, (Eddy Grant was also a mooted). No guitars on this track.

'Souls': Hugh telling us about ancient Mayan culture.

'Mad Hatter': Another tribute, kind of, relating to a warm-hearted eccentric whom Hugh befriended at a dinner party one evening. Other eccentric guests at the same gathering also feature.

Notable songs of the time not on the vinyl album:
'Vladimir & The Beast Part III': JJ and Dave's new chapter about the hapless Vladimir, this time based in Afghanistan in the Russian army.
'Head On The Line': An anti-drugs song from Hugh, as he says he'd given them up by then.
'In One Door': Probably about Hugh's relationship with the band at the time.

✪

Gareth Noon's review of *Aural Sculpture*:

Two years on from the Acousti-Euro-Electro album *Feline* and, in the words of the band, 'Behold, The Stranglers bring you Aural Sculpture'. It's a change of direction again, with the introduction of brass to divide fans' opinions. 'Ice Queen', the opening track, has a crescendo of trumpets and trombone to give us our first taste of it, and it's a good track. 'Skin Deep' is a poppy number and will provide the band with another hit, it's more uptempo than anything on *Feline*. Next up is 'Let Me Down Easy', a slower song with a great middle keyboard run from Dave and plodding bass from JJ, but is the weakest of the singles here. Another strong song next with 'No Mercy', with an oft repeated simple guitar line – well, simple if you can play guitar that is – with backing singers on too; another notable first for the band. The final track of side one is the strongest and my favourite here – 'North Winds', very strong lyrics, a great swirling, haunting keyboard and powerful vocals from JJ Burnel.

With The Stranglers, expect the unexpected ... the first two tracks of side two, 'Uptown' and 'Punch And Judy' feel like fillers, but then we get back on course with 'Spain', the highlight of this side, which starts with a slow drum intro with congas and castanets and slow bass line, plus a great clear vocal from Hugh. 'Laughing' is the next track, not sure if this is the band's sense of humour thinking they would be laughing all the way to the bank. They'd be wrong if it was; there are B-sides better than this! 'Souls' I think would probably have been the most suitable follow up single to 'Skin Deep', while the final song 'Mad Hatter' is probably the weakest of their career to date. Is that just their sense of humour or is the creativity waning?

Overall, *Aural Sculpture* shows The Stranglers moving on and experimenting with different soundscapes and styles but time will tell if the fans think it works and if they appreciate the change of direction. Personally, I doubt it.

1st December '84. 'No Mercy' is released as a single but fails to build on the foundation of 'Skin Deep', only making No.37 in the charts. Again available in different formats, 7", 12" AND as an ear sculpture-shaped picture disc.

An atmospheric shot of JJ, 1983. (Image courtesy of *Bernard Legon*)

Promo video for Stranglers singles. 'No Mercy': Plenty of surreal imagery here: faceless medical staff, sax playing surgeons, floating ears and Jet initially drumming with a surgical saw. Hugh climbs in and out of a giant ear as well, followed by an appropriately sized Q-tip. None of it is as daft as it sounds.

Friday 7th December '84. The Stranglers are on *The Tube* in Newcastle, playing 'Let Me Down Easy', 'No Mercy' and 'Uptown'. Jools Holland introduces them, holding in his hands the latest edition of *Strangled*.

21st December, '84. The band play Dusseldorf's Phillipshalle and, with a lot of English fans attending, the atmosphere is more akin to a football match than a rock concert. Friction in the crowd isn't exactly helped by Hugh's hammed up German early on, and the frequent crowd chants of 'England, England, England!' get annoying. The band had arrived to the rare sound of 'Aural Sculpture Manifesto' in German, evidence that Hugh certainly is capable of speaking the language without trying to sound like an 'Allo 'Allo! extra.

The set list: 'Midnight Summer Dream', 'European Female', 'Ships That Pass In The Night', 'Let Me Down Easy', 'Punch And Judy' (on which the brass trio sounds ropey), 'Peaches' ('... is she trying to get out of that Volkswagen?'), but with no change to the 'worse places to be' lyric, possibly because Hugh cocks up the preceding line. 'Skin Deep' is pretty woeful here, not a good choice to play live, and the backing vocals sound very out of sorts. 'No Mercy'. 'Uptown'. The gig is pretty much rescued at the end by a fine version of 'The Raven'; much more like it!

13 1985: CONSEQUENCES

Aural Sculpture sells a respectable number of copies in the UK, but fewer than the previous album, showing that however mild a gradient it may be, the band's popularity here is on a downward spiral. The album does help to establish them in Europe though – including, at last, Germany – and also Australia. To some, it's clear that The Stranglers are turning soft and becoming complacent, or more complacent, and the introduction of not only a brass/horn section, but *backing singers* too, for goodness sake, is simply too much to accept.

A mellower style is evident on *La Folie* and *Feline*, yet both still contain tracks *belonging* to the unique Stranglers sound; it would be a big ask for any *Aural Sculpture* tracks to be commended so highly. Laurie Latham's production on *No Parlez* was *crucial* in helping Paul Young's rise to stardom, but The Stranglers have reached such status already. Most of the frustrated fans don't blame Latham, the cause of the band losing their edge is down to the drifting apart of Hugh Cornwell and JJ Burnel – it just *has* to be. The band are growing up, growing restless and growing distant, while the fans are growing increasingly dissatisfied.

2nd February '85. Another national TV appearance, the band appearing on kids' Saturday morning show *No. 73*. They perform live, wearing sunglasses and in all black, playing next release 'Let Me Down Easy' and closing the programme with 'Uptown'. The brass trio on both songs are slightly too loud and Hugh's vocals too echoey but, all in all, it's good quality fare. 'Uptown' is quite startling in fact, with Hugh's opening line sounding suspiciously like 'I'm gonna grab my cock' rather than 'crop', and the song being danced to not only by Jim Lea and Noddy Holder of Slade, but comedian Sandy Toksvig and *Supergran* too, in amongst a load of kids and teenyboppers and weirdoes, also on stage, tucking in to buffet munchies. JJ looks likely to either break in to a grim smile or break a nose or two with his guitar if anyone gets too close.

7th February '85. The band appear on Dutch TV Show *Schoolplein* miming to 'Golden Brown', 'Skin Deep' and 'No Mercy'.

13th February '85. A 'packed to the gills' audience, as Hugh puts it, at Sheffield City Hall responds to each new Stranglers song with generally as much enthusiasm as the older ones, occasionally more so in fact. Even with a whole range of mistakes, duff notes and off keys, there is still something rather special about this gig. 'Something Better Change' is followed by 'Nuclear Device' – someone cocks up the ending, prompting Hugh to ask 'What happened?' afterwards. A person in the audience offers him a drink: 'I'll have that later, there's nothing like a Blue Nun to keep you ... religious,' quips Hugh.

'Uptown' gets a really good response, more so than old favourite 'Dead Ringer' despite Dave's vocals being superbly manic, as ever. 'No Mercy', then 'Nice 'n' Sleazy' which is accordingly brilliant, Hugh and JJ weaving splendid guitars. Thrown Away', 'Let Me Down Easy', 'Midnight Summer Dream', 'European Female' (with a sublime segue, though JJ really struggles to hit the song's higher notes), 'Ships That Pass In The Night', 'Golden Brown', 'Peaches' ('... she trying to get out of that Mercedes Benz?' and 'Like getting stuck in Sheffield, without a bloody prayer.').

'Death And Night And Blood' is cracking and 'Threatened' even more cracking! 'Punch And Judy', the finale where they all sing, is frankly very ropey. Hugh makes fun of the audience about their having no taste 'even when we play it wrong' to which JJ says '*You*' and he laughs and retorts 'No, *you* got it wrong ...' and then they *all* go and louse up the beginning to 'Hanging Around' AND Hugh gets one of the choruses wrong too! Then, 'I Feel Like A Wog' and 'Sewer' with Hugh in good spirits (when the first 'survive' in the lyric is due, someone shouts it from the audience, he responds 'No it isn't!' without disrupting the song). Before 'Nubiles', Hugh invites requests and pretends to hear someone ask for this. The Cocktail version is rubbish but then it's straight into 'Toiler' splendidly. The inspiring encore track 'The Raven' closes the gig.

16th February '85. 'Let Me Down Easy' is the new single, and that's exactly what it does, only making it to No.48 in the charts.

25th February '85. The first of five consecutive nights for the band at London's Dominion Theatre.

26th February '85. Tonight's 'Peaches' has, 'Is she trying to get out of that Mini Metro? Liberation for women, that's what I preach...' and 'I can think of a lot worse places to be, Like being stuck in a traffic jam on Tottenham Court Road on a Friday afternoon.'

27th February '85. And tonight's 'Peaches' features the stunningly profound changed lyrics of 'Like ... anywhere ... you can think of ... where you didn't like it.'

15th March '85. Some of the tracks from the band's Oslo Ice Stadium gig are televised, and JJ thoroughly enjoys Hugh's impersonation of *The Muppets'* Chef during 'Peaches' with him 'Waherder durder werder gerder scurder-ing' instead of the usual 'mmm mmm-ing' ejaculations.

24th March '85. To avoid causing another riot, The Stranglers regretfully cancel the gig scheduled for Bielefeld PC 69 in Germany due to an inadequate power supply there. All very disappointing, especially as the gig has sold out. Other gigs do take place in Germany during the coming weeks though, as well as in Belgium, France and Italy.

25th March '85. In Germany, at Cologne's Stadthalle Muelheim, the set list is 'Something Better Change', 'Nuclear Device', 'Uptown', 'Dead Ringer', 'No Mercy', 'Souls', 'Nice 'n' Sleazy', 'Let Me Down Easy', 'Midnight Summer Dream', 'European Female', 'Golden Brown', 'Strange Little Girl', 'Peaches', 'Death And Night And Blood', 'Threatened', 'Punch And Judy', 'Hanging Around', 'I Feel Like A Wog', 'Sewer', 'Nubiles', and 'Toiler'. After 'Uptown', Hugh spots a miscreant in the crowd, 'This chap here is gonna get his bum smacked, he's playing with matches, aren't you? He's playing with matches'. Someone shouts a suggestion involving a banana and inserting it up the man's 'behind' but there is no evidence such a procedure takes place.

His worse places to be on 'Peaches' is 'like stuck in Cologne in the summer' and before 'Nubiles' he lets rip: 'Everyone down here is smoking cigarettes ... You've got a lot to say for yourselves, haven't you?', which prompts shouting from the audience and someone throws a cig onto the stage. 'All I've said was you seem to be smoking a lot. That doesn't mean I want a cigarette,' Hugh says. There is a pause before his charm offensive, (well offensive, anyway) continues: 'So what's been happening in Cologne? I've got to say this is the best gig we've done so far in Germany. But no, what I'd like to say is it is the worst, it really is the worst. Never seen such a bunch of ugly people in my life. Yeah that's what I like to say, in fact I have never seen a bunch of uglier people, not even in America have I seen a bunch of uglier people! You're a bit plain, aren't you? You're a bit plain. If you let that wind you up then you gotta be really plain. You're full of shit, you should go to the toilet more often'.

6th April '85. A gig at the Messepalast in Vienna, Austria. 'Skin Deep' replaces 'Nuclear Device', otherwise it's the same set list as Cologne. After 'Skin Deep', a woman in the audience screams and Hugh remarks in a deadpan voice, 'Oh someone's getting a bit excited here'. The 'Peaches' worse places to be is ... 'on the Messepalast roof, I can't see where the fuck it is'. A toilet roll lands on the stage, prompting him to state politely, 'Someone's thrown a toilet roll there. None of us need to have a shit now, thanks very much for the toilet roll, we might need it later'. Before 'Nubiles' he asks, 'I hear Vienna has the highest suicide rate in the world, how come? And Vienna is named the lesbian city? What came first?' And amidst lots of shouting from the audience, he tries to have an argument with them: 'When we were here six, or, no, seven years ago ... Does anyone remember?' (Replies from the crowd). 'Bollocks! I don't believe you, you're all a bunch of liars. It's terrible! I didn't see you, I didn't see you, you got some proof you were here? We did 'Walk On By'? Anyone can say that!'

11th April '85. At the Planeta Tienoa in Rome, tensions between Hugh and JJ turn physical. Although it might seem relatively minor, it is significant to the future of the band. The exact circumstances have never been clear – Hugh has disputed JJ's claim that he had thrown some champagne at him after they had left the stage – but what is not in question is that JJ pushed Hugh against a wall, which was so thin he went *through* it. It startled Hugh sufficiently enough to worry about his well-being in JJ's company due to such unpredictable behaviour. It had come about over a disagreement regarding which one of them mistimed their jump during 'Hanging Around', but their relationship was cooling considerably by now.

JJ never denied or excused his actions, he just seems to regard them as less serious than Hugh does. That said, JJ is quite distraught about the incident and apologises profusely to Hugh soon after. The apology is accepted but the whole affair strengthens Hugh's resolve to forge a professional existence away from The Stranglers.

(Image courtesy of the author)

12th April '85. At the Palasport in Bari, Italy, serious problems are caused by the police's abrupt decision to limit the crowd capacity for the venue to 500 ... after more than 2500 official tickets have been sold. The band won't play until the police get their act together, which they eventually do, letting all ticket holders in. Stupid police or just a few crooked gobshites after backhanders?

29th April '85. 'Peaches' at Le Zenith in Paris has a new line from Hugh: 'I can think of a lot worse places to be, Like being stuck at five in the morning in Paris looking for some frogs legs'.

9th May '85. A short tour of Australia begins at Canberra University, with further gigs due in Sydney (three separate dates), Brisbane, Newcastle, Melbourne, Adelaide and finally Perth on the 18th.

10th May '85. It's a full house at the Hordern Pavilion in Sydney to see The Stranglers in good form and enjoying themselves, even with the unwelcome attentions of one phlegmy idiot who Hugh later rebukes for giving him AIDS to take back to the UK. His 'Peaches' line is 'I can think of a lot worse places to be .... can you? *Thought* you could' and his 'Nubiles' cocktail version contains wooing in wonderfully bad Aussie accent: 'Let me fack ya, and if you don't want it, do you mind lying down while I do?'

SPLIT

On 11th May, events, or rather non-events, at the Festival Hall gig in Brisbane (Queensland's state capital) convince one Strangler to quit the band. It isn't Hugh, it's Jean-Jacques, disillusioned at a missed opportunity to have a public dig at the current Queensland governor, their old friend Joh Bjelke-Petersen. JJ wants to stir it up onstage with some wry observations concerning the warped politician, but Hugh disagrees as he wants to *avoid* controversy. Thus, to JJ, Hugh had 'sold out' and probably lost his nerve too, while Hugh sees JJ's behaviour as immature and needlessly rebellious.

The gigs go ahead as planned, with little evidence of unrest in the band, but once the tour is over and they return home, Hugh flies out to Nice to visit JJ and persuade him the band is still a worthwhile cause. It works, JJ decides to carry on – in truth he doesn't need much cajoling – and the foursome remain intact, albeit with cracks slowly widening.

12th May '85. Newcastle Workers Club, Australia. Even with a less than 100% well Hugh, this is another lively, much appreciated gig. After the second song, 'Dead Ringer', he greets the audience warmly with 'G'day, g'day, g'day' but after 'No Mercy' complains about having 'a fucking awful throat'. 'Nice 'n' Sleazy' is performed well but it's clear Hugh is taking it nice 'n' easy with his tender vocal chords. 'Peaches' follows 'Golden Brown' and receives an even louder reception from the audience; the altered line is '... like being in a police van in the Sunshine State and it's pouring with rain all fucking day'.

27th May '85. The Pink Pop Festival takes place in Geleen, Holland. Appearing along with The Stranglers are Steel Pulse, King, Jason & The Scorchers, China Crisis and Chris Rea, and the compere is John Peel. Fan Eric Vonk explains that: 'Pink Pop is the oldest music festival in the Netherlands. The Stranglers' set was very short and no encores were played. The stage was then bombarded with fruit. Organiser and presenter Jan Smeets came on stage to tell the audience to apologise and to advise them to travel to London if they wanted to complain. Apparently The Stranglers were the most expensive band they had booked so far, paid 100,000 guilders in cash. The band flew back with suitcases filled with money'.

The set list is: 'Uptown' (Hugh greets the audience 'Friends! Dutch People! Lend us your ears!') 'Dead Ringer', 'No Mercy', 'Souls', Nice 'n' Sleazy, 'Skin Deep', 'Let Me Down

Easy', 'Peaches' (Hugh's worse place to be is '... like being on a festival having to use those horrible toilets'). 'Shakin' Like A Leaf', 'Punch And Judy' and 'Sewer'.

13th July '85. The Live Aid dual spectaculars take place here and in America. The Stranglers are far from the only notable absentees, but they are probably the most successful UK chart act not to be even invited.

26th July '85. At the Pansthinai Panathinaikos Stadium (also known as the Kallimarmaro Stadium, venue of the first modern Olympic Games in 1896), the band are third on the bill behind Depeche Mode and Culture Club on the first day of the Rock In Athens festival. The next day's bill includes The Clash and The Cure. It's a big cultural occasion for Greece and thus much of it is televised, with 'Souls', 'Let Me Down Easy', 'Midnight Summer Dream' and 'European Female' (both superb), and 'Skin Deep' and 'Golden Brown' (both not superb) aired.

Jet and Hugh are interviewed by a female reporter before their performance. Interviewer – 'Welcome to Athens and the first big rock festival in Greece. How did you decide to come to Athens?' Jet expounds: 'Well, we decided to go because we were offered a proposition which **enabled** us to go at a time – I think for the first time – when we are **free** to go. We did try to go to Greece once before and we were stopped somewhere in the south of France ...' Hugh chips in, 'It was about five years ago'.

22nd August '85. *Strangled* mag tells us that Dave Greenfield weds his fiancée today, Pam Leatherbury, at Cambridge Registry Office. Frankly, Dave doesn't look right in a grey suit and wearing a tie and carnation, but at least his good lady wore black.

27th August '85. Portrait Records release Hugh's solo single 'One in A Million' on 7"and 12". It's a charming, catchy song deserving of a chart placing if not *massive* commercial success. Alas, it doesn't get anywhere near it, peaking at No.78. Hearing the strong bass line spine which makes the vital hook, combined with Hugh's soulful, enchanting vocals, one could easily assume it's a Stranglers song, a strong one at that. Hugh is guest reviewer of the morning's newspapers on BBC *Breakfast Time* with Nick Ross and he's keen to tell the audience, 'The Stranglers haven't split up by the way ... a lot of people are assuming, just because I've got something out, that the band are splitting up'.

31st August '85. With Jet Black on drums and Chris Twomey on lead vocals, a 'new' band, christened A Marriage Of Convenience is formed, to release a cover of the very early Stranglers track 'My Young Dreams'. Tonight is the launch party, arranged by The Stranglers Information Service, at Ezee Studios, King's Cross, London (the single is out on the band's SIS label). Jet and Dave Greenfield attend, along with around 400 Stranglers fans.

19th December '85. In a surprising Stranglers-related guest appearance, JJ Burnel takes part in an event at the Heaven nightclub in London today. Carol Aid is another fundraiser for the Band Aid Trust and JJ sings 'O Come All Ye Faithful' with a couple of Page 3 girls, an unnamed fella and another unnamed fella who, we're told, was singer with Tight Fit. I can't be arsed looking his name up, sorry. Other pop stars there included Cliff Richard, Chris De Burgh, BA Robertson, Junior, Sandie Shaw, Lulu, Anita Harris, Flying Pickets and Jim Diamond. And Snowy White and Captain Sensible.

14 1986: SLUMBERTIME?

Although the band are said to be working on new material in Brussels late in '85, there is precious little by way of recordings as evidence. Therefore, for their fans, most of 1986 proves to be a frustrating time if they are hoping to hear new material or actually see them play live. Just like most of us mere mortals, rock stars deserve time off of course, they have their own lives to live and personal responsibilities to fulfil. And The Stranglers have shown themselves to be supremely hard working over the previous decade so a break is in order. Their deal with CBS enables them to enjoy some of the spoils of their healthy agreement with the label, and to ease up on their toils. Unfortunately, it seems that as a songwriting unit, they have eased up too much, becoming too easily self-satisfied. The aforementioned physical distance between Cornwell and Burnel is an important factor ... they aren't often in each other's company anymore, professionally or socially, and so their collaborations are few and far between too.

Naturally, each Strangler has hobbies and pastimes too: Dave Greenfield's is probably the most unusual (unsurprisingly), what with his enjoyment of fantasy role playing and membership of the Dark Ages Re-enactment Association in Cambridge. He and wife Pam liked keeping pet rats too, and Dave was into studying the occult, though never actually practising the Dark Arts. Pam will eventually take over *Strangled* duties too. Ever the astute businessman, Jet, in addition to keeping scrapbooks of the band's history and looking after much of the *Strangled* mag and SIS goings-on (until December '86), enjoys cooking and dabbling in joinery as well as working on advancements in drumming/percussion technology.

JJ, as well as achieving a very high standard of level in karate, spends time teaching it too. His guest appearances on other artistes' recordings and as a producer are mounting, as are Hugh's. And JJ takes over *Strangled* duties from Jet for a while. With respect to making music though, Hugh is probably the busiest, never far away from his next musical creation, either solo or for The Stranglers. As for his acting work, his agent Jackie Castellano will become his personal manager too. Her work as stylist eventually extends to the band, helping out their image also ('helping out' might not be the best description, changes to their wardrobe are never likely to go down very well with every Strangler).

March & April, 1986. The band work in Spaceward Studios on the next album, its anticipated release date sometime in the autumn, to be produced by The Stranglers and Mike Kemp, who replaces Laurie Latham. Kemp, along with Ted Hayton and Owen Morris, will also engineer. Though his experience lies in engineering rather than production, he is a very capable chap, already known to Jean-Jacques and Dave through earlier work at Spaceward.

The relationship with Latham has become strained, hence the separation. The band want more input on the new songs from Latham than he feels able to provide. It is, in a way, a compliment to his work, that they are happy to give him (incomplete) songs to work on, in anticipation that he can help transform them to finished high quality material. However, Latham isn't overly impressed with the idea or indeed with the quality of the demos presented. The Stranglers aren't too impressed with his response either.

May '86. BBC2 television cookery series *Floyd On Food* uses the wonderful 'Waltzinblack' as its theme tune, with snatches of 'Peaches' and 'Viva Vlad' regularly heard in the programme too. Chef Keith Floyd and Hugh Cornwell are, of course, old friends and now they hatch plans to record a Christmas single together, apparently extolling the cooking of alternative fowl to turkey for Christmas fare. Yes, they were serious, 'Give Geese A Chance' was a distinct possibility but thankfully the notion gets binned.

6th July '86. At Cagnes Sur Mer in France, the 12th Annual Bathtub Races take place, with JJ Burnel representing the band and being a fine evening host to fans. Over 30 fansinblackswimwear participate with JJ in the race which ends disastrously when the 'vessel', aptly named The Ravenlunatic, is turned clean over soon after entering the water.

23rd August '86. The single 'Nice In Nice' is released, it reaches No. 30, hanging around for five weeks. It's a good pop song, keyboards-led, receiving a decent amount of media airplay too, so the chart placing is dispiriting. The band actually wanted 'Always The Sun' to precede it as a single, as it was commonly regarded as the standout track on the album, but CBS had the final say. The wrong decision, it seems, and a sign that relations between band and label were not in great shape ...

JJ at Pink Pop Festival in Holland.
(*Image courtesy of Eric Vonk, photographer unknown*)

Promo video for Stranglers singles – 'Nice In Nice':
Even managing to look cool in yellow and black convict suits, this is generally a pretty standard film of the band performing, complemented with classy, understated animation as well as more cross-dressing, suggesting a certain bass player has quite a fetish for such things.

September 1986. *King & Castle*, a new ITV drama series starring Nigel Planer, graces our screens. Hugh and Planer's theme tune 'Rough With The Smooth' is brought out as a single. Given this programme is mainstream, aired during peak viewing time, and that Planer has enjoyed great popularity on screen and on vinyl as 'Young One' Neil, it's quite surprising that this pretty decent record does nothing in the charts.

13th September '86. The Stranglers play at La Louviere Euro Rock Festival in Belgium. Along with a few other ardent fansinblack, Bernie Nessbaum attends the gig on a Mead Gold Promotions coach trip arranged with SIS. He even taped it, saying:

> This is another Meninblack gig I bootlegged, the first live outing for 'Strange Little Girl' incidentally. It was an open air gig and we were all getting more than uptight due to the band

not coming on until after midnight. When they do appear, in bowler hats, JJ apologises in French and then English, for their being late, the reason is that they've had a guitar stolen. He's cheerful, a good rapport with the audience. It's raining heavily and so he asks if we're all wet, then adding 'I KNOW you're wet!' First track 'La Folie' is not a good live choice, mainly because the keyboards sound weak, but it's very well received by the crowd anyway. 'Nice In Nice' next, it's so-so, merging in to 'Punch And Judy', which is of similar standard but improved by Hugh greeting the audience in various languages and finishing with 'Wotcha' which is amusing. On 'Was It You?' the guitar sounds ropy and the brass section doesn't help. In to 'Sewer' which is naturally spot on.

Hugh is chatty, 'Do you realise this is the first international festival ever to be held on this day of the year in this actual place? D'you realise that? You don't realise how special you all are and how special we are, we're very international tonight – we've got bowler hats. Magritte ... very Belgian, bowler hats, and also very English' [René Magritte was a surrealist artist from Belgium]. For the next song, JJ announces, 'We need two girls really, this next song normally has two girls singing in it, and we've never tried it with two girls outside of the studio'. There are, alas, no volunteers so the backing vocals on 'Paradise' are provided by the brass trio.

The band storm through 'Always The Sun', 'Who Wants The World?', 'Shakin' Like A Leaf' and 'Uptown' to varying degrees of enthusiasm, and then 'Toiler'. Hugh decides to share a joke from his more tasteless repertoire, with JJ translating. 'This joke is about the Challenger Space Shuttle ... It went up and the last words on the flight recorder were 'Okay, if she wants to drive, let her.' [The Space Shuttle Challenger disaster happened in January '86, killing the crew of seven which included two female astronauts].

A cracking version of 'Tank' follows and then Hugh intros the final song, appearing to really go a bit off the wall during it before stating: 'It's time to bring the fresh fruit out ...' and so begins 'Peaches' with a whole range of new lyrics. 'Well I got the notion girl that you got some hair oil in that sun tan lotion bottle of yours. Don't spread it all over my peeling skin, it's gonna make my fucking hair grow all over my chest. Well there goes another one, just lying down in that oil slick. Well, my God, she's gonna get a tan, get covered in fucking oil. Is she trying to get out of that ... motorcycle? Looks like I'm gonna be stuck here the whole summer. What do you mean, the summer? There hasn't been one! Well, I can think of a lot worse places to be ... Thinks ... to himself...'.

Bernie's review ends with ... 'By the way ... the guy who pinched Hugh's beloved black acoustic guitar was a member of our coach party.'

11th October '86. The band appear on the kids' TV show *No. 73* again. Performing 'Nice In Nice' and 'Always The Sun', they're again joined, and probably annoyed by, various brats and presenters dancing and generally adding to the fiasco in which Dave is barely visible.

18th October '86. 'Always The Sun' is out, in various vinyl formats, but it only makes it to No. 30 in the charts, a huge disappointment. With frequent airplay over the ensuing years proving testament to its immense commercial appeal, The Stranglers' parade has most assuredly been rained on here. CBS has unwisely taken their time bringing 'Always The Sun' out and when they finally did do they didn't promote it enough, much to the band's, and especially Hugh's, chagrin.

Promo video for Stranglers singles – 'Always The Sun': Although it's a straightforward film of the band playing the song (and Dave Greenfield not engulfed by keyboards), it still causes a bit of media controversy with Hugh using a pistol to shoot an Aztec Sun icon. Pathetic fuss really. He was the only Strangler involved with the making/writing of the video and so the less than enthusiastic response from the others is not appreciated.

20th October '86. Complete with horn section and bowler hats, the band are on the road again, with the *Dreamtime* tour. It had been envisaged that the *Dreamtime* album would be out around now but some unexplained delay means the start of the tour pre-empts the record's release.

24th October '86. Edinburgh Playhouse – Chris Band's memories:

The band come on to some new non-Stranglers music and then they're straight in to 'No More Heroes' and even though the venue's seated, it really gets the audience going. Hugh goes: 'Good evening! Well, there we had *The Planets* by Holst because we all know that Edinburgh is the centre of the universe'. 'Was It You?' – first time I'd heard the brill linking of this into 'Sewer' which sees the start of one of many stage invasions. Hugh again: 'I'm afraid Buddy went! Whoever shouted for "Go Buddy Go", he went, he went a long time ago. He`s a fuckin million miles away!' 'Nice In Nice' then 'Punch And Judy', which works well live. I do like how cultured and polite the audience are, with someone shouting, 'C`mon ya cunt, "Five Minutes"!' ... 'Souls'. 'Always The Sun' – good performance of this one. 'La Folie' is one I never thought I'd hear live. 'Strange Little Girl', 'Nice 'n' Sleazy', 'Who Wants The World?' – a great version, the audience getting stuck into it too.

Next track is intro'd by Hugh: 'This is about big objects in America'. Yes, it's "Big In America", I think he's making fun of us. 'Nubiles' has a slight lyric change to, 'There's plenty to explore, I've got to lick your little gash, and nail you to the floor' and a big stage invasion, with lots of bodies cavorting around the stage, either dancing or 'doing the JJ' with the karate-cocked leg stance, before getting unceremoniously removed from the stage by one of the road crew, who we learn is called Al. Al McStravich, I wonder? Hugh: 'Right, now that's Big Al ten, the audience nil'. 'Shakin' Like A Leaf' next: they're playing quite a lot of new stuff, it's going down well. Then 'Uptown' with a slight lyric change 'I'm gonna pick a steed, who's been filled with speed ...'. 'Toiler' is followed by Hugh saying: 'Okay, I dunno if any of you are going to Spain for a holiday, but if you do, I think you should spare a thought for those poor buggers who live there'. During 'Spain' another big cheer goes up for yet more stage-invader action. Hugh says, 'Alan 51, audience nil. I tell you no one ever comes up and takes their clothes off during "Nice 'n' Sleazy" anymore. I mean it must be getting cold. No, you missed your chance, missed your chance, we've already played it'.

JJ joins in: 'I wanna know why it's only males? Is it the water? Is there something in the water? Why is it only guys who come up on our stages?' 'Peaches': 'I can think of a lot worse places to be ... like working in a porridge factory'. 'Tank' – with even more stage invaders causing a chaotic non-end to the gig'.

25th October '86. The second night at Edinburgh Playhouse suffers even more, thanks to stage invaders apparently convinced that the paying public want to see them acting like arseholes, rather than the band playing. Hugh's 'worse places to be' line is 'Speaks for itself …' and indeed it does. Earlier today, in one of their most unexpected guest appearances, the band are on *Roland Rat The Series* playing 'Always The Sun'.

27th October '86. The *Off The Beaten Track* compilation album is released on vinyl by EMI and reaches No.80. EMI owns the band's UA and Liberty back catalogues, the tracks here were originally only available on those labels. EMI's actions don't completely whiff of greed, though the use of an uninspiring band photo for the cover and no red logo, are definite minuses. Track listing: 'Go Buddy Go', 'Top Secret', 'Old Codger', 'Maninwhite', 'Rok It To The Moon', 'Love 30', 'Shut Up', 'Walk On By' (the longer version), 'Vietnamerica', 'Mean to Me', 'Cruel Garden', 'Yellowcake UF6', and 'Five Minutes'.

1st November '86. At the Gloucester Leisure Centre gig, Hugh seems unimpressed with life, at least this evening. The band play 'No More Heroes', 'Was It You?', 'Sewer', 'Nice In Nice', 'Punch And Judy', 'Souls' – after which he says 'Just think, you could have been sitting at home tonight watching some telly. What a silly mistake you made.' 'Always The Sun', 'La Folie'. He asks, 'Who was here last night?' and someone cries 'Yeah!'… 'Well you must be stupid, 'cos there was nothing on here last night'. 'Strange Little Girl', 'Golden Brown', 'Nice 'n' Sleazy', 'Who Wants The World?'.

Before 'Big In America', he enquires: 'Anyone here been to America? Well everyone in America thinks they've got things so much bigger than we've got. And it's true … cockroaches y'know, lunatic asylums, guns, murders … everything's bigger in America.' Brass actually adds to this song played live, but some fans would say it takes a lot to detract from it! 'Nubiles', 'Shakin' Like A Leaf', and 'Uptown', which really taxes his vocal chords as he puts great effort into it. Straight into 'Tank' then 'Toiler' which is pulsating, fast and *tight*.

The band exit then return for an encore … After going on about redesigning 'this monstrosity' – the building not the town – as they're gonna turn it into a car park, Hugh moves on to a rant about drinking habits … 'Any people here like getting pissed? Abroad? Well you're all wankers! A lot of people go down to Spain and get pissed and make absolute wankers of themselves, Okay? I'm sure you'll do exactly what you want to do, regardless of the fuck what I say'. Ironically, he slurs a couple of his words. He sings 'Spain' immaculately though, and then it's 'Peaches': worse places to be is again 'Thinks …' and followed by 'Duchess' and 'London Lady'.

3rd November '86. Wembley Arena hosts the band, the Holst *Planets* intro feeling most appropriate for a venue of this size where the stage sounds cavernous. The band is into the gig with a relish, the many fans reciprocating. After the tumultuously received 'No More Heroes', Hugh greets them with, 'Good evening. This is rather a large front room, isn't it?' to loud cheers. Then it's 'Was It You?', the brass section simply adds to the track which segues pleasingly into the classic 'Sewer'. Next, the catchy 'Nice In Nice', which also blends nicely, with a fanfare of brass, in to 'Punch And Judy'.

Hugh: 'It's not so bad this place is it really? Yeah, we almost got so pissed before we played, we could've come on absolutely pissed out of our brains. Our record company, right, left us the biggest bottle of booze you've ever seen in your life in our dressing room. I mean, talk about irresponsible ...' 'Souls' and 'Always The Sun' follow, with Dave's keyboards immense and with plenty of singalongers in the audience. 'La Folie' is deservedly welcomed with mass enthusiasm and JJ's vocals are perfect. 'Strange Little Girl' and 'Golden Brown' next, but Hugh's 'had enough of this slow stuff' and so it's the brilliant 'Nice 'n' Sleazy' next, followed by 'Who Wants The World?' which as always is fantastic. 'Big In America' rises a level in quality thanks to the suitably BIG brass accompaniment.

On 'Bring On The Nubiles', Dave's keys sound like a pinball on overload. 'Shakin' Like A Leaf' and 'Uptown' which isn't a bad track, but not good enough for this band. 'Tank', ah, this is more like it, never losing its explosive appeal. 'Toiler' is perfect, plain sailing, ho ho. They exit then soon return. Before 'Spain', we have Hugh's diatribe: 'We've been observing an interesting phenomenon recently. It's the English holidaymaker, the British holidaymaker abroad, especially in Spine, cos in Spine the thing to do, the hip thing to do, is to go on one of these 18 to 30 Holidays and get pissed out of your tree and er ... make complete arseholes of yourselves. The Great British Bulldog, will it never die?' After the song, he softens his tone: 'Anyone been watching any food programmes recently? Bloke from the West Country getting pissed every week, eating omelettes?' (a reference to his old mate Keith Floyd). His 'Peaches' line also alludes to him 'worse places to be ... like stuck watching an English food programme in the rain'.

Off again, and then another encore, Hugh commenting, 'We do requests actually ... bar mitzvahs, weddings, funerals, and requests...' A wave of shouts arrive in reply. 'Well that's very clever isn't it, I'm bound to understand what you want when everyone's ... I think this is a bad idea 'cos, nah it's not gonna work is it, it's not gonna work ... Okay, any advance on 'Ugly'?' but we get 'Duchess' anyway. They exit again, booed off in jest. Finally we get 'London Lady', the 22nd track of the night and perfect way to end a fantastic gig.

6th November '86. It's the first night of the European leg of the tour, playing at Utrecht Music Hall (Muziekcentrum Vredenburg). Eric Vonk attended:

The set list is practically unchanged, starting with the same intro music and 'No More Heroes' the first song. The band played the same venue a year before so Hugh asks: 'Do you remember us? The Stranglers? We were here last year? I don't remember a thing!' He later comments that the audience is looking 'very Dutch' and asks, 'Do you have your notebooks ready? And your pencils? Are you ready for the lecture?' (the Muziekcentrum looked like a university auditorium). Someone in the audience shouts 'Wanker!' in the hope of getting a similar reaction of long ago. It doesn't, though Hugh does tell us that the other night some American guests on the 'Terry Wogan Show' uttered the same word and had to be informed what it actually means. After 'La Folie', he remarks, 'An emotional use of lighters there'.

8th November '86. The long awaited new LP comes out today, Dreamtime, their ninth studio album and available in usual vinyl format and for the first time, compact disc. The word 'Dreamtime' derives from the natives of Australia, the Aborigines. Given that the previous album, Aural Sculpture, was a big success in Oz, perhaps the band chose the name so as to help build their fanbase there.

1986: SLUMBERTIME?

DREAMTIME
Released: 8th November, 1986.
Label: Epic.
Charted at No. 16.
Side One: 1 'Always The Sun', 2 'Dreamtime', 3 'Was It You?',
4 'You'll Always Reap What You Sow', 5 'Ghost Train'.
Side Two: 1 'Nice In Nice', 2 'Big In America', 3 'Shakin' Like
A Leaf', 4 'Mayan Skies', 5 'Too Precious'.
Horn Players: Alex Gifford (Sax), Hilary Kops (Trumpet),
Martin Veysey (Trumpet).
Pedal Steel Guitarist: B.J. Cole.
Additional Percussionist: Simon Morton.

In a few words – what the *Ford* are the songs about? Part 9
'*Always The Sun*': On the whole it's about optimism and our appreciating and loving the sun.
'*Dreamtime*': A Hugh song, tying in Aboriginal spiritual beliefs – 'dreamtime' being a sacred era – with successive Australian governments' prolonged maltreatment of their country's native inhabitants.
'*Was It You?*': From JJ, effectively a protest song about the current depressed state of the world.
'*You'll Always Reap What You Sow*': Though this is a JJ song, Hugh sings it as the band felt JJ's 'operatic' delivery didn't suit it very well. It refers to people getting what they deserve, and is possibly alluding to Hugh.
'*Ghost Train*': Hugh's song built on a JJ riff, about the band lacking direction but all seemingly trying to take charge of the controls.
'*Nice In Nice*': JJ's song, nothing to do with the ill-fated gig at Nice Uni, but in fact about his wife.
'*Big In America*': Not surprisingly, this is about things generally being bigger in America, though there are a couple of references to Hugh's ex-girlfriend and to cockroaches inhabiting TV sets.
'*Shakin' Like A Leaf*': A swing song thanks to JJ's influence, reportedly very different to how Hugh wrote it originally. As Russia and America were 'sparring' for world domination, the lyrics concern a general apprehension of life.
'*Mayan Skies*': A joint effort between Burnel and Cornwell, relating to Mexico and their people's suffering across history; the national flag of red (blood), green (the jungle) and yellow (the sun).
'*Too Precious*': Is about South Africa, its 'diamond economy' and the inequalities in wealth, power, influence in society there in these pre-Apartheid times.

Matt Brown reviews *Dreamtime*:

The album sounds of its time and the '80s was a time of excessive production techniques. Pop music generally had a huge sound, with big drums and all the bells and whistles of the newly emerging digital technology. While the production is a problem, rather than being overproduced, it seems to be more a victim of extenuating circumstances: producer Laurie Latham had departed and I imagine it sounded brilliant in the studio at high volume and through good quality monitoring equipment.

However, as the band had gone through the long process of re-recording all of the material, I believe plain old fatigue may have set in, explaining some of the problems. Take the closing track 'Too Precious' for example; it sounds great at high volume, the bass and percussion come across nicely and you can hear good detail in the mix. However, listening to it on more basic equipment, it seems muddy and the crucial bass is all but lost. Similarly with 'Dreamtime', 'You'll Always Reap What You Sow' and 'Mayan Skies' (the more melodic pieces on the album), there is a marked improvement in clarity when listening at higher volume (especially 'Mayan Skies', which has really great sonic textures, and inspired trumpet). 'Was It You?' has too much going on, with everything competing for space in the mix, making the listening tough going; a shame as it's a great song.

'Nice in Nice' is a fantastic pop song trying to get out of an overdone, over-egged 80's production – Hugh's twelve-string Rickenbacker sounds too thin and scratchy, while the super-compressed drums are too much. Production gripes aside, 'Big In America' has the most potential for being a classic quirky Stranglers tune, Hugh's vocal delivery and Dave's keyboards are outstanding.

'Shakin' Like A Leaf' – well, if you're going to have a brass section then put them to work on a catchy swing number like this! 'Always The Sun' sounds great at any volume and 'Ghost Train' is good too, but it should have been allowed to grow; it could have been a classic. Best moments for me are 'You'll Always Reap What You Sow', 'Big In America' and 'Mayan Skies'. Overall, my verdict of *Dreamtime* is turn it up and enjoy!

13th November '86. A brilliant gig from the band at Paris Le Zenith, and such is their popularity in France the concert is filmed and broadcast live in movie theatres around the country and on TV the following night. Hugh greets the audience: 'Good evening, or if you're French, *bon soir*. And if you're in the cinema then you're in the best place 'cos it's pissing with rain outside', before the band launch in to a nineteen song repertoire rapturously received by the audience.

18th November '86. The Madrid gig at La Estación de Perpignan is filmed, to be broadcast next year on Spanish television.

28th November '86. Dutch TV show *De Nachtshow*, recorded at Amsterdam theatre Stadsschouwburg, features the band playing 'Always The Sun' and 'No Mercy'. The Flying Pickets appear on the show, too.

6th December '86: The Stranglers are in 'the diamond capital of the world' – Antwerp, Belgium – being filmed for the 'Diamond Awards Festival 1986-'87' taking place over two days. A huge audience at the Sportpaleis sees the band perform 'Always The Sun' and 'Skin Deep'. Other acts include Bob Geldof, Duran Duran, Howard Jones, Chaka Khan and Alvin Stardust. Presented with an award by a rather tidy blonde, Hugh says, 'Well this is very kind of someone, I'm glad we didn't get a fist 'cos we wouldn't have known what to do with it'. Strange thing to say and it all does feel like an awkward appearance by a band who don't really belong there and who no one's taking much notice of anyway.

13th December '86. 'Big In America' comes out as a single, including as a shaped picture disc of a huge hamburger, smelling not of meat, but more of desperation on the part of CBS. The marketing ploy doesn't work well, the single peaking only at No.48 despite hovering around the charts for six weeks.

Promo video for Stranglers singles - 'Big In America': Lots of stars and stripes and too much red, white and blue as well as badly drawn cartoonery. The band are dressed stylishly though, including Alex Gifford on sax, but overall it's a cheap, gaudy affair, possibly matching the band's opinion of America itself.

PURPLE HELMETS' BIRTH

John Ellis:

> I had been out of the music biz for some time. I think I was driving a mini cab when I got a call from JJ asking me if I'd be interested in doing a session for a French singer called Laurent Sinclair. I agreed and went up to Cambridge to do the session. We all got talking about how great British beat music was in the sixties, bands like the Kinks, Them, and so on, and we thought it would be a good idea to do a record. I didn't hear anything for a long time and then JJ rang to say that there was a chance of doing a gig around the ideas we'd discussed. So we rehearsed and did the first show. Dave was a natural keyboard player for the band. I remember doing a big bikers rally and basically being bottled off when we launched into 'Doo Wah Diddy' by Manfred Mann.

10th December '86. The Purple Helmets' first ever gig takes place in Rennes, France, at the venue Salle de la Cité. The line up is JJ Burnel, John Ellis, Alex Gifford and Laurent Sinclair, the keyboardist of Taxi Girl with whom JJ has worked before. The Helmets is a pastime and not designed to worry fans that a Stranglers split is afoot. The set list is a collection of cover versions of personal favourites: 'Woolly Bully', 'Fire', 'Keep on Running', 'Tobacco Road', 'And The Beat Goes On', 'Never Knew', 'We Gotta Get Out Of This Place', 'Over Under Sideways Down', 'Baby Please Don't Go', 'Worried About You', 'All Day And All Of The Night', 'Can't Explain', 'Not Fade Away'.

15 1987: STATIC ON TOUR

For most acts, an album chart placing of No.16 hardly represents a 'flop', but the reality of The Stranglers' situation is that they and CBS were hurting at the poor sales performance of *Dreamtime*. The label has spent a lot of money on the band – though probably not enough on actually promoting them when it mattered the most – and they had hoped for better returns. To think that the relationship had all started so promisingly too. For avid fans, *any* new material is better than none which unfortunately means that this coming year will be even worse than last in terms of new Stranglers 'product'.

24th January '87. Recorded last autumn, Hugh Cornwell's 'Facts & Figures' single, effectively a protest song against nuclear arms and with the brilliant Jools Holland on piano, comes out on Virgin from the soundtrack album of a new animated film *When The Wind Blows*. The song is jaunty and pleasant but the lyrics are actually quite acerbic; this is another solo effort which arguably would have suited any recent Stranglers album. It reaches only No. 61 in the chart.

20th February '87. The second of two Stranglers gigs at the Cinerama in Tel-Aviv, Israel, this one broadcast on local radio. A fine gig it is too. Set list: 'Always The Sun', 'No More Heroes' after which Hugh welcomes the crowd: 'Shalom shalom shalom, that means "Hello" and it also means "Peace" [The Israeli's probably knew that], and it's the end of the Sabbath, and I think we're all gonna get a piece tonight!'. 'Strange Little Girl', before 'Was It You?' when Hugh announces, 'So I just wanna say "Holy shit!" cos I've never said that on live radio before'. JJ's bass almost punches an entrance into your ears, it's damned fine.

Then, 'Golden Brown' and a stupendous 'Sewer' – the sound has flesh and bone to it. Hugh's not happy though: 'Well there seems to be some real unhip people down there you know, these spitting. That was ten years ago, the really hip thing now is to get AIDS, it really is ...'. 'Nice 'n' Sleazy' follows after 'Stop the spitting, just go out and get AIDS, it's much more hip,' announcement from Hugh. 'Nice In Nice' then 'Who Wants The World?' and Hugh has brightened up a bit: 'I had an amazing revelation today, I went down on the beach right, Saturday, the sun was shining, went down on the beach to get some sun … the place was packed out. So you don't have to worry about being invaded on a Saturday cos there's no room for anybody more'.

'Punch And Judy', 'Big In America', Souls', 'Nubiles', 'Shakin' Like A Leaf'. Before 'Uptown' we have: 'Okay, let's go racing, place your bets', followed by 'Tank' and 'Toiler'. Hugh asks: 'Was anyone here on Wednesday?' Pathetic, about ten people, absolutely pathetic. The rest of you, you just waited until people told you it was good before you came, that's really pathetic. You're not scene leaders, there's only ten scene leaders here, ten scene leaders. The rest of you are following, like sheep …' 'Peaches' worse places to be is '… keep it to yourself …'. Best and last song is 'Hanging Around'.

28th February '87. The band feature on the UK TV show *Almost Saturday Night Live* playing 'No More Heroes' (one edited version, one full) and forthcoming new single 'Shakin' Like A Leaf'.

7th, March '87: 'Shakin' Like A Leaf' comes out, CBS again making it available in various formats including a picture disc in the shape of a television. It reaches just No.58 in the charts.

22nd & 23rd March '87. Consecutive nights at Glasgow Barrowlands, with fanatical followers loving the gig and literally rocking the joint, Hugh praising tonight's crowd for making the stage wobble more than last night's. It's not all positive though, he's again riled for being spat at.

31st March '87. The last of three sold out nights at Hammersmith Odeon, and some of tonight's gig will be used on a forthcoming live album release.

April '87. The Stranglers embark on their North American *Dreamtime* tour, starting with two dates in Toronto and one in Montreal, on the 9th, 10th and 11th. Then it's down to Washington DC on the 13th and a series of gigs in America. It gets a tad complicated as lucky Jet develops a case of shingles.

28th April '87. The Metro in Chicago gig is buzzing and Hugh seems positively pleased to be there. Not too surprisingly, the older material gets a better audience response than the newer but, overall, it's a keenly received gig. Interesting too that it's a clean version of 'Nubiles'. Following the opener 'No More Heroes', Hugh says his hellos: 'Good evening, good evening … now you're all on the radio or as we call it in the United Kingdom, the wireless. Now it's your chance to tell them to er …' a loud 'Fuck off!' from the crowd interrupts him and he laughs, 'Well, I wouldn't have quite said that ….' He later explains Jet couldn't be there as he's drying out in the Betty Ford Clinic and so Robert Williams has stepped in and is doing a fine job. 'Toiler' is particularly good this evening,

Hugh really crooning and the audience loving it too. Conversely though, he delivers 'Grip' as if he's bored out of his tree, fortunately Gifford's excellent sax really boosts it.

ROBERT WILLIAMS

Captain Beefheart drummer, and *Nosferatu* collaborator, Robert Williams has got a call requesting he be Jet's temporary stand-in - or 'sit-in' - and so he joins the band for five dates: Cincinnati, Columbus, Milwaukee, Chicago and Minneapolis. He actually goes to the trouble of making his own way to play in San Diego too, only to discover on arrival that the band are already playing, Jet having sufficiently recovered to pound the skins again.

May '87. Their US tour ends on the 10th at the Warfield Theatre in San Francisco. Now back to Europe and a very interesting summer in store.

4th July '87. Eric Vonk describes The Stranglers' appearance at the Roskilde Festival in Denmark:

> The First Roskilde festival took place in 1971 and it has grown to be one of the biggest festivals in Europe. The line up for this three day festival included Echo and the Bunnymen, Iggy Pop, The Pretenders, The Mission, Sonic Youth, Black Flag and Van Morrison. The Stranglers' set list leans heavily on *Dreamtime* and *Aural Sculpture*, as well as classic hits and some cool album tracks, where 'Toiler' to me sounds particularly great. They can't really go wrong with that one anyway.
>
> Before 'Always The Sun', Hugh addresses the crowd in (I think) Swedish. After it he tells the festival goers, 'I see the sun is getting down, you all are gonna get very dirty now are you? I wish I could stay the whole weekend, I hope you're as stoned as I am! Fucking out of my brains! Better watch out for the acid here though. And the angel dust has cocaine in it. What else is there? Oh wait, I just heard there's none of that out here, which is great news'.
>
> Before the band starts a rather fast version of 'Spain', our Hughie says, 'We're going out to Spain later, fuck you lot! It's gonna rain later, In an hour or so, so you might as well go home. We are going to Spain and get some real sun!' and he stays silent after 'worse places to be' in 'Peaches'. A good gig, sometimes a bit hurried, but faultless at the same time. Perhaps they were hurrying to get to Spain to join David Bowie.

6th July '87. In Madrid, The Stranglers support David Bowie at the Estadio Vicente Calderon ...

7th & 8th July '87. ... and they also support the Thin White Duke at the 'Mini Stadium' in Barcelona, that's the Mini Estadi, close to the famous Camp Nou football ground.

30th August '87. Sunday night of the Reading Festival with The Stranglers second to headliner Alice Cooper. The band don't disappoint and with parts of the gig to be used for a forthcoming live album and a BBC *Radio One* broadcast, it's a sign that they still register and still *matter*. But the penultimate song of the set is a new cover version (The Kinks' 'All Day And All Of The Night'), which provides evidence to the critics that the band's own creative flow is drying up. The festival is at a time when the onset of AIDS causes panic here, and so, with that in mind, the organisers have arranged for thousands of free contraceptives to be distributed. Two stages are erected for the festival, quite close to each other.

The Stranglers perform on the left stage and Alice Cooper will play on the right stage. During The Stranglers' set, a very large beast, presumably the Alice Cooper drum technician, begins sound-checking the other stage's drum kit. Whatever his reason for doing it, he will regret it when JJ Burnel gives him a good going over after The Stranglers' gig ends. Set list: 'No More Heroes', 'Was It You?', 'Sewer', 'Nice In Nice', 'Punch And Judy', 'Souls', 'Always The Sun', 'Strange Little Girl', 'Golden Brown', 'North Winds', 'Big In America', 'Nice 'n' Sleazy'. 'Who Wants The World?', 'Nubiles', 'Shakin' Like A Leaf', 'Uptown', 'Tank', 'Toiler', 'Spain', 'All Day And All Of The Night'. 'London Lady'.

Interspersed between songs are some comic gems from Mr Cornwell. As a plastic bottle lands near him on stage he intones: 'Now look, it's very nice of you to give us some drinks, but we've got some already, so you can hang on to it.' Later, 'So I hear that 21,000 free condoms have been distributed over the last few days' ... cue *Monty Python* Eric Idle nudge-nudge voice ... 'So some of you have been lucky and some of you haven't been so lucky! So if there's 30,000 people here, and 21,000 condoms handed out then that means there's nine thousand wankers out there!' Also, two ropey jokes. Q: 'Why did the Mexican throw his wife off a cliff? A: Tequila!'. And, Q: 'What did the Mexican fireman christen his two sons? A: Hose A and Hose B!'.

19th September '87. Another unusual gig for the band, this time at the Bol d'Or motorcycle endurance race held in Le Castellet in France. Hugh: 'Okay, my first impression of this evening ... What is this an impression of? *Nyaaaaarp ... nyaaaaaarp ... nyaaaaarp...* Okay what's the answer? No it's not a motorbike, it's a Kawasaki'.

20th September '87. A gig at Lyon's Bourse du Travail in France, beginning poorly with 'No More Heroes' and all the instruments sounding like they need a boost of power; the keyboards being especially insipid. And Hugh delivers it like he's bored already. Once the song's finished though, he brightens up a bit: '*Bon soir, bon soir, bon soir. Ca va, ca va bien?* Lyon Lyon Lyon ... Well I haven't had a decent meal in Lyon, EVER. There's better food in Brussels'. 'Was It You?' follows, merging into the outstanding 'Sewer', after which he remarks, 'I always love coming to Lyon, it's always full of smiling faces and smiling anuses, I love it here, it's lovely, lovely'.

JJ then translates and sounds as confused as everyone else, whatever nationality. 'Nice In Nice', 'Punch And Judy', 'Souls', 'Always The Sun', 'Strange Little Girl', 'Golden Brown', 'North Winds' (very good but spoiled again by weak-sounding keyboards), 'Big In America', 'Nice 'n' Sleazy', 'Who Wants The World?', 'Nubiles' (which is also powerfully good), 'Shakin' Like A Leaf'; 'Uptown', 'Tank', 'Toiler', 'Spain' (Hugh cheekily

157 • 1987: STATIC ON TOUR

recommending it as a holiday destination for the French), 'All Day And All Of The Night' (the guitar sounding very ropey), 'London Lady', 'Peaches' (his worse places to be, 'like the Bol D'Or for 24 hours'), and then final song, the regal 'Duchess'.

JJ pictured at the Reading Festival, 1987.
He later gave Alice Cooper's roadie what for.
(*Image courtesy of Greg Gregori*)

16 1988: M.I.B. M.I.A.

1988 will ostensibly turn out to be a case of The Stranglers 'Missing In Action' almost, though that certainly isn't the plan. No, the plan has been for the next album to come out late this year and so, to that end, the wonderfully versatile Jet Black has built a recording studio complete with control booth and 16-track machine and desk, in Jean-Jacques' back garden. Theoretically, it will make things easier for them all, though JJ lives in Cambridgeshire while Hugh (and Jet) live on the other side of England, in the West Country, so Hugh especially will have plenty of travel and upheaval to endure, being the chief creator, so to speak.

Rightly or wrongly, he is feeling more of the new writing pressure than his three colleagues and, as a knock-on effect, is feeling increasingly disillusioned and unappreciated too. Though they had spent winter weeks in the studio creating what they considered to be strong new material and there was a general positive air in the camp, Hugh nonetheless believes his ambitions for the band are much stronger than the others, as if they are satisfied with what success they have already achieved.

For the album, a new producer will be needed as Mike Kemp isn't interested. The band opts for Owen Morris, who has worked as an engineer on *Dreamtime*. Despite the disheartening sales figures, the band are pleased with *Dreamtime* and the presence of the brass section, Alex Gifford in particular, seems to have reinvigorated them. Also of relevance is that American audiences are known to be keen on brass in Stranglers music, therefore the signs are promising that a big impact in the States is still possible. Hugh and JJ write together for the new album but generally work independently, believing it to be an established formula proven by the quality of the songs on *Dreamtime*. How they arrive at such a conclusion is a slight puzzle as the album has clearly underperformed. Were they that confident, arrogant even, to believe the declining sales had nothing to do with a perceived decline in the quality of their music or that record buyers were going off them? Perhaps it is more a case of their wanting to avoid facing some harsh truths and realities.

1st January 1988. The Stranglers appear on two television shows today, *Make A Date* and *Wogan*, miming to the imminent new single 'All Day And All Of The Night'. The first studio is very smoky and so Jet wears a gas mask and looks menacingly fantastic. On Wogan, in a great performance which includes choreographed moves from the brass trio, they're introduced by the lovely Dawn French. Hugh wears a red nose on top of his head and JJ has one attached to his mic.

7th January '88. Desperate to repay their label's faith in them, and because they have no new material ready, the band choose the cover version of The Kinks' classic as their new single. Had they not proposed this to CBS then the unprecedented four singles lifted from *Dreamtime* would probably have been FIVE: an altered version of 'Was It You?' has been mixed in readiness. The original picture sleeve of 'All Day And All Of The Night' is abruptly withdrawn by a nervous CBS, showing as it does a photo of call girl Monica Coghlan, who is at the centre of a political scandal involving the deputy chairman of the Conservative Party, Cecil Parkinson. And a second sleeve has to be redesigned too, because the first contains too much nudity, giving CBS the willies again. The band are on *Top Of The Pops* with 'All Day And All Of The Night' and mercifully the single proves to be a big success, charting for seven weeks, peaking at No. 7.

Promo video for Stranglers singles – 'All Day And All Of The Night': Another pretty average effort, here the band perform to the song along with the brass boys, with interspersed shots of an attractive lady showing how temperamental she can be. And occasionally the footage of the band is shown in negative form. Humdrum video of a humdrum cover version!

12th January '88. Promoting the single, the band appear on the Kid Jensen-hosted TV show *The Roxy* along with Lloyd Cole.

21st January '88. They're on Dutch TV show *Kippevel*, Leonard Cohen is a guest too. *Kippevel* ('chicken skin' in English) is hosted by Jan Douwe Kroeske; he interviews JJ and Hugh about the influence of sixties bands like The Doors on the punk movement, covering old hits, and their current record 'All Day And All Of The Night'. Footage of The Kinks playing it is shown, followed by The Stranglers' promo video. Then we get a part of The Doors' 'People Are Strange' followed by archive film of The Stranglers at the Paradiso in 1977 and the JJ kicking through a wall incident.

20th February '88. *All Live And All Of The Night*, a new album from the band, is out but it's not much to get excited about really, being a live compilation with the studio cover version of The Kinks' cover added on. The live cuts are taken from concerts at Le Zenith in Paris, Hammersmith Odeon and last year's Reading Festival. The track listing, described in the blurb as 'the best versions of what many consider their best live set' (though there are only twelve songs), is 'No More Heroes', 'Was It You?', 'Sewer', 'Always The Sun', 'Golden Brown', 'North Winds', 'European Female', 'Strange Little Girl', 'Nice 'n' Sleazy', 'Toiler', 'Spain' and 'London Lady'. Despite it looking rather cheap – Okay, it's a gatefold sleeve– there is no doubting the quality of the songs and it gets to a creditable No. 12 in the charts.

March & April 1988. A few gigs are played by The Purple Helmets, including at the Central London Polytechnic and Dingwalls in London, the Pink Toothbrush in Rayleigh, Essex and The Astoria, London – where the gig is filmed for video release.

5th May '88. The Helmets play an unannounced warm up gig tonight at La Locomotive in Paris, followed by two scheduled nights there.

7th May '88. A new single from Hugh called 'Another Kind Of Love' and a spankingly good, if slightly familiar promo video with it (it's a little similar to Peter Gabriel's ground-breaking *Sledgehammer* vid. Not too surprising as filmmaker Jan Svankmajer created both). Alas, despite that and the fact that the song is very catchy, the single only reaches No. 71 in the charts. The video is shown on ITV's *The Chart Show* and while it plays, a caption beneath mentions Hugh has recently been acting in a few roles, including as Frank Sinatra in 'One For My Baby'.

8th May '88. The Purple Helmets hold a private gig for friends and family at Spaceward Studios; it's recorded, to be released as *The Purple Helmets Ride Again* LP. It's a good old effort at some good old rock 'n' roll, nothing like The Stranglers, but still with plenty of quality.

24th May '88. A gig arranged by The Stranglers Information Service at the Marquee Club has Polyphonic Size playing with the Purple Helmets, which just sounds morally questionable.

29th May '88. A scheduled benefit gig at Wembley Arena involving The Stranglers and various others is cancelled due to lack of ticket sales. This unsatisfactory state of affairs is down to inadequate promotion and organisation on the part of the, er …, organisers, the not very aptly named 'Action Against AIDS'.

13th June 1988. The band headline a punk festival at Düsseldorf's Phillipshalle, in West Germany, possibly something of a surprise seeing as punk daddies The Ramones are on the bill too. Another part of the city of Düsseldorf, unfortunately, plays host to international football matches in the 1988 European Championship finals. And England, followed by a large number of notorious hooligans, are in the tournament. There are plenty of German hooligans too, and consequently a tense atmosphere seems to pervade this gig. This tension is most likely down to the presence in the crowd of German skinheads and right wingers, neo-Nazis and similar lowlife.

The Stranglers enter the stage to 'Waltzinblack' before launching with 'Always The Sun' and Hugh then sounding deliberately like a crap tour guide: 'Good evening, good evening, we're The Stranglers. Well Düsseldorf, the centre of, erm …, civilisation as we know it in today's Germany. Well in fact for tonight, at least tonight.' Then 'Spain' which is politely received, almost as if the crowd suspect they're at the wrong gig but don't want to show it. The same with 'Uptown', but then 'Toiler' is greeted with relief by the audience, almost like an old friend. It is of course a gem.

'North Winds' blows in with gusto, a fine choice of song for a German gig and, like Hugh, JJ is on top singing form, the almost operatic harmonies are odd but, in a way, brilliant. After it, Hugh teases the audience: 'Right now, you haven't heard this one before have you? ... How do you know, you don't know what we're gonna play? Just keep your fingers crossed'. Two beats in and then whatever it is, is aborted … 'Someone out there wasn't keeping their fingers crossed, I said keep your fingers crossed, for God's sake!' Next is a first, it's 'Vietnamerica'… Jet's drumming is too loud and it's all rather slow and cumbersome but it still possesses some magicinblack.

'Strange Little Girl' and 'The Raven' follow, both oozing with majesty from Dave's keyboards, then it's 'Peasant In The Big Shitty', another live rarity, and a real treasure it is too. Next up, 'All Day And All Of The Night' and sharp guitar work from Hugh and even if their version is possibly better than the Kinks' original, it still shouldn't be a Stranglers recording, in my not so humble opinion. 'Shakin' Like A Leaf' is boogie-worthy and original but again it doesn't befit The Stranglers. 'Big in America' isn't one of my favourites either but it's well done here.

Who Wants The World?' is disappointing, surprisingly, but 'Tank' is as barnstorming as ever. A fine 'Was It You?' eases in to the best gig-closer there is, 'Sewer', Jet's drumming particularly awesome here. And then some prick in the crowd throws a teargas canister, the band leave the stage and don't come back, though Alex Gifford does reappear to give a not-at-all-inappropriate recital of 'The Last Post'. The same night, there is serious disorder elsewhere in the city, involving English football hooligans fighting, wrecking and torching bars.

18th June '88. While The Stranglers appear at the Amnesty International Festival at the Milton Keynes Bowl, Hugh Cornwell's solo album *Wolf* sneaks in to the Top 100 Album chart at No. 98. Probably not much to the liking of fans of more 'traditional' hard-edged Stranglers music, nonetheless the lowly status for the album seems to be a less than pleasant surprise.

Moody shot of Hugh, 1983. (*Image courtesy of Bernard Legon*)

WOLF

Side 1: 1 'Another Kind Of Love', 2 'Cherry Rare',
3 'Never Never', 4 'Real Slow', 5 'Break Of Dawn'.
Side 2: 1 'Clubland', 2 'Dreaming Again', 3 'Decadence',
4 'All The Tea In China', 5 'Getting Involved'.
Musicians: Hugh Cornwell, Graham Broad, Simon Clark,
Steve Dawson, Mani Elias,
Alex Gifford, Haywoode, Jools Holland, Gus Isadore,
Clive Langer, Melanie Newman,
Ian Ritchie, Chris Sheldon, Pete Thomas, Don Weller.

[Possibly one of the longest ever 'Thanks to' lists, Hugh expresses his gratitude to over 100 people, including the rest of The Stranglers and the Bank Of Scotland).

Robert Endeacott's review of *Wolf*:

Sadly, the production and especially the musical arrangements dilute and weaken the quality of the songs, which too often seem obscured by too much synthetic sound and too polished production. It's a mediocre pop album as a result, it's safe, soft, sanitised rock lacking any real power or soul. Some quality songs are smothered here. First track, 'Another Kind Of Love' is as catchy as a cold or indeed JJ's 'Crabs' and I'm still not really sure why it wasn't a hit, the vocals are good, it's lively and it's different yet commercial. Then comes 'Cherry Rare' which is average, unexciting in fact, it smells like a filler. Back on track with 'Never Never' – appealing vocals and a good beat even though it seems to be electric drums, unless it's just over-production and '80s typical'. 'Real Slow' could easily be a Paul Young offcut! It's too buffed, too synthetic, too '80s *ordinaire*'; nothing that bad really about it, just not much good either. 'Break of Dawn' is a slow one, with lovely female backing vocals from Haywoode to lift it to half decent level.

Side Two starts with 'Clubland', which is a less than great song improved by fine guitar work which, in turn, is then spoiled by overuse of the drum machine. 'Dreaming Again' is very pleasant, mellow as mellow can be, with a Mike & The Mechanics-type guitar repeat going on in the background. That's not a criticism. It's a decent track, just not overly inspiring. Next song 'Decadence' sounds like it could be from a soundtrack for a cheap UK TV movie rip-off of *Miami Vice*. Pretty lame, not helped by incongruous brass. 'All The Tea In China' is a surprise little gem with some lovely understated keyboard behind simple but pleasing guitar melodies. Final track is 'Getting Involved' which again feels like a filler track that has more great guitar sounds wasted on a quite boring melody.

Nosferatu has a few weaknesses but blandness certainly isn't one of them, I'm sad to say that on the whole *Wolf* IS. I think much of that is down to trying (and failing) to create highly refined sounds when pure good old rock 'n' roll rawness would suit Hugh's abilities much much better.

July '88. The band play at the Paleo Festival in Nyon, Switzerland on the 19th, and around this time another single from Hugh's album Wolf is released. Very pleasant as it is, 'Dreaming Again' fares poorly, like the album, reaching just No. 97 in the charts.

November '88. Trying to cash in again – a.k.a. flogging a dead horseinblack – EMI release the compilation LP Rarities. It's actually reasonable value but, regardless, it doesn't even chart. The nineteen tracks are 'Choosey Susie', 'Peaches' (UK radio airplay version), 'Mony Mony' and 'Mean to Me' (by Celia and the Mutations), 'No More Heroes' (edited for UK radio), 'Walk On By' (edited for UK radio), 'Sverige' ('Sweden' in Swedish), 'N'emmenes Pas Harry' (French 'Don't Bring Harry'), 'Fools Rush Out', 'Bear Cage' (12" Mix), 'Shah Shah A Go Go' (12" Mix), 'The Meninblack (Waiting For 'Em)', 'La Folie' (edited), 'Rok It To The Moon', 'Shut Up', 'Old Codger', 'Yellowcake UF6', 'Vietnamerica', 'Love 30'.

27th November '88. The Purple Helmets perform at London's Hippodrome as part of a benefit concert for John McCarthy, the journalist being held hostage after his kidnapping in the Lebanon in 1986. JJ Burnel and co. had nothing to do with the abduction.

17 1989: THE TWILIGHT

The bleakest period ever for many fans hoping for more Stranglers action this year, very little happening on the new releases front and not much more to see on the gig circuit either. Hardly inspiring either is the SIS release in 12" format of 'N'emmenes Pas Harry', a straightforward reissue of the 7" single released nine years ago. A glimmer of hope, though, comes later in January with a remix of a brilliant old single, causing followers to wonder if the idea will catch on so as to include more Stranglers songs from the past to make fresh assaults on the singles charts.

20th January 1989. The Purple Helmets play at Le Truck in Lyon, France, and their set list has expanded: 'Woolly Bully', 'Over Under Sideways Down', 'Don't Bring Me Down', 'We Gotta Get Out Of This Place', 'Baby Please Don't Go', 'Can't Explain', 'What You Gonna Do About It', 'Keep on Running', 'Do Wah Diddy', 'All Day And All Of The Night', 'Louie Louie', 'Tobacco Road', 'I'm A Man', 'I Wanna Be Your Man', 'Brand New Cadillac', 'Money'.

28th January '89. Liberty Records, owned by EMI of course, bring out 'Grip '89' in red vinyl 7" and extended version on 12". 'Grip '89' is a remixed version of '(Get A) Grip (On Yourself)', almost a refined and souped-up dance version, and on the reverse is the sublime 'Waltzinblack'. The 12" edition is quite an impressive package too, with not only the extended version of 'Grip '89' added to the above – called 'Grippin' Stuff' – but 'Tomorrow Was The Hereafter' too. The remixes of the original song are really very appealing, the extended mix a sonic pleasure too. It charts for three weeks, peaking at No. 33. It's a signal for the February compilation album from Liberty, *Singles (The UA Years)*.

18th February '89. *Singles (The UA Years)* is out, peaking at No. 57 for a couple of weeks; it's a straightforward collection of all the band's singles up to the release of 'Strange Little Girl'.

April '89. Jean-Jacques Burnel brings out a solo album and plays a couple of dates in France to promote it. *Un Jour Parfait* is French release only, with most of it sung in French and the album specifically aimed at the more poppy market there. Although Dave Greenfield (and Alex Gifford and Chris Lawrence) play on it, *Un Jour Parfait* is far from Stranglers-typical. It's not easy to describe genre-wise, it has a gentle Euro disco vibe mixed in with a strong sense of melancholy, soaked in majestic keyboards. There is some good dance music, if that's what floats your bateau. Two French gigs to back it up, in Lyon on April 5th and Bourges on the 6th.

7th June '89. In the second part of the mini 'Four Nations Tour', The Stranglers play at Dublin's national stadium. Tomorrow night is Cork; tonight they open with a very ropey 'All Day And All Of The Night' and Hugh struggling with the higher notes and not doing much better on guitar, but it all swiftly improves when it blends in to 'Bring On The Nubiles'. Hugh asks the crowd, 'Are you ready for the Derby? It's the Derby on Saturday, are you ready for it?' I wouldn't bet on it, hoho' before 'Uptown', and afterwards, 'Well we were in Belfast last night, I dunno if you're as lively as they were, I'm not sure about that'. His 'Peaches' worse places to be is '... like... or even... and there again...'. New song 'Where I Live' makes an appearance, with JJ singing, almost operatically.

Before 'Shakin' Like A Leaf', Hugh for some unknown reason remarks, 'Okay hands off cocks and on with socks' and after a fantastic 'Sewer' he complains, 'Listen, what is all this spitting for Christ's sake? Would you spit at your grandfather, would you spit at your grandfather? Spitting at me is like spitting at your grandfather Okay? Show some respect!' He's not as pissed off after 'Hanging Around', possibly because it's near the end of the gig: 'Here's my impression of an Irish accent – "Oi'll see you later, Oi'll see you later"... Is that good?' It is rather good, yes, like most of the concert.

10th June '89. Chris Band's review of The Stranglers' gig at Livingston Forum Exhibition Centre:

> Excellent gig, though Dave's keyboards are sounding like a Casio calculator. A great crowd and Hugh's in to it straight away too, even though the first track is 'Uptown'. Hugh says, 'Well this is more like it, this is a GIG!' and it's strange but 'Uptown' actually makes a good opener. 'Peaches' next, and the brass is good here, real mucky. New lines include, 'Is she trying to get out of Livingston?' 'Oh buggeration!' and '...worse places to be, Like... on the M8? I dunno'. Before the next track Hugh says, 'And now for something completely different...' and it's 'Someone Like You' which doesn't sound completely different or original either.
>
>   After, Hugh seems to be touting for the Spanish Tourist Board, 'I see Spain beat West Germany today. The first tennis champion – Spanish'. He does enjoy singing 'Spain' though. Then he tells us, 'Well you're all on *Radio Clyde* tonight. Well, not tonight, but ... tonight you'll be on *Radio Clyde* but not tonight, if you understand what I mean.' 'Always The Sun' – same old Always innit? 'Nice 'n' Sleazy' has very jazzy and steamy brass, combining greatly with Hugh's lead. 'Where I Live' – 'salright. 'Golden Brown' – s'also alright. 'Hanging Around' – brass doesn't bring anything to this track. Before 'Nuclear Device', Hugh comments, 'I've never seen so many men in an audience before, are there any women in Scotland? Or arre they all at home coooking your dinner?' in a near-acceptable Scottish accent.

11th June '89. Wales tonight, at the Newport Centre. During the encore, Hugh has another rightful whinge at whoever's doing some more gobbing and does his 'Would you gob over your grandfather?' routine [depends if he gobs on me first, I suppose]. He has a joke argument with the crowd too, wondering aloud how long it is since the band last played there. While some punters shout for 'Five Minutes', he states confidently that it's actually much closer to ten years than five minutes.

12th June '89. The Stranglers play at the Brixton Academy in London. Most of the time, Hugh Cornwell doesn't seem too keen on performing. It is possible, I suppose, that the regular chants of 'Jet Black, Jet Black' from the crowd cause him to be feeling a wee bit bored and underappreciated. He gets over it, praising the crowd just before last track 'No More Heroes': 'I've never seen anything like that, there's a real … um … example of humanity right here at the front here. This week we went to Ireland, Scotland and Wales and I did a study. I gave a glass of water to the front and it wasn't passed round … you've gone dead quiet … amazing, dead quiet. Anyway, it was not passed round, you come out to Brixton and it actually gets passed round, that's humanity for ya; funny that, innit?'

Autumn '89. A collection of new tracks recorded in JJ's garden studio and co-produced by the band and Owen Morris, is presented to CBS's Muff Winwood by The Stranglers. They are very pleased with the quality. To their great disappointment, he says he likes the songs, but believes they need stronger production. Somewhat dejected at the rejection, the band must re-record the tracks, with the famed Roy Thomas Baker now producing. He has previously produced Queen and so was deemed the perfect choice to enable, *empower*, The Stranglers to break America. Were it so simple … Hugh apparently got on well with him, though the relationship between JJ and RTB was not as smooth, he thought.

Roy Thomas Baker's production methods include demanding numerous recordings be made of the guitar parts. This is a relatively new process to Hugh and JJ, plus JJ supposedly dislikes being told what to do. The recording sessions of the final version of the album take place in Hilversum, Holland at the renowned Wisseloord Studios. Dutch engineer Emile den Tex assists Roy Thomas Baker. One of the new songs is 'Too Many Teardrops' and it is this song which prompts Dave and JJ to criticise Hugh for trying to make the whole album a solo project.

9th October '89. The Purple Helmets play tonight at London's Marquee in what will turn out to be their last ever gig.

18 1990: AND NOW THE END IS ...

Initial signs for Stranglers fans for 1990 looked promising in terms of Stranglers activity with a new album due and a tour promoting it, and whichever singles came from it. What most fans are unaware of though, is how dispirited the band are, the rejection of the new material late last year has hurt. Also, a tiresome knock-on effect is the album and tour being delayed for around six months. Those instructions to re-record tracks – which they felt didn't need re-recording – not only frustrate the band but also, in their opinion, weaken the material as the emotion and *soul* invested into the originals is impossible to recreate.

January 1990. *Rapido*, BBC2's popular culture show hosted by Frenchman Antoine de Caunes, airs an interview with the band at Shepton Mallet Pavilion where they're rehearsing for the forthcoming tour. The Stranglers are polite but there is an air of disinterest about it all. In the past, such attitude would have been expected, but not now, they aren't young 'punks' anymore. Hugh answers a question on the band's reputation: 'In France they treat us like intellectuals don't they? Whereas here we're sort of mischievous yobs ... I suppose'. Jet: 'One recent journalist described us as misfits and I think he was probably right, we don't fit in to the system of things and so I suppose we're noticeable'. JJ: 'We started when most bands are retired'. Were shock tactics ever used? Hugh: 'You can shock anyone if you think about it'. Jet: 'I don't think the public are shocked by The Stranglers, I think they're titillated by The Stranglers, not shocked. I mean, everybody goes out and buys the shocking daily tabloids for titillation, not to be shocked, y'know'.

On to the new album ... the cover is a photo of the band in various guises as eminent world leaders, how did that happen? JJ: 'I think it was one of those ideas you have on a drunken late evening when you're exchanging ideas. I do this [dress up in women's clothing] in my spare time'. Hugh: 'John loves doing those sort of things, so Benazir Bhutto and Margaret Thatcher, that was no problem, we had more problems finding someone prepared to do erm, whoisit, Arafat, yes that was very difficult'.

The new single '96 Tears', another cover version, why? Hugh: 'Well we're good at covers, we admit that. Each song we've covered has been successful and this song was mooted as a possible cover, with lots of long discussions between us and Roy Thomas Baker and our management. We listened to it and it seemed perfect for us and it's got that lovely keyboard and strong bass line. It's very simple so it fitted in with the other songs on the album, it fitted perfectly'.

February '90. The new tour begins in Bristol on the 17th, and a guest addition to the live line up is long time contemporary John Ellis, there to help with the more complex lead guitar work on the new album. His input will add a new layer of fine guitar work to many of the songs and his energy will help freshen up proceedings too. As with the introduction of the brass section to Stranglers gigs all that time ago, such a new sonic contribution might not be to all the fans' liking but even some of the classics will have added spice and intrigue now.

15th February '90. Another appearance on Top Of The Pops for the band, this time to push the new single '96 Tears', another hit that isn't a Stranglers original, reaching No. 17.

Promo video for Stranglers singles – '96 Tears': The band perform the song, while an apparently wired pot-bellied jester fucks about, trying to annoy them. He looks quite sinister actually, but the video makes little sense and isn't particularly striking to watch either.

20th February '90. Poole Arts Centre. The emphasis seems to be more about putting on a technically proficient show than providing good old rock 'n' roll entertainment. The band seem bored, like they're just picking up their fee almost. Scant interaction between them on stage either. Guest guitarist John Ellis standing stage right, close to Hugh Cornwell, and JJ Burnel standing way over to the left. It's nothing spectacular or special to report, which in a way sums up the audience too, showing little enthusiasm throughout and seem as bored as the band. The 'extra' musicians take a break before 'Walk On By' and Hugh is slightly chattier when audience requests begin: 'Well all the other blokes, John Ellis, Chris and Richard and Alex are all indisposed at the moment, I dunno what they're doing so we'll have to do something, just the four of us I suppose. No we can't do "My Old Man's A Dustman", not anymore, we've never done "My Old Man's A Dustman", we've never done it, you're mixing us up with another band'.

23rd February '90. The scheduled gig at Leicester De Montfort is called off due to a bomb scare.

24th February '90. After that unanticipated day off, The Stranglers are back in action at Brixton Academy. Hugh seems distracted and in truth it's generally another indifferent concert. Set list is 'Shah Shah A Go Go', 'I Feel Like A Wog', 'Straighten Out',

'Shakin' Like A Leaf', '96 Tears' (after which Hugh comments on England cricket, 'Okay you might like to know that we're whipping the West Indies, they were 150 for 8 just now, yeah!'), 'Someone Like You', 'Sweet Smell Of Success', which he introduces with 'The Stranglers go Latin, believe it or not', and which contains a brief but incongruous John Ellis guitar solo. 'Always The Sun' rarely changes, it's nearly always, always, al-ways the same! 'Ships That Pass In The Night', 'Peaches' – with new worse places to be… 'like down in Brighton, picking up a sign I carry saying Jesus'. 'Where I Live', 'School Mam', 'Let's Celebrate', 'Tank', 'Uptown', 'Was It You?', 'Sewer', 'Golden Brown'. Hugh mentions that the Jet Black Fan Club is here again, they're brilliant and travel all around the country for him, plus they're going on *Mastermind* to answer questions on their specialist subject of Jet Black. After 'Walk On By' we get, 'Now, can you tell me the Theory Of Relativity? Answer – 'Jet Black, Jet Black!' Following are 'Strange Little Girl', 'All Day And All Of The Night', 'Grip', 'Nuclear Device', 'The Raven', 'Duchess', and final, 26th track of the evening, 'Punch And Judy'.

March '90. The Stranglers' new album is out, it's their tenth studio album and is cunningly titled *10* to mark the occasion. If the album sleeve is anything to go by then the listeners are in for a treat as it is one of the most original designs ever created for an LP, with The Stranglers dressed as ten world leaders of the era: Yasser Arafat, Rajiv Gandhi, Pope John Paul II, Mikhail Gorbachev, Margaret Thatcher, George Bush, Fidel Castro, Muammar al-Gaddafi, Benazir Bhutto and Joshua Nkomo. For Bush (Hugh), JJ and Hugh wanted to draw a pair of glasses on the face to make him look more stupid, but CBS lost their nerve again and vetoed it as they didn't want to upset America.

Hugh and JJ in Japan in 1979. (*Unknown*)

10
Released: March, 1990.
Label: Epic.
Charted at No. 15.
Side One: 1 'Sweet Smell Of Success', 2 'Someone Like You', 3 '96 Tears', 4 'In This Place', 5 'Let's Celebrate'.
Side Two: 1 'Man Of The Earth', 2 'Too Many Teardrops', 3 'Where I Live', 4 'Out of My Mind', 5 'Never To Look Back'.

Horn Section: Alex Gifford: Saxophone. Chris Lawrence: Trombone. Sid Gould: Trumpet. (Trumpet Solo on 'Sweet Smell Of Success' by Stuart Brooks). (Conga Player on 'Sweet Smell Of Success': Simon Morton). Overdubs: Southern Belle on 'Where I Live': Pamela G. 'Let's Celebrate': Tere Thomas Baker.

Reading Festival, 1983. (*Unknown*)

In a few words – what the *Ford* are the songs about? Part 10.
'Sweet Smell Of Success': Written by Hugh, JJ AND Dave, this is Hugh's view of the band having achieved great success but always wanting more without as much work being put in towards it.
'Someone Like You': Hugh's song about his new girlfriend. Dave uses a Farfisa keyboard on the song, it sounds very similar to a fairground organ, as does the next track.
'96 Tears': Supposedly one of the most recorded songs ever, the original hit belonging to ? And The Mysterians (that's the right, spelling honest). It was producer Roy Thomas Baker's idea for The Stranglers to cover it.

'In This Place': JJ's song, about a personal relationship.

'Let's Celebrate': Developed from JJ's riff, Hugh's words, about different ways of celebrating.

'Man Of The Earth': A story from the perspective of an office worker wanting to live in the countryside to get away from it all.

'Too Many Teardrops': Hugh's song about how he was feeling at the time, he was struggling and hurting, though 'teardrops' might be an exaggeration.

'Where I Live': JJ's song about his home life in Cambridgeshire.

'Out of My Mind': a neat play on words, it's about tripping, an out of body experience, and about a woman you can't get out of your mind, in this case Hugh's current girlfriend.

'Never To Look Back': JJ's song, suggesting that he had a fresh outlook on life and that he needed to change his own personal course as his past had been too *stormy*.

✪

Album review by Guy Westoby:

10 suffers from a too-big production and generally unimaginative songwriting. The brilliant cover, with the band dressed as ten world leaders, promises more than it delivers alas. Opener 'Sweet Smell Of Success' should set the scene for the main strength of Dave's keyboard skills being right up in the mix, but the track is too cluttered by piano, bongos and trumpet. The tempo remains high for 'Someone Like You', with a simple but effective keyboard riff and clever guitar. Completing a catchy starting trio is the cover of '96 Tears', the infectious brass/keyboard interplay working really well. But it all goes downhill with the dreary and uninspiring 'In This Place' which just doesn't fit with the overall feel. That it's followed by 'Let's Celebrate', the LP's best and most upbeat track, highlights the disparity between it and the rest of the album. 'Let's Celebrate', with instrumentation and vocal work all melding successfully, closes Side One strongly.

Side Two kicks off with an overproduced 'Man Of The Earth'. Next, 'Too Many Teardrops' tries to get things going again with Dave's keyboards driving the song forwards but unfortunately the album's momentum nosedives with the abject 'Where I Live', showcasing JJ's worst vocals on record and some irritatingly overcooked drums. A nondescript 'Out Of My Mind' follows with unsubtle drums overpowering the song's vague psychedelic feel. 'Never To Look Back' closes the album, and it's a good sentiment given the previous two tracks! Improved vocal work by JJ and Dave's swirling keyboard combine effectively to deliver the best track on this side but the album on the whole is a big disappointment, intra-band tensions seem to influence the quality. Not their best album by some way but still enough there to keep fans interested.

1st March '90. Fan Steve Bullock was at the Wolverhampton Civic Hall gig:

I remember the atmosphere of pessimism prior to the gig, people were feeling pretty let down with the direction the band had taken over the last two albums. The band do their best to put on a professional show but there's a distinct lack of emotion or real *feeling*. After 'I Feel Like A Wog', Hugh asks us, 'Where do I go to get a bit of action? You know there's no one on the street out there, it's dead out there... dead out there, where are they? Must be in here'.

After 'Straighten Out' ('That was nice enough wasn't it?') and before 'Sweet Smell Of Success', Hugh says, 'I bet you never thought you'd see The Stranglers with a pair of congas on stage ... well rub your eyes'. Following 'Ships That Pass In The Night', he provokes the most enthusiastic audience reaction of the whole gig by asking, 'So what's new in Wolverhampton then, Wolves are doing well aren't they, going up this year probably?' But soon, the night gets depressing as JJ abruptly halts 'Where I Live' because some idiot in the crowd throws a drink at him. JJ: 'Okay, you're so brave, you throw water at me. I could get electrocuted, whilst I can't play'. I remember JJ was gesturing in a 'come and have a go' fashion and then he says, 'Come on tough guy ... tough guy', it all lasts about 30 seconds, with the crowd egging him on too. A couple of tracks later, Hugh notices the audience is thinning out: 'Okay, they've started leaving back there, that's it, that's it, that's good, that's good. I mean it is, it's finished, the gig, I mean if you weren't here I'd be in bed by ten for God's sake'.

2nd March '90. Jim Radley was in the sell-out crowd for the gig at Bradford's St George's Hall:

This tour was initially planned to start last October '89, but the delay with 10 meant it needed rescheduling. The band appear at around nine and by now the crowd is near frenzied. 'Walzinblack' kicks in over the PA then the house lights drop and a shadow figure is seen behind a large backlit canvas on the stage pretending to call the opening of 'Shah Shah A Go Go'. The canvas drops and JJ Burnel is revealed, the rest of the band then appear and we're into the first track of what is to be an excellent set list.

Hugh's new 'Peaches' line is 'I can think of a lot worse places to be, like Bingley or Shipley'. The new material sounds a lot better live than it does on the album. I'm seated up in the balcony and it's a tad chaotic, especially for a young un like me! A fight breaks out and it gets dangerously close to the edge of the balcony. Bouncers charge in from the side while the band play on. JJ asks what the hell is going on, thinking the bouncers are trying to throw punters over the balcony. The set continues and the crowd is getting more and more excited; a bit later a stage invasion occurs, starting with one fella climbing up a speaker stack at the side of the stage then on to the rigging like a little monkey. Chimp boy gets quite high and other punters join in, a large speaker swaying dangerously close to the crowd as a result. People get on stage, dancing with the band who don't seem unduly bothered. The end of the gig arrives in some kind of beautiful chaos.

5th March '90. The band usually receive vociferously wild receptions in Scotland, and Edinburgh Playhouse is no exception. In the crowd too was Chris Band:

A freezing cold night, and I had persuaded a bunch of mates to go along. We had pretty decent seats too, though we'd have preferred to stand. The gig kicked off with 'Shah Shah A Go Go', superb opener segueing into another wonderfully powerful track, 'I Feel Like A Wog'. And then Hugh greets us all: "Allo, 'allo, 'allo 'allo Edinbrrrrr ... you know why it's called Edinburgh, don't you? Cos its bloody freezing up here, it's Edinbrrrr!'.

Next is 'Straighten Out' which also goes down brilliantly simply because it's done brilliantly. Hugh says, 'It's getting warm in here!' 'Shakin' Like A Leaf' followed by a Hugh intro: 'And now for something completely new. Came out today, still new I suppose...' and '96 Tears'. Then 'Someone Like You' with, 'Come on, you're not sweating enough! Let's get some sweat on those bodies!' 'Sweet Smell Of Success' next, which is surprisingly very good, particularly where the guitar, bass and keyboards all come together. The addition of Ellis' guitar really adds to the impact. 'Always The Sun' – the crowd aren't as shout-a-long as usual on this. 'Ships That Pass In The Night' – pretty damned funky with the horns complementing the driving bass and guitars. 'Peaches' has a couple of lyric changes: 'Is she trying to get out of Edinbrrrr?' and, 'Still, I can think of a lot worse places to be, like down in the street, or at the end of a street or even a cul-de-sac'.

'Where I Live' – some very nice guitar work from John Ellis at the end here. Works very well, and shows off his fluid playing nicely. But all the gig positivity seems to go to pot with 'School Mam', with a school bell at the start, as Hugh sounds bored to shit now! Then it's 'Let's Celebrate' followed by 'Uptown' and 'Tank' with more interesting Hugh pronunciations where we get 'dreyv' instead of 'drive'. Then comes 'Was It You?' into 'Sewer' which is epically fantastic as always. Before 'Golden Brown', more Jock-mocking from Hugh, 'Edinburrrrr, we were up in Aberrrrdeen yesterday. By the Rrrrriverrrrrrr Don.' JJ interjects – 'It's pronounced Edin-boigh'. Hugh – 'Edinb-boigh? Oh, och aye! Right. Rrrrrrrright!'

Next, 'Walk On By' – stunning – followed by nearly as good versions of 'Nuclear Device', 'Duchess', 'Five Minutes', 'Grip' and even 'All Day And All Of The Night'. During that, a fella in one of the balcony boxes to the left of the stage manages to get from up there to the top of the speaker stack and down on to the stage next to JJ. He's quickly 'escorted' off by security while Hugh says, 'It's alright, he`s just explaining the theory of relativity to John'. Last is 'Punch And Judy', one of the worst choices of song to end any Stranglers concert with! Great gig though.

6th March '90. Carlisle Sands Centre gig. Steve Bullock:

Not a bad gig musically but again more emphasis on technical ability than entertainment. A few notable comments from Hugh, starting with, 'Good evening, anyone remember the Market Hall?', to which the crowd cheers. Hugh: 'What a shithole!' Hugh 'kills' another rat soft toy thrown on stage while on 'Peaches' he says, 'I can think of a lot worse places to be, like down in the street, down the road, or even at the end of a cul de sac'. I always wonder if he was being deliberately profound with the cul de sac comment.

13th March '90. Portsmouth Guildhall. 'Shah Shah A Go Go' is a solid opener straight into 'I Feel Like A Wog' with some trademark John Ellis guitar-noodling over the intro. The whole guitar sound is pretty powerful when the two lead guitars come into play together. Hugh says hello: 'Good evening, two oldies but goldies. Wonderful, wonderful. Portsmouth, Portsmouth. I saw you lot in Poole, you were in Poole the other week. Poole! That's another horrible place ...' Next, 'Straighten Out' and Hugh gets lyrics on the second and third verse a bit mixed up, not that it detracts from the song overall. 'Shakin' Like A Leaf' – the brass section give a great performance with much gusto, then '96 Tears', On 'Someone Like You', Hugh says: 'Okay, how about something new for a change? You can handle it'. Ellis takes the solo on this one, and very fluid it is too, a technically excellent guitarist.

'Sweet Smell Of Success' and Hugh says: 'Jet Black's going to get down and get funky now. Never seen that before have you? Quite disgusting'. 'Always The Sun', then 'Ships That Pass In The Night' and Hugh, 'So what's been happening in Portsmouth then? Fuck all eh?' but then a ladies underwear garment lands on the stage ... 'What's this? Well something's been happening ..., heh heh heh!' Fittingly it's 'Peaches' next and lyric changes of 'Is she trying to get out of Portsmouth Harbour?' and 'I can think of a lot worse places to be, like Gosport ... or even Southampton', finishing with the odd addition of 'Then pop it into the oven and it will be done in half an hour'.

'Where I Live'. 'School Mam' ('Back to school,' says Hugh, ringing the bell to signify that it's time for the lesson to begin). After, it's 'Let's Celebrate' then 'Uptown' and 'Tank' or as Hugh pronounces it, 'Tenk'. 'Was It You?' crosses into 'Sewer' and interesting lyric addition of 'I tell you what I'm gonna do, when I've remembered the words ... I'm gonna make love to a water rat or two'. 'Duchess' – the keyboards are really prominent here, swirling along like a well-oiled machine and showing how brilliant Dave is with the arpeggios. 'Grip' follows briskly, then 'All Day And All Of The Night' and final track 'Punch And Judy'.

18th March '90. The band play a professional but uninspiring gig at the Hexagon in Reading, better known for being a World Snooker venue. A few gems from Hugh to a relatively quiet audience: 'And he's potting the black, and he's going for the black, and he's missed it. Good evening Reading, no snooker tonight I'm afraid. But instead of Pot Black we've got Jet Black'. In 'Peaches'... 'I can think of a lot worse places to be. Can you? Oh **really**?' and during the encore, 'I can't believe they have snooker in here. Where do you all go when they play snooker? Watch it on telly?' and regarding soft rodent toys: 'I have here a throttler to be claimed. Where's all the rats then, we're running out up here. Very quiet here really, are you on drugs or something? Why are you so dopey? Are you on drugs? Fuckin' wake up!'

19th March '90. A kind of homecoming for the band at Guildford Civic Hall tonight. 'Shah Shah A Go Go' is pulsating as always thanks to the storming keyboards and guitar intro, with Hugh's vocals 'different' as well due to more strange enunciations. 'I Feel Like A Wog' is equally mesmerising, with jazzy, psychedelic keyboard and guitar adding a new layer. Whether it all works perfectly is questionable but it would be extremely hard for them to spoil a song of this calibre. However, Hugh does sound like he's merely going through the motions and not enjoying it, though 'Straighten Out' is splendid, and after it he asks, 'Well that was a bit slow wasn't it? I reckon that should have been a bit faster, don't you think?' and so next up is 'Shakin' Like A Leaf' and the brass trio enter the fray. Very funky, if you like that sort of thing.

'96 Tears' is quite boring, as is 'Someone Like You' which is like a weaker version of the same song. A few in the crowd chant the 'Jet Black/million pounds' ditty. 'Sweet Smell Of Success' is jazzed up quite pleasingly but there's no disguising the rather mundane lyrics and vocals. Dave's keys sound souped up impressively on 'Always The Sun' and John Ellis' guitar 'chimes' add a pleasant texture to it. 'Strange Little Girl' goes down well, so to speak, but then we have 'Peaches' on which JJ's bass sounds like a weak and wet fart! '... worse places to be... like Woking' is well received by the Guildford crowd, while another toy rat having the squeak squashed out of it late on too is a bonus. JJ sings impressively on 'Where I Live' but he cuts it short and apologises as the band apparently can't hear everything on stage. The crowd doesn't have a problem though. Hugh chips in with, 'Proves we're not miming, doesn't it?'

'School Mam' and then 'Let's Celebrate' follow, then 'Uptown' and a blistering 'Tank'. 'Was It You?' next and it's a decent brassy thrash, and the great guitar-led transformation into 'Sewer' on which Dave's keys make it more *Doors* In The Sewer'. Hugh asks if anyone here is from Woking, or creepy Crawley? He answers his own question – 'Just lovely Guildford people.' Later: 'Well all I can say is that they've completely destroyed Guildford. I mean, what happened to that lovely town that I used to know? They've completely destroyed it, they've turned you into another Amersham or something. Or a Welwyn Garden City or something. It's disgusting, all those horrible new buildings ... awful! Awful, why didn't you do something about it? Awful, it's got no character anymore. And YOU let it happen, cor, pathetic!'

21st April '90, 'Sweet Smell Of Success' single released, a definite misnomer which only reaches No. 65 in the charts.

Promo video for Stranglers singles - 'Sweet Smell Of Success': It's a stylish video and ties in well with the cover for 10, with various world leaders and a Pope dotted around a casino while the band plays the song and some people dance and a dandy young fellow gets chased by two penguin suited heavies.

LABEL DISILLUSIONMENT

The release of only two singles from 10 is 'a shame' to Hugh, a third has been planned in 'Man Of The Earth', but CBS shelve the idea even though a sleeve has already been designed. The label's reasons are apparently on grounds of cost and because there is 'nothing happening' in the US for the band, which Hugh believes is proof that CBS don't really know what they are doing and clearly aren't sufficiently supportive of the band.

22nd May '90, The Stranglers are playing in Zagreb, Yugoslavia. Steve Bullock watched:

Hugh and John Ellis dance round in circles during the intro to 'Shah Shah A Go Go', and. JJ is also pretty energetic. The most notable thing about this performance is that it was really obvious that JJ and Hugh kept away from each other for the whole gig, no eye contact and a substantial distance between each other, Hugh and JE at one side of the stage and JJ the other. Hugh changes a line in 'Peaches' to 'I can think of a lot worse places to be ... like... Belgrade' but all in all it's an uneventful gig, the crowd just want to hear music rather than chat from Hugh, possibly because they couldn't understand him.

Band at FR3 Studios in France.
(*Unknown*)

28th May '90. A gig at the Phillipshalle in Düsseldorf, Germany. Hugh, after a powerful-as-always 'I Feel Like A Wog', reveals a little more about the song; 'Hello, good evening, that's about a very unsavoury character we once met in Hamburg believe it or not, called Pimpo'. Later, crowd watching, he comments, "We got some serious smokers down here. Have you got shares in Philip Morris or something? There's a lot of cigarettes going down here. I can't see with all that going on. You got shares in Philip Morris? Puff, puff... go on, get six out, come on let's get you smoking. Six at a time, come on'.

Following 'Strange Little Girl': 'Okay our brass section are having birthdays this week ... So ... yeah ... those young lads are growing up finally. Wish I could say the same thing. Now they've got a little present for you, which ... uh ... we hope you're going to enjoy. If you don't... sod ya'. The three lads then blow some bloody awful noise together, trying to create German oompah band sounds or something as unholy. But then JJ starts the intro to 'Peaches' and the audience is saved from more punishment. Hugh's new line is, 'I can think of a lot worse places to be... like stuck in a one way system in Düsseldorf centre' and later, for their second encore, he finally gets a bit chattier due to the crowd's enthusiasm. 'Never in my experience of coming to Düsseldorf have I ever experienced such a commotion. I'm going to ring the Chamber of Commerce about it right now, first thing tomorrow morning. Disgusting behaviour, all this noise. You're just a bunch of rowdies aren't you? German rowdies, I thought so. I had a suspicion earlier. Look this is not a request show ... I've got a request ... Go home' and then 'Grip' enters the proceedings, followed by 'Duchess' the finale and Hugh saying, 'Thank you very much, goodnight'.

29th May '90. The Espace Foire in Lille, France is the venue for tonight's Stranglers concert. After the conjoined 'Shah Shah A Go Go' and 'I Feel Like A Wog', Hugh tries to coax some energy in to the audience, 'A little medley! You're very still tonight … Lille. I'm from Lille, I stand still'. Someone in the crowd shouts, 'Wankers, wankers' to which he responds, 'Ooooh, I love you' before launching into 'Straighten Out'. Later, 'Peaches' has 'I can think of a lot worse places to be, like trying to find the Espace Foire with a badly bad road map'. Very late on, JJ has a word or two with the fans, *'Vous êtes trop folie'* [roughly, 'You are all mad'] and after explaining why there's no 'Go Buddy Go' – *'Buddy est parti'* – before the band finish the gig with 'All Day And All Of The Night'.

30th May '90. No pun intended but it's a big night at Le Grand Rex in Paris tonight, and reputedly the best gig of the whole tour. That's probably not saying much though. Tension is in the onstage air, and during the gig Hugh does all the French talking rather than JJ which is just odd. JJ swigs liberally from a crowd member's Jack Daniels bottle throughout. It's the standard 10 tour set list but at times the performance near crackles with friction between Hugh and JJ even though they barely acknowledge each other's existence. The 'Meninblack' tune heralds the band's arrival and then it's started, the fuse-lit opening of 'Shah Shah A Go Go' crossing in to 'I Feel Like A Wog', arguably the band's best ever choice of starters. Hugh alters a chorus line in 'Wog', 'Don't ask me to be your gollywog' and he verbalises his guitar sound instead of actually playing it. Also odd. And the 'Peaches' change is 'I can think of a lot worse places to be … Like you do, Frenchman'.

11th August '90. A date many Stranglers fans will never forget, regardless of whether they attended the gig tonight or not; it is memorable … for the wrong reasons.

The Stranglers at Alexandra Palace. Mark Luff attended:

> I'd gone to the Brixton Academy gig in February and also again there in March. This tour had been well attended but I did get the feeling that die-hard fans were thinking the brass section had outstayed their welcome. This gig was also the fifth anniversary of the Town And Country Club. It started with a foghorn sounding and searchlight going from one side of the stage to the other to add to the build-up of tension, and when the crowd sussed it was 'Toiler' then the place erupted. To say it was lively near the stage would be an understatement so I eventually moved a little to the side which was an Okay view but poor sound quality. On the huge stage are Hugh Cornwell, Jean-Jacques Burnel, Jet Black, Dave Greenfield and John Ellis, plus the brass section of Chris Lawrence, Richard Sidwell and Alex Gifford.
>
> Though there are a couple of guitar notes sounding just off key, Hugh's vocals are perfect on 'Toiler'. He looks miserable but then jokes with the crowd at how long it is since the band played there, as they never have. 'Something Better Change' with JJ on vocals of course, with a softer delivery here. He looks happy enough but there is minimal interaction between the band members. '96 Tears' and the crowd's really enjoying the gig and the brass addition to this track really adds to it. 'Someone Like You' – the crowd remains lively but this is relatively weak and JJ's 'high pitched' backing vocals do not help. He grins at friends in the crowd and Hugh asks the audience how old 'Ally Pally' is today, and 'You don't know, do you?'

'Sweet Smell Of Success' next, complete with fine bongo introduction, and maracas, tambourine and backing vocals from the brass boys. JJ does a few of his leg stretches while Dave Greenfield looks as uninterested as could be, an electric fan blowing his hair all over in his makeshift watchtower made of keyboards and synthesisers. Hugh and John Ellis partake in a little guitar 'sparring' together, leaning towards each other when plucking particular notes. As JJ kicks and dances through 'Always The Sun', Ellis studiously plays lead guitar, while Hugh's little solo on Spanish guitar is faultless. 'Strange Little Girl' is a perfect rendition, and then 'Hanging Around' and as the first keyboard notes vibrate the air, at the front the crowd is a pulsating sea of people, mainly men. As JJ sings the backing vocals, Hugh glances at him. It's only a glance but it feels relevant somehow.

'Let's Celebrate': some clued-up fans begin chanting this before Jet's intro gets going. Hugh's guitar work is immaculate, he looks absolutely intent on giving as perfect a performance as possible. Dave's psychedelic keyboard flow here is also excellent, as 'Jet Black, Jet Black, Jet Black!' chants rise from the crowd. And a huge cheer as his bass drum beats, along with Dave's 'harpsichord' keys, heralding the arrival of their greatest hit 'Golden Brown'. JJ is shirtless now.

'No More Heroes' follows, with big time pogoing and fists aplenty punching the air. Before 'Nuclear Device', with a slight smile on his face, Hugh tells us it's 'Time to go to Australia'. This is one of the songs where Jet really proves he's the sonic spine of the band, the solid cornerstone, the heartbeat, but it's all spoiled a bit by the silly knee-slapping dance from the brass trio. Still, maybe that proves the band doesn't take themselves too seriously. Maybe.

Next is 'Duchess' and Dave's wizardry excites even more, and JJ's bass is deep, moving and brilliant at the same time. 'All Day And All Of The Night'. Hugh says: 'Come on, time to go home now …' and he smiles but it's a strained smile. 'Punch And Judy' – a great sax solo from Alex Gifford, front of stage and just about in the faces of close spectators. And then that's it, all over. I'm wondering what's going through Hugh's mind, knowing what I know now, and I can't help thinking 'If only …' … if only they'd talked to each other, sorted things out, resolved their issues, then most of us wouldn't have wasted so much time since hoping for a reunion or at least peace and goodwill in our timeinblack'.

12th August '90. Hugh Cornwell telephones Jet Black, then Dave Greenfield and finally Jean-Jacques Burnel, to inform them that he no longer wishes to be a Strangler. He has quit the band. It's said that Jet reacts quite sympathetically to Hugh's not entirely unexpected news, while Dave certainly hasn't seen it coming, nor has JJ, so the conversation between Hugh and he had been the hardest and most emotional, it being the end of a long relationship between Hugh and the band and of course the partnership of Cornwell and Burnel. Meanwhile, 'guest Strangler' John Ellis remembers, 'There were no clues about Hugh jumping ship, but I do remember him saying something like see you in another life when I said goodbye to him at the end of the tour. The first thing I knew about Hugh leaving was when the management phoned me to tell me and ask if I was interested in becoming a permanent member. I have no idea how the other three reacted when Hugh left. Personally, I wasn't surprised. Also, it was obvious he was the creative driving force in the band and the last few albums had not been well received, plus he wanted to explore his acting. So I guess there were people around him advising him to move on, and JJ's behaviour gave him the push he needed'.

19th November '90. The Stranglers' *Greatest Hits* album is released and will spend almost a year in the charts, peaking at No. 4.

SUMMING IT ALL UP

This is me, Robert, talking now. Much as I'd like to tell you that I was tearfully shocked and distraught about effectively the split-up of my favourite band, the truth is it came only as a slight surprise; it had seemed inevitable for some time. And much as they were 'my' band, much as I regarded them almost as friends, and much as I could argue the quality of their music over any other band going, I felt their output had been waning for a while. And I was tired of 'having' to buy numerous versions and formats of singles that I could barely afford and wasn't massively keen on in the first fucking place.

Unless you were in the 'inner circle' of The Stranglers, if indeed there actually was such a thing, then those were the days of slow and 'foggy' communications (and I was oop North remember, where southerners believed cars were powered by coal and there was no such thing as colour television) so much of the news and gossip remained secret. Of course, it hurt when Hugh left, but I was quite sure it would be temporary and there was a way back wasn't there? This unfortunate situation was like splitting up with a girlfriend who you didn't **really** love anymore, where 'I love you but I'm not IN love with you' sort of drivel is the overriding feeling.

However, back in 1990 I was 25 years old and emotionally immature (still am probably) full of mixed up feelings and not quite sensible opinions (yes, still am probably), so Hugh deserting The Stranglers didn't have that much of an impact on me then as it did in later years. (Maybe there I should say does in later years). I mean, why couldn't they just have a temporary break from each other? Why not announce that the split was 'indefinite' and so wasn't absolutely final? Why not declare that all the teddies and rattles thrown from the respective Cornwell and Burnel prams were in fact retrievable?

Someone, maybe the elder statesman Jet Black, should have arranged a meeting with Hugh and JJ and told them in no uncertain terms to sort their selves out, to settle their differences and to not let personality clashes ruin their friendship and working partnership. And to GROW UP for fuck's sake instead of hurting each other and their friends & colleagues and the fans too, the fans who, let's face it, had a great deal of influence in helping them realise their quest for fame and fortune.

The Stranglers are still going, they are still capable of brilliant new music and they are still one of the best bands in concert you could hope to see. And they are always different and original. Hugh Cornwell also has many moments of brilliance, and he too nearly always provides fantastic gigs for his faithful fans. Many of those faithful fans still follow The Stranglers too.

Is it possible that the four original members will meet up again, in happy circumstances? Is it possible that somehow Hugh could work with Jean-Jacques again, with the approval of Baz Warne don't forget, as he is a superb front man and vital to the existence of the band. Yes of course it is possible. Of fucking course it is! I doubt it's plausible though but I would be delighted to be proven wrong.

BIBLIOGRAPHY

A Multitude Of Sins – Hugh Cornwell.
Inside Information – Hugh Cornwell.
Melody Maker.
Much Ado About Nothing – Jet Black.
New Musical Express.
New Pose fanzine.
No Mercy, The Authorised And Uncensored Biography – David Buckley.
Punk – Dorling Kindersley.
Punk Diary, 1970–79: An Eyewitness Record of the Punk Decade – George Gimarc.
Punk Rock, An Oral History – John Robb.
Record Mirror.
Sounds.
Strangled enthuzine.
The Men They Love To Hate – Chris Twomey.
The Palace And The Punks – Tony Hill.
The Peel Sessions – Ken Garner.
The Stranglers, Song By Song – Hugh Cornwell & Jim Drury.
ZigZag.

ABOUT THE AUTHOR

Robert Endeacott was born, bred and still lives in Leeds, West Yorkshire, England. He arrived in 1965 and is an April Fool; he doesn't give a damn who knows it.

Also written by Robert Endeacott: One Northern Soul. Fanthology (with Graeme Garvey). No More Heroes. Dirty Leeds. Disrepute – Revie's England. After Extra Time (Dirty Leeds Uncut). Scandal FC. And the forthcoming Operation Red Card.

■ ■